The Barren Sacrifice

Studies in Violence, Mimesis, and Culture

SERIES EDITOR
William A. Johnsen

The Studies in Violence, Mimesis, and Culture Series examines issues related to the nexus of violence and religion in the genesis and maintenance of culture. It furthers the agenda of the Colloquium on Violence and Religion, an international association that draws inspiration from René Girard's mimetic hypothesis on the relationship between violence and religion, elaborated in a stunning series of books he has written over the last forty years. Readers interested in this area of research can also look to the association's journal, *Contagion: Journal of Violence, Mimesis, and Culture.*

The Barren Sacrifice

AN ESSAY ON POLITICAL VIOLENCE

Paul Dumouchel

Translated by Mary Baker

Michigan State University Press · *East Lansing*

♾ The paper used in this publication meets the minimum requirements of ANSI/NISO Z39.48-1992 (R 1997) (Permanence of Paper).

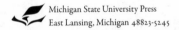 Michigan State University Press
East Lansing, Michigan 48823-5245

Printed and bound in the United States of America.

21 20 19 18 17 16 15   1 2 3 4 5 6 7 8 9 10

LIBRARY OF CONGRESS CONTROL NUMBER: 2015934711
ISBN: 978-1-61186-183-9 (pbk.)
ISBN: 978-1-60917-470-5 (ebook: PDF)
ISBN: 978-1-62895-242-1 (ebook: ePub)
ISBN: 978-1-62896-242-0 (ebook: Kindle)

Book design by Charlie Sharp, Sharp Des!gns, Lansing, Michigan
Cover design by David Drummond, Salamander Design, www.salamanderhill.com
Cover image is a detail from *Intrusion d'en Haut* by Arcabas (Jean-Marie Pirot) ©2015 Artists Rights Society (ARS), New York / ADAGP, Paris, and is used with permission.

g green press Michigan State University Press is a member of the Green Press **INITIATIVE** Initiative and is committed to developing and encouraging ecologically responsible publishing practices. For more information about the Green Press Initiative and the use of recycled paper in book publishing, please visit *www.greenpressinitiative.org*.

Visit Michigan State University Press at *www.msupress.org*

For René Girard
and
Jean-Pierre Dupuy

Contents

ix   Acknowledgments

xi   Introduction

1   CHAPTER 1. Solidarity and Enmity

31   CHAPTER 2. The State, Violence, and Groups

61   CHAPTER 3. Territory and War

87   CHAPTER 4. The Traitor and Reason

115   CHAPTER 5. Indifference and Charity

143   CHAPTER 6. Social Justice and Territory

169   EPILOGUE

181   Notes

197   Bibliography

205   Index

Acknowledgments

T his book would never have seen the light of day without the help,
support, patience and encouragement of Benoît Chantre, peerless
editor and perfect interlocutor. Lucien Scubla read, generously com-
mented, and severely criticized the first version of the manuscript. Thanks
to him, this book is much less imperfect than it would otherwise have been.
Finally, I would like to thank, for their criticism, comments, advice, and
often long discussions, Mark Anspach, Mary Baker, Maria-Stella Barberi,
Daniel Bell, Daniel Bougnoux, Luisa Damiano, Jean-Pierre Dupuy, Antoine
Garapon, Reiko Gotoh, Marcel Hénaff, Sergio Manghi, Geping Niu, Masa-
chi Osawa, Wolfgang Palaver, Stefano Tomelleri, Shigeki Tominaga, Hiromi
Tomita, and Kozo Watanabe.

Introduction

According to modern political philosophy, the primary function of the state is to protect its citizens. It is to protect them from one another and to defend them from outside enemies. Yet violence against civilian populations, genocides, ethnic cleansing, and massacres are perpetrated mainly by states and, to a large extent, against their own citizens. In Cambodia, Rwanda, Turkey, Russia, Argentina, and Chile, the state became for a time the worst enemy of those whom it was its job to protect. Likewise, the Nazi regime began by turning its fury against *its own* citizens, such as communists and other political enemies, liquidating those it judged "inadequate," before directing its genocidal madness to the outside. That states are violent in their relations with other states and that they sometimes use force against their own citizens is commonplace and all too frequent. Here, however, we are talking about something else. The scandal comes from the contradiction between the official function of the state, namely, protection of its members, and policies that target the extermination of a very large number of those members.

Of course, there is no veritable *contradiction* between what a theory teaches and what states sometimes do. At the very most, there is tension and a paradox in the original sense of the term.[1] The state's protective function is nonetheless not simply theoretical. By prohibiting private vengeance and reserving for itself the right to use violence to resolve disputes, the state takes on the role of its citizens' defender. There are even good reasons to think that this role is constitutive of the modern state, the holder of the "monopoly of the legitimate use of physical force," as Max Weber wrote.[2] The massive violence that states commit against their own citizens is consequently a singular perversion of political order. Designed and instituted to maintain domestic peace and defense against outside enemies, the state suddenly turns against those whom it should protect and makes their destruction its goal. Surprise in the face of this paradoxical reversal is the starting point of this inquiry into the relationships between violence and politics. How can we make sense of the fact that states undertake to destroy those whom it is their vocation to defend? Could genocides, ethnic cleansing, and government-backed massacres simply be unfortunate accidents and political failures? Or is it possible that these murderous inversions of the state's primordial function are phenomena the risk of which is deeply inscribed in modern political institutions?

We have to take seriously the classical thesis according to which the primary function of the state is to protect us from our own violence, but how does it manage this? The violence that individuals inflict on one another is what makes the state necessary. Thus, as Hobbes—one of the finest representatives of this political tradition—saw long ago, it is by violence that the state protects us from violence. We generally think of the state's violence as the force that it uses, when necessary, to coerce members of society to comply with their pact of reciprocal nonaggression. However, where does this superior force come from? The unanimous transfer to a single sovereign of our right to defend ourselves creates the institution that violently puts an end to violent disorder. By renouncing our right to violence (and vengeance), we give the state the monopoly over violence. What we transfer is what we have "renounced," in other words, our violence. The unanimous transfer transforms the violence: *it makes it legitimate*. Thus, the state's coercive power no longer seems to be real violence, exactly, or rather, it becomes *good violence*, the purpose of which is peace, in opposition to *bad violence*, which creates disorder.

The holder of the monopoly of legitimate violence has authority that is moral in the strict sense: the authority to differentiate between good and bad violence. The state does not create this difference, which is prior to it, but it institutes it in a special way: it monopolizes the authority to make the distinction. This monopoly is new. It is specific to the modern state. Social contract theories generally contrast the state with a "state of nature" in which each individual has the freedom to decide which violence is legitimate and which is illegitimate. The theories then argue that if all people do not divide violent acts into the categories of good and bad in the same way, the distinction between the two could cause disputes rather than be a means of resolving them. When we each claim to make this difference for ourselves, we are quickly in disagreement because we are each convinced that our own violence is good and everyone else's bad. Distinguishing between these two forms of violence in a common, public manner is essential to the modern state. It makes it possible for the state to protect us by using good violence to put an end to bad violence.

This is correct: the division between these two forms of violence is the foundation of modern politics. Yet the premises of the argument are false. Exacerbated moral individualism, of which social contract theories fear the political consequences, does not historically precede the modern state: it follows. In feudal and archaic societies, no one determines the division between good and bad violence on one's own. Socially, the division between legitimate and illegitimate violence results from the interplay of the many solidarity and hostility obligations that gather individuals into opposing groups: families, clans, tribes, lords and vassals, nobles and peasants. The modern state erases these divisions, and ensures that the uncentralized moral authority to differentiate between good and bad violence is replaced by the monopoly of legitimate violence.

Yet what establishes the state's moral authority and the division between good and bad violence is the unanimous transfer to the sovereign, by the citizens, of their right to protect themselves, in other words, the transfer of their own violence. The unanimous violence of all, united in the person of the sovereign, separates good violence from bad. What founds the moral authority of the state is also what gives it its strength. The distinction between legitimate and illegitimate violence rests on the monopoly of violence. "Eliminating a violent act is not, in itself, a political act. Greater violence suffices,"[3] wrote Claude Bruaire at the beginning of *La Raison politique*. On the contrary, the greater violence that puts an end to violent disorder is the political action par excellence, the one that is at the origin of all political order.

Thus, we can define as political all *violence that legitimizes itself.* Violence that is legitimate because the person who exercises it is a representative of the state's (legitimate) authority is either military or legal violence. Violence that fails to legitimize itself is criminal. Political violence is violence that becomes legitimate through the simple fact that it occurs. It is a form of violence that others than those by whom it is committed identify with or recognize themselves in. It is a form of violence that gathers and rallies, and receives the support of those (or at least some of those) who are not its victims. Such violence gives moral authority to those who exercise it. The source of the moral authority is none other than the "transfer," to those who commit the violent act, of the violence of those who approve the violence and recognize it as justified, legitimate, and good.

All political power, monopolistic or not, whether it is that of the state or that of insurgents opposing the state, is based on shifting the violence of those who recognize the power in question to acceptable targets. Redirecting violence toward victims other than those originally targeted is what gives rise to political power and protects members of the state from their own reciprocal violence. In other words, this is what establishes the political community, the reciprocal friendship of its members. Political violence, whether it is that of repression or terrorism, is the return of violence to the space pacified by the monopolistic violence of the state. This return constitutes a failure of the mechanism by which violence is unanimously shifted onto substitute victims. This is why the eruption of private conflicts, jealousy, and personal rivalry within political violence, such as civil wars, social clashes, ethnic uprisings, and even state repression, is not an accident or malfunction, but one of the fundamental aspects of political conflict. Exploitation of political violence for private purposes indicates the failure of the transfer mechanism.

The failure of the unanimous shift of violence is inseparable from a challenge to the moral authority of the state, to its monopoly of legitimate violence. For example, the violence of terrorism challenges the official difference between good and bad violence. This loss of unanimity leads to a confusion between legitimate and illegitimate violence. It is at the same time an attempt to redraw, but differently, the lines between the two forms of violence. Repression, state violence, is an attempt to respond to this loss of difference. Its goal is to reaffirm the original distinction between good and bad violence. However, even in this case, violence, especially when it is more extreme, blurs and weakens the difference that it seeks to reestablish. All political violence is thus simultaneously a challenge to the existing distinction between good and bad violence and an action that is designed to restate that same difference.

The State and the Sacrificial Mechanism: Reason

It is through violence that the state protects us from violence. It is through the exercise of superior force that it prevents us from tearing one another apart, and that superior force comes from shifting the community's violence to acceptable targets, to sacrificial victims. This rereading of the classical conception of the modern state suggests that it is a variant of the sacrificial mechanism described by René Girard.[4] Indeed, the similarities are striking: the unanimous transfer of violence that puts an end to disorder; the fact that this unanimity gives birth to a moral authority that promulgates rules designed to keep the peace within the community and separate *good* violence from *bad* violence; the shift of the violence to acceptable victims. In his analyses of sacred kingships, Girard suggests that the first kings were victims waiting to be sacrificed who found a way to take advantage of the gap in time separating the point when they were selected as victims and the moment when they were to be put to death.[5] Sacred kings played the roles of victims, but they would have gradually managed to shift the violence that was directed at them and aim it at others. This is how they would have established kingship as a political regime.

In a sense, I am simply extending this Girardian analysis of sacred kingship to the modern state. However, the modern state has special features in relation to the sacred with which I am trying to link it. Three of them seem especially crucial. The first is *rationality*. In this case, the transfer of violence is not the result of a blind mechanism experienced through misapprehension. On the contrary, the means by which it is accomplished are consciously designed and rationally motivated, even though their veritable nature remains partially dissimulated and the sacrificial aspect of the operation goes unnoticed.[6] The transfer to the sovereign of each person's violence, of each person's right to engage in self-defense, is supposed to result from a rational decision. We each renounce our violence and receive in return the peace and security that make it possible to pursue our personal goals. The rationality of the agreement that founds the state is, second, inseparable from its *secular* nature. The rational contract by which individuals come together and submit themselves to the power that protects them desacralizes the state. It says that the state has no transcendent source, and that its origin and purpose are to be found with the people who establish it. Compared to the sacred that is engendered by the sacrificial mechanism and to the office of the sacred king in particular, its secular nature, the fact that it is "human, only human," is the second characteristic feature of the modern state. In principle at least, modern politics abandons the illusion of transcendence.

The third special feature of the modern state is that it has a *"monopoly of the legitimate use of physical force."* Until the modern state emerged, sovereigns, kings, emperors, "sons of heaven," and representatives of God on earth were, at best, never more than those who were able to exercise supreme violence—in other words, those who were able, in the end, to subjugate the violence of others. Having a monopoly of legitimate violence is not simply having violence that allows the sovereign to destroy those who oppose his or her sovereignty; it is also to be the source of the difference between legitimate and illegitimate violence. In the world of the sacred, no one ever has that monopoly because the place from which rules distinguishing between good and bad violence flow is an empty space: that of the dead victim. Even though sacred kings may occupy that space during the time when their death is postponed—a period that they sometimes manage to extend almost indefinitely—they never manage to gain the monopoly of legitimate violence. In the last analysis, the reason for this is that *in the sacred world, it is impossible to have the monopoly of violence.* This is, at least, the way it seems we have to interpret the hypothesis of the mimetic crisis and the sacrificial mechanism by which it ends. This means that there can be no ultimate winner of the violent conflict within the community. Lasting peace can be achieved only if violence has a self-regulating mechanism.

Since all political violence legitimizes itself, in order to have the monopoly of legitimate violence, it is necessary and sufficient to have the monopoly of violence. To acquire the monopoly of violence is automatically to acquire the monopoly of legitimate violence. It is thus important to see what transformations of the sacrificial mechanism have made it possible to establish such a privilege.

Having the monopoly of legitimate violence is to claim to state, or create, the difference between good and bad violence. Wanting to, or thinking one must, invent the difference between good and evil is so eminently modern that it is almost a definition of modernity. This goal, this pretension, suggests that there is a close link between rationality and the monopoly of legitimate violence. Thus, as Kant saw clearly, the practical reason of the individual, who is autonomous because he or she adopts his or her own moral laws, imitates the social contract. Like the sovereign's legitimacy, the moral subject's autonomy depends on the unanimous agreement of an ideal community. Rationality, secularism—which is another way of understanding moral autonomy—and the monopoly of legitimate violence are closely related in the theory and practice of the modern state.

According to modern political theory, reason founds the monopoly of legitimate violence, and the rational agreement of society members gives birth to the state. Because they are rational, members of society renounce their violence and bestow upon the sovereign the monopoly of legitimate violence, the necessary power, which makes it possible for the sovereign to protect society members from one another and from outside enemies. The Girardian reading invites us to inverse this founding relationship and suggests that the monopoly of legitimate violence is what provides reason with its claim to be violence's Other, thus making itself "Reason." *The difference between reason and violence, on which we would like to base the unanimous agreement of members of society, does not precede the action that establishes the political order, but flows from it.* Reason, conceived of as violence's Other, depends on there being a monopoly of legitimate violence. If there is no such monopoly, the difference that defines Reason also fades away.

This is why, when the monopoly of legitimate violence yields under the blows of political violence, the distinction between violence and reason disappears. There is no longer any difference between the recommendations of violence and the prescriptions of reason. Recourse to violence then looks to individuals not only like a rational option, but also, very often, eminently reasonable. According to Hobbes, in the state of nature, in other words, in the absence of a sovereign power, "there is no way for any man to secure himselfe, so reasonable, as Anticipation; that is, by force, or wiles, to master the persons of all men he can, so long, till he see no other power great enough to endanger him."[7]

"Indifference"

The starting point of chapter 1 of this book is an observation that is frequent among authors who have studied large-scale collective violence: many of those who commit such crimes neither have strong ideological motives nor act under the threat of severe punishment if they refuse to participate. It is as if no special reason were needed to commit unspeakable violence and atrocities against defenseless groups of people! The Hautefaye crime,[8] which I analyze, illustrates what may seem to be an entirely opposite attitude. The murder in the Dordogne in August 1870 of a young noble by a group of enraged people, who accused him of being a "Prussian" and who tortured him for two hours before finally burning him alive in a bonfire, occurred before a crowd of several hundred people who had come out for a fair. For the most part, people simply continued going about their business while the tragedy unfolded before their eyes. They did not participate in the violence, but they also did not make the slightest attempt to come to the victim's aid. Between participation in atrocious violence that apparently has no major reason or grounds, and refusal to help those in danger, there may not be much distance. In both cases, we find the same "indifference" to the fate of others.

This "indifference" is not so much a psychological disposition as a fundamental sociological phenomenon. The attitude of Hautefaye's fairgoers reveals a change in the ties of solidarity among agents. It reflects the existence of new social rules. The transformation of the bonds of solidarity, from which this "indifference" flows, protects us from violence up to a certain point because it limits violence's capacity to turn into a frenzy, as can be seen by the fact that the great majority of those present did not participate. However, it deprives us of the protection that used to be offered by traditional solidarity rules, as can be seen by the fact that the great majority of those present did not consider it appropriate to come to the victim's aid. Like the sacred according to Girard, "indifference" is ambiguous, ambivalent. On one hand, it isolates and separates agents, thereby creating an obstacle to the contagion of violence, but on the other hand, because it isolates and separates agents, it abandons them to their fates and turns each into a potential sacrificial victim. Yet *the change in social ties that makes this "indifference" possible also thwarts the mechanism that engenders the sacred.* It prevents what is, according to Girard, the normal resolution of the mimetic crisis: the spontaneous convergence of all on a unique victim. This is the central thesis of the first chapter, and the rest of the book will demonstrate some of its many consequences. Indeed, this same transformation of social ties is also what makes possible the emergence of a monopoly of legitimate violence, and favors the adoption of exchange as a rule of conduct among those who owe nothing to one another, in other words, among those who are not linked by reciprocal solidarity obligations.

Understood in this way, indifference corresponds to what Hannah Arendt called "the banality of evil," an inability to imagine and put oneself in the shoes of others, which she discovered in Eichmann's attitude. During his trial, the SS bureaucrat seemed in fact more concerned by the little slights he had suffered from his Nazi colleagues than by the fate of millions of people whose transportation to death camps he had organized.[9] Nancy Scheper-Hughes finds the same indifference at the heart of the "genocidal continuum" of "peacetime crimes," which is how she refers to certain forms of everyday structural violence with respect to which we demonstrate the same carefree attitude as those who, in genocidal situations, take a laissez-faire approach.[10] The same indifference makes both large-scale and small-scale violence possible. Her analyses point to what will be one of the recurring themes in the present book: the fact that there is continuity between ordinary everyday violence and the "extraordinary" violence of political conflict. They also suggest that the transformations of the social bonds that limit the escalation of violence are not unrelated to the murderous excesses of modern political violence. In the world of politics, as in the realm of the sacred, crises occur when there is a malfunction in the mechanism through which violence protects us, and we are then threatened by the very violence that normally protects us. However, unlike what happens in the sacred world, in this case the crisis does not automatically lead the community back to peace. Violence's self-regulatory function fails.

The State and Groups

Chapter 2 turns to the way that states' violence against their own citizens has been framed in political philosophy. I take as a point of departure the *Discourse on Voluntary Servitude* by Étienne de La Boétie, who was first to formulate this issue in modern terms, in the way later taken up by the liberal and democratic tradition. I then analyze liberal contractualist tactics for warding off that danger. They are based on two central ideas: that of individual "subjective" rights and that of a rational agreement among society members that founds political power. The individual and subjective rights that are supposed to protect citizens presuppose that groups, which are sometimes called intermediary groupings, have been excluded as political players. Yet all crimes against "humanity" and states' crimes against their own citizens are group crimes in both senses of the word. They are perpetrated by organized groups, and they are committed against persons who, while they are in a sense "isolated," are identified as victims on the basis of the social category or group to which they belong. This is a strange "contradiction." Modern political theory refuses to recognize the political pertinence of groups, thereby denying the importance of what empirically defines one of the major problems to which it claims to provide a solution: the violence of political power against those subject to it!

Group crimes reject the separation of persons that is characteristic of subjective rights. They infringe on the rights of individuals by reducing persons to members of an execrated group. They throw them out of the group of "friends" and expel them into the group of "foes." At the same time, they redraw the border between those who have rights and those who do not. The two operations are closely linked. Drawing the boundaries separating the groups is inseparable from the fact of establishing the rights of the members of one of the groups." This is what is shown through a rereading of Hobbes. According to him, the modern state is established by excluding the existence of groups within it and by opposing another state that is a "homogenous" group of the same type. The exclusion of groups is simply one with the sovereign's monopoly of violence and with the separation of individuals that is characteristic of modern law. However, the peace established by the sovereign's monopoly of legitimate violence is possible, according to Hobbes, only in the shadow of an enemy outside the state, an opposing group that is more or less of similar size.

The role of the relationship between "friend" and "foe" groups in the foundation of the state is essential, but remains difficult to see in the work of the author of *Leviathan*. In Carl Schmitt's work, on the contrary, this opposition becomes the essence of politics. Yet the modern state as described by Hobbes, in other words, the one that excludes groups from within it and makes enmity coincide with the state's inside-outside separation, is, according to the author of *The Concept of the Political*,[12] only one of the possible forms that politics can take. It is only one specific case, among others, of what Schmitt considered a fundamental dichotomy: the "friends-foes" opposition. However, despite himself to a degree, and though he did not distinguish them clearly, Schmitt discovered in the modern state two types of political enemies: interior and exterior. He was thus led to acknowledge the existence of two different forms of warlike clashes, of which one is more violent than political opposition, which he had earlier described as the supreme form of hostility. It is as if there were a necessary doubling of the dichotomy that defines politics, a double "friends-foes" relation.

A detour through anthropology can shed light on this difficulty. In stateless societies, the space in which there are ties of solidarity and hostility is always divided into at least three areas. This threefold division reflects the existence of two types of friendship/enmity relations: adversarial and hostile. Adversarial relations oppose "equal" groups in conflicts in which the violence is subject to rules. Hostility is a relationship of unrestrained violence that authorizes the extermination of "Others" who are too different. René Girard's sacrificial hypothesis suggests an explanation for this doubling of enemy relations. In contrast with the measured, ritualized clashes between adversaries, the exterminating violence of hostility resembles that which destroys the sacrificial victim. The doubling of the enemy relationship is an expression of the sacrificial principle. Like sacrifice, the twofold enemy relationship is part of the mechanism that protects us from our own violence by directing it onto victims who are far from the heart of the community. Like sacrifice, the relation of extreme hostility helps to ensure that the rivalries characteristic of adversarial relations remain measured; it prevents their violence from becoming uncontrollable. We can at least entertain the idea that this is the case in stateless societies because exterminating hostility is generally exercised against the enemies the furthest from the community, those who are the most exterior and "foreign." In contrast, it is often for internal, terrorist, subversive minority or ethnic minority groups, for the "foreigners" who live among us, that modern states reserve the greatest violence. It is they whose right to have rights is taken away, and who are refused even the feeble protection of international law. How can we explain this inversion?

Territory and the Failure of the State's Simplification
of the Space of Hostility

The establishment of the monopoly of legitimate violence leads, first, to a simplification of the enmity relationship. The threefold division of the solidarity/hostility space that we see in stateless societies is replaced by a twofold division that expels "foes" and confines "friends" inside the state, which it defines as coinciding with a *territory*, a mixed concept composed of physical space and cultural proximity. It has to be considered a fundamental political category. The modern state where there is rule of law and in which the government has the monopoly of legitimate violence does not define itself as a community, but rather primarily as a territory over which it exercises its power in a homogenous manner. The simplification of the "friends-foes" relation leads the distinct adversarial and solidarity relationships to blend into a single relationship. It leads us to think about the relationships between agents within the space pacified by the state in terms of rationality and law. The simplification of the "friends-foes" relation also corresponds to an effort to exclude sacrificial violence from relations between persons. Both inside and out, the modern state claims to employ only legitimate, rationally justified violence. In this sense, we can say that the modern political system is an attempt to renounce sacrificial violence while not entirely renouncing violence.

However, modern states' efforts to definitively simplify the solidarity/hostility space have failed. The threefold division always resurfaces. In international relations, we can see a structure that is quite similar to the hostility and solidarity spaces in stateless societies. In the center, a first circle is delimited by the nation's land. It is the domain of law where conflicts are resolved without recourse to open violence. It is surrounded by a second circle, defined by the alliance of nations, which is the realm of the "friends-foes" political relationship as Schmitt sees it. Colonies and *terra nullius* form a third circle, where the relations of hostility are completely different, and where entire populations can be freely exterminated. In fact, as groups get further away, the moral assessment of the conflicts opposing them changes. Spatial and cultural distance becomes the sign of a rationality deficit, which justifies recourse to more intense violence. This connection between the two forms of distance makes three different types of "realms" coincide. Those who are furthest from us in the physical realm are the most foreign in the cultural realm and the most distant in the moral realm. This threefold distancing defines them as "Others," and their excessive otherness deprives them of rights, so we can exercise uncontrolled violence against them.

The doubling of the enmity relationship also resurfaces closer to home in conflicts opposing modern states. Thus, Clausewitz distinguishes between "armed observation," which is, properly speaking, "the continuation of policy by other means," and "war of extermination," which targets total destruction of the adversary. Carl Schmitt also distinguishes two types of war: political wars, which are limited clashes, and moral wars, which are characterized by their violence and inhumanity. In fact, for both authors, the excessive violence of some warlike confrontations is due to the fact that they are *moral wars* that transcend politics. They discredit the enemy group and make it "a monster that must not only be defeated but also utterly destroyed."[13] *Moral wars* disobey the logic that makes the enemy the most distant in physical and cultural space, and the most foreign in the moral space. In such wars, physical and cultural proximity does not exclude maximum moral defectiveness.

According to a recent book by René Girard, the Clausewitzian distinction between two types of war has itself become unstable.[14] The transformation of political enmity into moral enmity is now the normal evolution of armed conflict and in Europe has characterized military clashes since the Napoleonic Wars. This gradual fading away of the difference between "armed observation" and "war of annihilation" indicates, according to him, the disappearance of *war* as an institution designed to limit violence, and its replacement by even more deadly forms of conflict. According to Carl Schmitt in *The Nomos of the Earth*, it is the existence outside of Europe of an "unoccupied" space where it was possible to give free reign to violence that long limited the violence of European wars.[15] The doubling of the "friendsfoes" relation was still playing its normal role, but at the planetary scale in a conception of the world in which Europe was the center. It is the disappearance of this sacrificial space outside of nations' borders that explains, according to him, the intensity and violence of the wars in the twentieth century.

These two analyses are in fact complementary. The advent of wars of extermination in Europe went hand in hand with obsession with the enemy within, with hatred of the "Other on the inside," whether communist, bourgeois, or Jewish: the enemy that absolutely had to be tracked down and

destroyed. The order that used to distribute the two forms of the enemy relation in accordance with physical and cultural distance has now disappeared.
The most dangerous enemy is also the closest. The mechanism designed to
shift violence away from those close to us and onto faraway, sacrificable victims has ceased to function.

The Traitor and Reason

Going back to the example of the Hautefaye crime, the purpose of chapter
4 is to discover what distinguishes political violence from ordinary violence,
what separates political antagonism from everyday animosity. Only its
self-justifying capacity defines an instance of violence as political. Political
violence is violence that legitimates itself through violence, through the fact
that it occurs and through the violent reactions that it provokes. This is why
it always challenges the state monopoly of legitimate violence. All political
violence shifts and redraws the line separating "friends" from "foes," and at
the same time changes the physical and moral borders of the state. Consequently, it inevitably leads to the creation of a "friends-foes" division among
those who used to be "friends."

This is illustrated by the traitor in Jean-Paul Sartre's *Critique of Dialectical Reason*.[16] When traitors appear, the enemies who are most "Other" have
returned inside the state, in other words, in the space closest to "friends,"
and since these enemies are the most "Other," it is permissible to exercise
the greatest violence against them. Traitors are both the closest, most similar
enemies, and the furthest, most foreign foes. This is why they are also the
most dangerous, the ones who have to be eradicated at all cost if we want to
succeed in conquering the outside enemy. The figure of the traitor reverses the
logic of territory. The latter placed the most dangerous enemies outside and
at the furthest distance; they were the ones against whom the most extreme
violence could be used. Traitors, like sacrificial victims properly speaking,
come from closer to home—in fact, from too close to home, because they are
literally part of the community, which is why they, unlike sacrificial victims,
fail to protect us from our violence.[17]

Analysis of the Cambodian genocide shows how the traitor figure
emerges in a state's violence against its members. It shows that it is at the

point of new foundation, which is the point when the traitor is eliminated, that political antagonism and ordinary reasons for animosity tend to converge and intertwine. This is a radical failure of politics, an inability of violence to legitimize itself and transform into political violence that rallies and brings together. The disappearance of the monopoly of legitimate violence, the failure to get the violence of "friends" to converge on the same "foes," leads the former to tear one another to pieces, and "rational actors" to use political violence for their private advantage. This example and others show that reason does not escape the play of violence. It is thus not of itself and by nature that reason is the "Other of violence." Public reason's capacity to resolve disputes through compromise, through recourse to just, equitable solutions, rests on the peace imposed by the sovereign's superior violence. Outside of the area pacified by the holder of the monopoly of legitimate violence, reason fails to escape violence. It turns into an instrument of ever more systematic, ever more *insane* violence. Contrary to what we would like to believe, reason does not transcend the political order for which we would like it to be the foundation. Only mastery of reciprocal violence by stronger violence, and its shift to acceptable targets, allows reason to emerge as the "Other of violence."

Exchange and Charity

Chapter 5 returns to the theme of the first: "indifference." What creates an obstacle to the convergence of violence onto a unique victim and prevents the traitor from uniting the whole community against him or her is "indifference." More specifically, the conditions that make such indifference possible are what lead to the genocidal inflation in which more and more victims are required as they become "worth" less and less. By systematically destroying the traditional solidarity relations in Cambodian society and radically fragmenting the relationships among individuals, the Khmer Rouge established the conditions for complete indifference to others. By abolishing money, in other words, exchange, they instituted the convergence of private conflicts and political animosity, thus eliminating any way for people to defend themselves or improve their lot, other than through political rivalry. On one hand, they destroyed the conditions for transfer of violence, and, on the other, they reduced the means of expressing conflict to only one form, thereby ensuring that clashes would always escalate. This failure in instituting political modernity suggests *a contrario* the conditions for a more successful ground-laying, an institution of politics that effectively protects people against their violence by expelling it outside the community.

In line with the thesis defended by René Girard, we can think that, historically, Christianity has played a fundamental role in the transformation of solidarity/hostility relationships that made it possible to establish social indifference and create a monopoly of legitimate violence. In order to see this, we have, however, to conceive of Christianity as a set of practices rather than as a system of belief. Indeed, it is neither necessary nor useful to interpret Christian Revelation in an essentially cognitive manner, as is sometimes suggested in *Things Hidden since the Foundation of the World*, and as many commentators and critics of Girard have tended to do since then.[18]

Conceived of as actions rather than as beliefs or psychological or moral dispositions, charity and forgiveness have been the primary agents of the change in behavior that, in the West, has gradually reduced violence's effectiveness in spontaneously leading back to peace. Charity, for example in the parable of the Good Samaritan, is the recommendation that we should not reserve our aid for those with whom we are related by reciprocal obligations. We should extend it to all. This recommendation is not a negation of traditional obligations, but rather *excessive* in relation to them. However, it inevitably weakens those obligations because it does not divide agents into opposing groups: those with respect to whom we have duties and those with respect to whom we do not. Charity recommends giving those who are in need precedence over those with whom we are linked by exclusive obligations. Forgiveness transforms a transgression, namely, the rejection or abandonment of the duty to take vengeance, into an ideal of excellence and perfection. Consequently, it *naturalizes* vengeance. It transforms the obligation to take vengeance into a sin, in other words, into a "weakness," a spontaneous reaction that is all the more difficult to suppress when the affront is major. This has made it possible for forgiveness to accommodate vengeance and live with it. Rather than rejecting vengeance out of hand, forgiveness gradually undermines it by condemning it all the more strongly when the wrong is benign. Charity and forgiveness, taken as model forms of behavior, have destroyed, little by little, the traditional obligations of solidarity and violence. They have disarmed them and reduced their capacity to structure communities into distinct groups.

Yet neither charity nor forgiveness presupposes the victim's innocence, the nonguilt of the person who is forgiven or the merit of the person with whom we share. Forgiveness teaches us not to make our enemies our victims, but it does not proclaim their innocence. Charity recommends that we should help even those with whom we have no reciprocal obligations. As actions, charity and forgiveness suffice to break the unanimity against the victim because they place care for the other above any obligation to commit violence. They also have the advantage of being able to spontaneously deconstruct violent unanimity in a retrospective manner, so to speak, once it has already occurred, once we are beyond the moment of mimetic enthusiasm that founds it and in which those who forgive today may have participated yesterday. Because forgiveness and charity do not directly address the beliefs of agents but aim to reform their actions, they are models of behavior that give people the possibility to act otherwise, without first having to change their beliefs. In fact, the evolution of the relationship between action and knowledge is the opposite in this case, and just as killing victims is proof par excellence of their guilt in the crazy logic of their torturers, it is the practice of charity and forgiveness that creates the possibility of the victims' innocence.

Charity and forgiveness free people of their traditional obligations. They give them a moral justification that authorizes them to not fulfill those duties. In this, these virtues are ambiguous because traditional obligations are very often in contradiction with individuals' interests. If it were possible, each would abandon them, not as a whole and in all circumstances because they are sometimes useful, but from time to time, when convenient and safe. Charity and forgiveness provide agents with an "ideal" that allows them to resist their obligations without being at fault. They provide an excuse that makes it possible to renounce solidarity obligations when they go against self-interest. This is why it is impossible to reduce the historical consequences of these values to actions that have been done out of charity and forgiveness. On the contrary, what has played at least as big a role is the way that, by weakening traditional obligations, these virtues have made new forms of interaction possible.

First among the new forms of interaction is exchange, conceived of as a rule of behavior among those not bound by any reciprocal solidarity obligation. Exchange can play this role because, as Adam Smith saw, it is a law unto itself. In fact, modern exchange can be established and exist only among those who are not linked by any reciprocal obligation, solidarity, or duty to commit violence. This is why it can perform its function properly only in the shadow of the monopoly of legitimate violence, within the space pacified by that violence. Unlike charity, exchange replaces rather than exceeds traditional obligations. Consequently, it establishes the indifference that it tends to turn into a virtue. Owing nothing to others gradually becomes an obvious truth that each accepts as a basic given of life in society. This rule of behavior creates opportunities for new conflicts, which are fertile soil for new "legitimate" violent acts that establish new groups, which in turn challenge the state's monopoly.

Social Justice and the End of Territories

It is in relation to these new conflicts that we have to understand the development of the idea of social justice in modern states. Social justice is a response both to conflicts and to the indifference that exchange engenders. It can be considered the result of a "marriage" between the ideal of charity and exchange conceived of as a rule of behavior. It is also a new attempt to reduce the solidarity/hostility space to two areas, in other words, to make all members of the state "friends" and to expel from the territory the conflicts introduced by class struggle. It refuses to assign guilt and recognizes only victims who have the same rights as everyone else: their rights have been violated, but by no one in particular. The paradoxical nature of this justice, which recognizes neither crimes nor guilt, could be considered a sign of inconsistency. However, we should instead see in it the result of an effort to reject all sacrificial temptation and to prevent the reappearance of "domestic enemies," of which the state has to be purged.

Heir of the social contract tradition, a theory of justice like that of John Rawls is based on the idea of *conditional* rationality and solidarity, in other words, on the idea of a form of solidarity the only condition of which is the other's disposition to engage in solidarity in return. Conditional solidarity corresponds to the ideal of a community that claims to exclude only *those who exclude themselves* by refusing to engage in solidarity. Yet this "universality" can exist only among "friends" who are the "same." This is because, in the last analysis, it is the guarantees and exclusions characteristic of the state holding the monopoly of legitimate violence that establish the "condition" of conditional reciprocity. Finally, *those who exclude themselves* are always those whom the state excludes. Indeed, Rawls recognizes this implicitly since, according to him, social justice can exist only within a closed society, a territorial society that institutes a fundamental moral difference between those who are inside and those who are outside the state. However, as Seyla Benhabib notes, those whom a state declares to be foreign are, by definition, subject to laws of which they are not the authors.[19] They *do not exclude themselves.*

Territories and Sanctuaries

Thus we are back to square one, the point of departure. The purpose of social justice is to achieve the goal that has been implicit in the modern state from its beginning: to transform into "friends" all those living within its borders. Its objective is for none to be in need, no matter what the reason or circumstances. In this sense, it extends to all of the state's territory the perfect solidarity characteristic of the first circle of solidarity. Because it reduces the question of justice to need, thus separating it from the question of whether some people cause the unhappiness of others, social justice establishes fraternity among all members of the state. Historically, this domestic order has always required a certain relationship with an "outside." Initially, it required the presence of an adversary outside the state, a political enemy in Schmitt's sense. From the beginning it has also required the presence of "Others" who are even more "external" and "foe" than political enemies. This requirement has grown in importance as the role of earlier structures has diminished within the state. Despite these efforts to expel enmity far from the community, the "foe," in the framework of the class struggle, reemerged within the state. However, this "inside" was also an "outside" because the international social clash crossed borders and rejected the division of the world into opposing states. We needed two wars, genocide, the Holocaust, and the nuclear threat to manage to fit this transnational animosity into the territorial mold. The "European Civil War," to borrow the title of the book by Ernst Nolte,[20] finally gave birth to a clear territorial divide: the East/West division that took the physical form of the Iron Curtain. This conveniently simple opposition has now disappeared.

Recently, we have replaced the figures of traitor and class enemy, which social justice tried to eliminate, by those of terrorist and illegal immigrant. They are indeed enemies within, but they also indicate a change in the relationship between the interior and exterior. They suggest the end of territory as a principle structuring violent oppositions, and, consequently, a deep transformation of the state as the holder of the monopoly of legitimate violence. We need only look around ourselves to see that the territorial system is being replaced by that of sanctuary, in other words, by private rather than public organization of shared space, the homogeneity of which yields to a separation between safe places and places abandoned to violence and disorder. The topology of territory is that of a surface on which all parts are in contact and the whole is isotropic, since each part of the territory is just as much a part as any other. In contrast, the topological model behind the sanctuary structure is that of a network, made of hubs and linking spokes. Depending on the place, the network of sanctuaries is more or less dense, communication between protected places more or less strong, but everywhere the space between the links in the net is less politically important. This fragmentation of territory means the state is giving up the monopoly of legitimate violence to a certain extent and, at the same time, renouncing the ideals of equality and social justice that used to give it meaning and stability. Indeed, the transformation of hostility rules is inseparable from the transformation of solidarity rules. Reorganization of the political space goes hand in hand with a new moral economics of violence, of which the fundamental concepts are security and "collateral damage."

It also means, as René Girard has rightly seen, the end of wars properly speaking and their replacement with what we can call "states of violence":[21] long-term conflicts that do not oppose "equal" adversaries, but multiple powers, some of which are private, others public, some national or regional, and others international. Contrary to wars that have a beginning and end sanctioned by international law, and that consequently remain ritualized conflicts to a certain extent, "states of violence" have neither a beginning nor an end clearly marked in time. Just as the difference between the two forms of the enmity relationship (adversariality and hostility) are no longer embodied in physical distance, now there is no clear separation between times of peace and times of violence and conflict.

The new division of international space into protected sanctuaries and zones more or less abandoned to violence and disorder suggests the *end of politics* as we have known it for the last four or five centuries. The primary players in the military clashes raging today include not only states, but also terrorist organizations and private security firms. Either involuntarily in the former case or voluntarily in the latter, states partly abandon conflict management to other actors. This new division of the labor of violence is gradually undermining its properly political dimension, in other words, violence's capacity to legitimize itself. Initially, it leads to a dissociation of the space where the violence occurs and the place where it has political value. Thus, al-Qaeda finds its legitimacy in an international Muslim community that supplies it with fighters, rather than in the populations within which it exercises violence. Similarly, the military action of the allies and private security companies in Iraq and Afghanistan is legitimate only in the eyes of their countries of origin and suppliers of funding. This dissociation of the location of where violence happens and the place where it is considered legitimate prevents it from occurring where it can play its political role of rallying and bringing together. Thus violence has lost the positive value that made it something other than a simple exercise in destruction.

In fact, this dissociation was already the case of colonial violence, which was legitimate in the eyes of the people in the colonizing countries (and settlers), but not in the eyes of local populations. The only thing that has changed is the structure of the international space resulting from globalization and the development of new technology that makes it easier to act from afar. This transformation of the international space is not something exterior to the dynamics of the system. The colonial expansion and the economic and technological developments that later made decolonization possible are direct consequences of the evolution of the territorial political order. The disappearance of the third circle of the space of violence, in other words, an absolute periphery to which violence could be exported without ever returning to the center, signifies that shifting the location of violence is no longer a way to protect the community.

◆ ◆ ◆

The violent acts that states commit against their own citizens are thus not contingent accidents that occur outside of the modern political order. They are, on the contrary, events whose occurrence is deeply inscribed in its structure. They reveal failures of the mechanism that established the modern political order: the transfer of violence onto acceptable victims. These repeated failures were in fact inevitable. The process of abandoning traditional bonds that, by destroying groups, has made it possible to establish the monopoly of legitimate violence necessarily leads to the emergence of new "friends-foes" groups that challenge the territorial division of friendship and enmity ties. In consequence, this was just as inevitable as the crumbling of this order itself, which we are seeing today.

The establishment of the monopoly of legitimate violence at the heart of the modern political order supposes the disappearance of conditions that make possible the normal resolution of the mimetic crisis: the convergence of the violence of all against a single victim. The modern political order is possible only when the sacrificial mechanism that establishes the sacred has become impossible. *The political order thus corresponds to the moment when sacrifice, understood in the strict sense, becomes barren.* However, the modern political order is based on an economics of violence that has the same nature as sacrifice: the shift of violence onto acceptable victims, even though the transfer of violence is less economical in this case. This is why it is not surprising that political violence has so often been thought about as belonging to the category of sacrifice: sacrifice for the nation, for the working class, for whatever cause, so long as it goes beyond and transcends the individual. For, like sacrifice, political violence is a form of violence designed to protect against violence; it justifies itself by its intended end. *One of the fundamental theses of this book is that this "sacrifice" demanded by political violence has become barren today: it is now unable to protect us from violence or give rise to a stable order.*

CHAPTER 1

Solidarity and Enmity

In Kibungo, N'tarama, Kanzenze and the town of Nyamata, anyone who publicly opposed the genocide, by word or deed, risked being executed or condemned to kill a victim on the spot. Everybody had to participate in some way, to be involved in the killings, destruction and looting, or to contribute monetarily. Still, I repeat: no one was seriously threatened with physical harm for reluctance to use a machete.... Compared to your neighbour who killed every day, you could seem lazy or recalcitrant and, really, no competition, but you did have to show yourself worthy by reddening your hands that one time.

—Jean Hatzfeld

This quotation,[1] taken from the study Jean Hatzfeld conducted in a prison on Rwandans who had been convicted of genocide, suggests that there was, with respect to the supposedly universal (since everybody had to take part in some way) participation in murdering Tutsis, some space for, perhaps not refusal, but at least *abstinence* and *reticence*. What is the nature of this space? What makes it possible? How can one withdraw while not opposing; how is it possible to be "recalcitrant," lazy, or "no competition" in the massacre game, and what does that mean exactly? What is the signification of such "passive" participation in collective violence?

Participation and Abstention

According to the killers' accounts in *Machete Season*, during the genocide it was impossible to oppose the massacres publicly or to defend a Tutsi without running the risk of either being executed oneself or being forced to kill—perhaps the very person whom one was trying to protect—in order to prove one's loyalty to the common cause. However, it was perfectly possible to demonstrate reticence, to be "recalcitrant." Anyone could essentially avoid the common "task" of murder by invoking other obligations or some special weakness, or even by paying someone to kill in his or her stead. Christopher Browning reports quite similar information concerning policemen in the German reserve who, at the beginning of the Final Solution, before the huge death camp industry was established, committed mass murders of Jewish civilians.[2] None of the uncooperative policemen were ever seriously punished or threatened for refusing to kill so long as the refusal did not take the form of political opposition. If it was portrayed as the result of a certain "weakness" of character, a personal inability with respect to large-scale murder of civilians of all types, old people, women, children, the refusal was accepted. So long as it was presented as a failure or fault flowing from a lack of courage, nonparticipation was tolerated and had no serious consequences. In Rwanda, as behind the front lines of Operation Barbarossa, it was possible to be a "massacre slacker."

The essential was to show that one was worthy, in other words, that one approved of the genocidal policy, or at least one had to not show one's disapproval, even if it meant revealing oneself to be especially weak, incompetent, or clumsy when carrying out orders. So long as one was in agreement "in principle," refusing or being uncooperative resulted in no serious punishment. The presence of "incompetents" enhanced, by comparison, the prestige of those who were motivated and efficient. According to Hatzfeld and Browning, it is clear that there was also rivalry among many of those carrying out orders, the executors, with respect to "doing the job well," carrying out their killing "work" in an exemplary manner. Fulfilling the "violent duty" was given a positive value and well considered, though those who tried too hard were often criticized.

Afterward, murderers often say that they had "no choice," that they were forced or even threatened with death. This is possible, but the data collected by Browning, Hatzfeld, and others[3] suggest that many who could have abstained without placing themselves in grave danger nonetheless participated in the slaughter of innocents, who were often their neighbors or even their relatives.[4] We also know that the massive executions of Jewish civilians sometimes turned into shows that soldiers on leave and civilians attended, and that the latter sometimes asked the killers if they too could "try their hand." Researchers confronted with this kind of information wonder why so many ordinary people found it so easy to help murder those they had been living with for years. The incomprehensibility is all the greater since the mass murderers were generally neither bloodthirsty fanatics nor trained killers. They were neither true-believing Nazis nor members of the Interahamwe Militia. Why did they agree to do it? Why did they so easily comply with the norm that transformed a mass crime, if not into a moral imperative, at least into a socially acceptable practice?

Here, we have to resist the temptation to express moral indignation, which obscures understanding. Of course, we wonder why so many ordinary individuals agreed to participate in massacres when refusing was relatively danger free and would have had no dramatic consequences. However, this way of framing the question is misleading. It leads us to think that what was in question was an abstract individual choice. This is the question that, scandalized, we ask the murderers after the fact. The question reflects our misunderstanding, but not the context in which the murderers made their decisions. They often answer that they had no choice. We know that this is false in a sense because they could have abstained without placing themselves in serious danger. Yet, perhaps in another sense, they are telling the truth. That they had no choice would then mean that the response was automatic, that the question did not even arise.

As Harald Welzer shows, mass murderers make the decision to kill in a context that is completely different from the one familiar to us. It takes place in a world where extermination has become socially acceptable and is praised by moral authorities.[5] The real question is actually: How are social norms changed to make the unthinkable acceptable? What collective alchemy transforms violence against defenseless innocents into a duty, a quasi-moral obligation? The question of individual choice does indeed arise, but with respect to those who actively reject or oppose the violence, not with respect to those who, from near or far, participate in and endorse the massacres.[6] It also does not arise with respect to those who simply managed to get out, to avoid participating while they could.

Indeed, the actions of those whose refusal is limited to a form of *abstinence* or reticence to commit violence are entirely consistent with the moral space defined by massacres. Those who are "lazy" or uncooperative neither contradict nor reject the genocidal policy: they simply admit their personal failure, their inability to put into practice the social imperative of massacre. They do not reject genocide. They simply want to avoid the sordid task of murder. They want to avoid getting their hands dirty. They are massacre free riders. Their abstinence excludes neither indirect participation nor reaping the benefits of the crime. It is not a challenge to the violence, but an admission of personal weakness. Moreover, it is judged, tolerated, lightly punished or not, depending on the "moral" criteria of the situation, such as elimination of European Jews or extermination of Rwandan Tutsis. What is permitted, what can be excused, is non-participation, but *not opposition to the goal.* It is acceptable that an individual admit his or her inability to kill because by recognizing his or her failure, he or she does not defy the murderous norm but rather reasserts its well-foundedness. Accepting the goal, or at least not rejecting it openly, is the fundamental condition for nonparticipation. The possibility of avoiding getting involved in massacres, in the act of killing, exists only within the space defined by agreement with genocide. This is why the question does not arise, why it is never asked of those who cite their "weakness" to escape the labor of murder. Those who avoid participating in this way do not reject genocide: they adopt a different individual strategy within the range defined by the duty to commit genocide.

Am I My Brother's Keeper?[7]

In *The Village of Cannibals* Alain Corbin analyzes an instance of collective violence that occurred in Dordogne in the midst of the Franco-Prussian War. On August 16, 1870, at a time when things were beginning to go badly for

France, a fair was held in Hautefaye. At the fair, before a crowd of nearly eight hundred people, a young noble from the local area, Alain de Monéys, was tortured for two hours and then burned alive in the public square. He was accused of being a Prussian, a spy, and a terrorist working for the enemy because a number of barns in the area had been burned not long before. At first sight, the event has all the features of the mechanism by which the sacrificial crisis is resolved, as described by René Girard in *Violence and the Sacred*: a spontaneous phenomenon of collective violence that converges on an arbitrarily chosen victim and purges the community of all its hatred and frustration. Indeed, at the end of the chapter that he devotes to a detailed reconstruction of the murder, Alain Corbin notes that "René Girard's analysis of the mechanics of victimization comes to mind."[8] However, while there are striking similarities between what occurred in the village of Hautefaye and the resolution of the sacrificial crisis as described by Girard, there are also significant differences.

On that day, when Alain de Monéys arrived at the Hautefaye Fair, he was challenged by peasants who accused his cousin, Camille de Maillard, of having cried "Vive la République!" Alain, though he was a sickly man, had just had his "weak constitution" exemption from military service rescinded in order to enlist in the emperor's troops and fight against the invader. He refused to accept that his cousin could have said something "so unpatriotic" at a time when the empire was in danger. It was this rejection of their accusation that attracted the crowd's anger onto him. In fact, a few days before, Camille de Maillard had said things in the public square that were much more scandalous. He had announced to all within hearing that "The Emperor is done for . . . he is out of ammunition."[9] Peasants who were outraged by this pessimistic (though accurate) analysis of the military situation had asked him about this on the sixteenth, as he arrived at the Hautefaye Fair. Quick to sense the danger, de Maillard had decamped immediately. Alain de Monéys, who arrived after Camille had fled, really was therefore a substitute victim, one onto whom the violence was shifted since the original target was no longer available. He was chosen arbitrarily simply because he was related to Camille de Maillard. He was accused of collaborating with the enemy even though he was preparing to join the army. His only fault was probably that he did not run away fast enough, or that he thought that he did not need to run away.

Alain de Monéys was soon accused of having cried "Vive la République!"

himself, and the crowd, persuaded that this time they had a real "Prussian" in their hands, attacked him. He was hit and beaten. At one point there was an attempt to hang him, but then there was a change of plan. Corbin's theory is that hanging would perhaps have been too quick, for de Monéys's suffering was to last two hours. Finally, unconscious but perhaps still alive, he was burned in a bonfire around which participants gave patriotic speeches. As one of the witnesses said during the enquiry: "the way those lunatics saw it, everyone had to have a hand in torturing the victim. One person struck the man, then stood aside so that somebody else could have a turn, and so on until they'd all had a shot."[10] At the beginning of the incident, the village priest jumped over his garden wall with a revolver in his hand to try to get Alain de Monéys away, but he quickly saw that if he persisted in trying to protect him, he would suffer the same fate. He thus abandoned the victim, and had wine brought from his cellar, which he himself served to all who asked! A little later, Alain de Monéys, already injured but helped by a few faithful friends, managed to climb the stairs of the mayor's house, but the latter barred him from entering. Shortly afterward the door of a bar was shut brutally in his face when he tried to take refuge. He was rejected everywhere and by all—it indeed seems that there was a unanimous opinion against the "Prussian," the "Republican," the universal enemy of all the peasants, who were faithful supporters of Napoleon III, had sons on the front lines, or were themselves soon to leave for a war that was going badly. He was the scapegoat victim on which all hatred and resentment converged.

This was certainly the case, but the unanimity was not as clear as it seems at first sight. To begin with, there were the friends who accompanied de Monéys, supported him, helped him, and tried to protect him throughout his ordeal. Of course, they were brutally pushed away from time to time, but they were not attacked directly. They were fended off like irritating flies, but not pursued like enemies. There were also, and above all, some six hundred people who did not take part in the killing, but who also did not take action on behalf of de Monéys. Indeed, it is estimated that, on that day, there were around eight hundred people at the Hautefaye Fair, and that around two hundred participated directly in the lynching. What were the others doing? They were either watching with more or less interest, or simply going about their business.

In Hautefaye, thus, as in Rwanda and in the reserve units of the German police, it was possible to not participate. However, to oppose, as the priest briefly tried to do, was to run the risk of becoming a victim oneself. The friends who tried to help and protect Alain de Monéys did not try, like the priest, to be obstacles, to confront the crowd. They pleaded before it, constantly repeating that Alain de Monéys was neither a traitor nor a "Prussian," but a young nobleman from the area, a municipal councillor known for his generosity, that they had only to ask and everyone would testify to his good heart, and so on. They did not reject the policy of violence against "Prussians" and enemies of the empire, but argued that Alain de Monéys was innocent. Finally, it was clearly quite possible to remain a spectator, fascinated or indifferent, and to turn one's eyes away to continue discussing the cow that one was trying to buy or sell.

As analyzed by René Girard in *Violence and the Sacred*, the functioning of the mechanism for resolving the sacrificial crisis excludes the possibility of such distance and such indifference to the victim. At the climax of the crisis, the killing that brings back peace requires "unanimity less one": the convergence of all hatred onto a single victim. During the crisis, violence gradually invades all of the community. It eats away at differences among individuals and transforms them into doubles with nothing to distinguish one from the other. It is at the point of the most extreme violence, when differences among individuals have disappeared, that there is a convergence on the victim. At that stage, there should no longer be any indifferent spectators or defenders of the victim.[11] Why did Alain de Monéys' friends never completely abandon him? If violence is mimetic and contagious, as Girard argues, why was the contagion limited in this case to two hundred participants, around a quarter of those who were present?

Was it because of the composition of the crowd, because of differences among the individuals assembled for the Hautefaye Fair that could have created obstacles to mimetic contagion and prevented the violence from propagating to all? In fact, the crowd was relatively homogenous. There were neither many women on the Hautefaye fairgrounds that day nor many children because, as Corbin notes, a fair is something for men old enough to engage in trade. Most of the people were peasants, landowners, tenant farmers, craftsmen, and minor noblemen or their representatives. Thus it seems that among those present there were no major differences isolating certain people into closed subgroups that could explain the containment of

the violent contagion. Why did only some persist in hatred against Alain
de Monéys, while others just went about their business? Why, despite the
efforts of the "fanatics" to ensure that all played a part in torturing the victim,
did so many remain indifferent to and outside of the violence?

In his analysis of the tragedy in Hautefaye, Alain Corbin insists on the
fact that most of the participants in the fair did not know one another. They
came from a number of places in the surrounding area. The center of the village, located close to the fairground, had around fifteen houses where some
forty-five people lived. Nearly all of the eight hundred people assembled that
day thus came from elsewhere, and while some of them had met or glimpsed
each other before, few really knew one another. At the trial that followed the
incident, it was revealed that the twenty-one accused, who were considered
to be the leaders, did not know one another and did not know the victim.[12]
Corbin insists on this, rightly, to show that the murder "was not . . . the work
of the inhabitants of Hautefaye"[13] and that the "kinship structure of the vicin-
ity has nothing to teach us, nor is there much to learn from an understanding
of the tensions that existed within the village community."[14] The crowd at the
Hautefaye Fair was neither a harmonious village community nor one that
was torn apart by hatred and jealousy, but the anonymous crowd of those
who meet to trade. The enquiry also established that the accused were normal workers, some were heads of families and none had had any clashes with
justice. The violence was therefore also not the work of unemployed vaga-
bonds or criminal elements, but of ordinary people that chance alone had
brought together and transformed into murderers. But why did the event
leave so many others in peace?

According to Alain Corbin, the Hautefaye tragedy was a *political crime*.
The reason it was so shocking to people at the time is because "after nineteen
years of universal suffrage, murder and mayhem had ceased to be acceptable
forms of political expression."[15] In the eyes of Alain Corbin, the murder of
Alain de Monéys was a singular, isolated manifestation of an obsolete form
of political violence, a vestige of a world of violent behavior that had virtually
disappeared and was gradually giving way to new forms of collective violence.
What forms?

> The "modern" form of urban carnage, perpetrated by troops armed with
> rifles and artillery.

The nineteenth-century form of mass killing, the response to obses-
sive fears of frenzied mob violence, was a disciplined affair, inspired by
images borrowed from the battlefield. Death was now instantaneous. It
had shed those traits that once linked it to torture. Its ritual was simplified.
Its narration became elliptical. Its traces were quickly erased. This new, permissible, understated form of bloodbath was calming and reassuring. Too
little attention has been paid to the fundamental importance of mass killing in nineteenth-century French history. The violent events of 1831–1835,
June 1848, December 1851, and May 1871 have rightly been perceived and
analyzed as episodes in a single revolutionary process. The crushing of mass
movements has been interpreted as a manifestation of repressive will and
nothing more. Yet it is as if no regime could establish itself firmly until it
had proved its capacity to bathe in the blood of the monster: the angry
populace, the frenzied mob.[16]

Corbin says that Hautefaye is a "monadnock," a geological remnant from a
strange past, a manifestation of the ancestral monster, the deranged crowd,
that modern violence is going to try to overcome. It seems to me that, on the
contrary, while the Hautefaye murder did indeed echo the past, it was not so
far from the modern forms of collective violence that Corbin is trying to distinguish it from. Alain de Monéys's torture certainly had archaic, primitive
features, but it was also "modern" in many ways. What made the Hautefaye
tragedy, with its special mixture of indifference and violent passion, possible
is precisely what makes possible modern, regulated, orderly massacres, which
follow a simplified ritual.

A Modern Crowd

The most crucial of the modern aspects of the Hautefaye crime concerns those
who committed it: it was the deed of an anonymous crowd. The murderers
knew neither their victim nor one another. At the time of the gathering, at the
beginning of the incident, they were individuals from various different places
who had come to take part in the fair. Of course, some of them knew Alain
de Monéys, since he was singled out because of his cousin, and there were also
the friends who tried to defend him. However, all of them were anonymous

individuals in the sense that nothing distinguished them from other members of the crowd. No one was anyone in particular, whom a difference would have separated from the others so as to confer some form of ascendance or authority. During a fair, the differences among individuals in other contexts disappear. All that remains are sellers and buyers. When the violence began, neither the mayor's authority nor that of the priest could stand up to the crowd. Distinctions that in normal times ensured the influence of some over others had disappeared. However, even before the violence erupted, the network of differences that normally separated and organized individuals within society had yielded to another form of relationship. People had come there to buy and sell. Commercial exchanges were the only ties that bound them, and they made them all equal and separate. The relationships were temporary, had their own limits, and, once ended, left each as free as before. The crowd was modern because it brought together isolated individuals rather than people linked to one another by reciprocal solidarity obligations.

The solidarity obligations that link each individual to certain others, whether or not those other people are there, impose on a real or potential crowd an invisible structure that resurfaces when a conflict breaks out. This invisible structure then splits the crowd into opposing groups, clans, tribes, villages, or nations, to which each sees himself or herself as belonging. It is because the Hautefaye crowd contained no structure of this type, no division to separate it into different camps, that the violent convergence occurred so quickly. In fact, it preceded the violence. The least opportunity for conflict, an insult (even an imaginary insult) targeting the emperor, was sufficient to make all turn together against a single victim. This pretext for violence also reveals the level of association where the crowd found its unity: the nation, the emperor. In other words, its unity was in the "imagined community" whose horizon and capacity for inclusion were situated beyond any real, concrete relationships among those present.[17] This suggests that there were no forms of unity at lower levels, for example, nobles versus peasants, or the people of Hautefaye versus people from elsewhere, which could have broken the crowd into opposing groups. This is why the convergence was so rapid, from the beginning of the incident. The choice of victim preceded the violence, as is the case in a ritual sacrifice, but it did not, as is the case during the sacrificial crisis, result from the spontaneous convergence of "mimesis of the antagonist."[18]

The absence of links of solidarity also explains why, at Hautefaye, it was possible to remain a detached spectator and abstain from participating in the conflict. There is no sense in calling out "Quick, quick! Come! They are killing one of ours!" if there are no "ours." If there are no ties both uniting individuals and dividing the crowd into opposing groups, there is no reason to call for help. Each is left to himself or herself; no one is expected to come. Unless one has nothing better to do than to join in the game of murder, why would one intercede? Because violence is fascinating? Of course, but it is also frightening. The traditional ties of solidarity impose duties of violence and assistance that extend beyond the space and time of the original conflict. Those duties require individuals to abandon their usual occupations to respond to a greater emergency. A sufficiently dense framework of traditional solidarity ties ensures that no one can be a spectator. You have to come, take part, fight, be for or against. It also guarantees that, unless there is some accident, those who come in aid of the victim will not find themselves alone like the priest, isolated in the face of a crowd of "maniacs." Solidarity obligations procure allies.

In Hautefaye, the situation was completely different. Each could continue to do whatever he or she was doing or watch the event from a comfortable distance; they could enjoy the show or deplore the excess of violence. In the absence of solidarity ties, no one was required to help or intervene. Moreover, there was nothing to ensure that those who tried to defend the victim would not be condemning themselves to the same fate as him, that anyone would come to help them either. Individuals not bound by solidarity ties have many reasons not to intervene. They may be afraid, they may have something better to do, or they may be secretly happy about what is happening to the victim. It does not matter. Once individuals are freed from their traditional obligations of help and violence, each is free to join in the violence or to walk away. However, because the disappearance of reciprocal ties of solidarity transforms us all into isolated individuals, it makes it improbable that anyone will help the victim. The normal reaction is to not get involved. This is why the question of personal decision is relevant only in the case of those who actively oppose the violence.

Traditional ties of solidarity have an ambiguous relationship with violence. On one hand, they protect those who are attacked because they provide them with support. They can, in consequence, dissuade potential attackers because they increase the stakes, so to speak: solidarity ties make it more difficult to engage in violence and make aggression more dangerous for the aggressor. On the other hand, and for the same reason that they provide each with allies, they prevent the conflict from remaining contained. Solidarity ties ensure that a violent conflict never concerns present adversaries exclusively, but always threatens to spread to others and to include more and more individuals and groups. While solidarity obligations assemble individuals into different groups, they at the same time create oppositions among the groups. On one hand, solidarity obligations can function like preventive measures by creating obstacles to unleashing violence, but on the other hand, once violence has begun, they facilitate and accelerate the contagion of the conflict.

Yet the absence of solidarity ties proves to have an equally ambiguous role. First, it takes the protection of the group away from the individual. Each individual could, if he or she wanted, remain indifferent to the fate of Alain de Monéys. No one had, properly speaking, an obligation to help him. Each was free to refuse to participate. No one was forced to be associated with the violence, either to help the victim or to attack him. Absence of solidarity ties abandons the victim to violent attackers. It does not prohibit anyone from helping him; it only makes it implausible that one would do so. Simultaneously, withdrawal of the protection of the group, because it abandons the victim to the violent attackers, reduces the violence's capacity to spread. Weak solidarity ties mean not only that violence's only means of spreading is through the agents' spontaneous mimetism, but also that they create obstacles to violent contagion in that they isolate people from one another. In comparison, in traditional societies, sacred obligations strengthen mimetism by imposing duties of vengeance. Disappearance of the ties of reciprocal solidarity dissociates conflicts from the community, and abandons conflict to its spontaneous evolution because the lack of ties limits its contagious power. While solidarity ties prevent the outbreak of violence but facilitate its spread once a conflict has begun, when there are no such ties, conflicts and violence are freer to arise but spread with much more difficulty.

However, it will be objected that the people brought together at the Hautefaye fair were not simply buyers and sellers. They were also heads of families, landowners, tenant farmers, merchants, and craftspersons. They were citizens, and some were perhaps already conscripted and would soon be leaving for war. They were municipal councillors, mayors, and forest rangers. Would it not be false to assert that they had only commercial ties? Were they not integrated into a society structured by domination relationships and subject to obligations more complex than the temporary ties established by anonymous exchange? Certainly. However, the fair created a kind of abstraction or, better, an *épochè*, a bracketing of these dependent relationships. The network of ties and obligations had not disappeared entirely, but for the instant its effects were, so to speak, suspended and existed only through the need to reactivate the relationships later. In his explanation of the Hautefaye tragedy, Corbin employs the category of ritual. He is certainly partly right. The fair was an economic ritual and ancient festival. Like carnivals, with which they are often associated, fairs are a space and time in which usual norms are suspended and where normal social authorities no longer really have complete hold. There is a certain externality to fairs in relation to time and the usual rules of society. However, the "ritual" in this case can also be considered a form of experimental mechanism. From this point of view, the Hautefaye fair was not a social experiment, but resembled a scientific experiment. The fair made real and embodied for a time the abstraction that is the economic market, a system of exchange in which producers and consumers are perfectly equal and where nothing links them with one another other than commercial ties. These ties last only the time of the transaction, which, once finished, frees them of any mutual obligation and leaves them just as free as before.

This reduction of individuals to economic atoms has to be considered a "mechanism" that limits violence and reduces its contagion. However, it limits it in a very special way. It places no boundary on its intensity, quite the contrary. This social arrangement can very well accommodate the most extreme violence. Rather than prohibiting violence, it allows it to ignite, to burn itself up and to finally exhaust itself because it remains contained and does not spontaneously spread to ever more numerous groups and individuals. The ties of solidarity that link people are by definition reciprocal, but they are not necessarily symmetrical. The obligations of some are not unavoidably the mirror image of those of others. While a father owes aid and support to his children, in return they owe him aid, support, and obedience. This is indeed a case of reciprocity, but not of symmetry. In contrast, when ties of solidarity are abandoned, the absence of reciprocity, paradoxically, introduces perfect symmetry among agents. If there is no tie of solidarity between us, I owe you nothing and you owe me nothing either. Our situation is perfectly symmetrical. This symmetry produces a homogenous, isotropic space, where there is no specific location marked by a difference. In this monotonous topology, a topology without topos, one might say, violence sinks as into quicksand, and never manages to spread far from its place of origin.

How does this brake on violence function? Abandoning solidarity obligations limits the contagion of violence to the effects of mimetism alone. The convergence of all against a single victim is a possible configuration of mimetism, but it is not the only one. Just as in the scapegoat mechanism, we are dealing with the spontaneous operation of mimesis, which entails that as the number of people attacking a victim grows, the more attractive the violence becomes. However, what stops the contagiousness of violence in this case and prevents it from spreading to the whole community *is mimesis itself*. Agents, freed of their solidarity obligations, get involved in conflicts and rivalries that bind them to other specific individuals and engender what, following Kant, we can call our "unsocial sociability." The detachment of the "spectators" with respect to the violent incident occurring under their noses is simply a result of the fact that they have something better to do.

It is not simply the fact that each is busy selling a cow, finishing an exciting conversation or transaction, seducing the barmaid, protecting her café from rioters, concluding a deal, or observing the fascinating display of violence from a comfortable distance, and so on: the individuals are also linked, engaged in rivalries that are important to them and that they are not willing to give up without reason. However, those rivalries divide them more than they bring them together. The absence of internal structure, which explains the speed of the crowd's convergence against a single victim, also makes it possible to understand why the violence is only weakly attractive. In a sense, the violence occurs too quickly to be integrated into the conflicts and rivalries that motivate the individuals. This is why it repels as much as it attracts, creates fear as much as it mesmerizes. Since it is displayed to individuals who have no duty to get involved, it reaches its maximum range relatively quickly. It is not easy for it to contaminate those who are too preoccupied by their own private conflicts, their own personal rivalries. The model of their "own" desire, which fascinates them, distances them from the new violence that suddenly erupts into their world.

As I have tried to show elsewhere, here, as in the case of the scapegoat mechanism, we are dealing with a self-regulatory mimetic phenomenon. No conscious rule, no constraint exterior to conflictual mimetism itself prevents the violence from spreading. What prevents the violent incident from contaminating all of the community and causing it to tear itself apart is the fact that there are so many different points of convergence. In other words, this is a special figure of mimetism specific to modern societies that I call "scarcity" in *The Ambivalence of Scarcity*.[19] The social organization of scarcity prevents unanimous convergence of violence against a single victim. When there are no solidarity obligations to force individuals to pay attention to the original conflict and impose on them veritable duties of violence, each will prefer to pursue the objects of his or her own desire, which we generally refer to as "personal interest."

Indifference and the Banality of Evil

In her report on and analysis of the Eichmann trial in Jerusalem, Hannah Arendt coined the expression "the banality of evil" in reference to a fundamental aspect of the SS bureaucrat's attitude to his victims and the way he saw his participation in the Final Solution.[20] She considered that a certain thoughtlessness, a lack of imagination, which created an incapacity to put himself in other people's shoes, in the place of those who suffered the consequences of his actions, was one of Eichmann's characteristic features. During his trial, it seemed that this central player in the extermination of European Jews had never paid much attention to the evils that he inflicted on others. What mainly marked his memories of the time were jurisdiction conflicts with other Nazi bureaucrats who encroached on his prerogatives, and also his superiors' attitudes toward him. Eichmann was not really interested in the people he was sending to their deaths.

Some have taken the "banality of evil" as a psychological thesis. They have understood this absence of thought, this failure to imagine the sufferings of others, as a special disposition of the individual named Eichmann, which would explain the facility with which he planned the deaths of millions of people, of whom, he claimed to feel no special hatred. Others have seen the expression as a way of rendering the crime banal and, finally, exonerating the murderers. I think, on the contrary, that what we have to see in it is an expression of surprise by Arendt, and an *antisacrificial observation*.[21] The "banality of evil" should be seen neither as a moral affirmation about evil—there is nothing "banal" about an evil such as the murder of millions of people—nor as a hypothesis about the authors of such crimes, such that they would suffer from certain intellectual or cognitive deficiencies. The expression "the banality of evil" expresses Hannah Arendt's astonishment when she fully realizes the disproportion between the size of the crime and the individual who committed it.

What struck Arendt during Eichmann's trail was the complete disproportion between the criminal and the crime, between the mean-spirited petit bourgeois eager for promotion in the rigid edifice of bureaucracy, and the monstrous horror of which he was one of the main artisans. "The banality of evil" does not mean that the evil committed by Eichmann was banal, all in all, an ordinary crime. It instead refers to the banality of the criminal, to the fact that there was nothing in the simultaneously grotesque and insipid individual that could lead one to suspect the immensity of the crime of which he had made himself guilty. Eichmann was only a very ordinary man, whom even his monstrous crime did not manage to transform into someone more interesting. The theme of the banality of evil expresses surprise in the face of what we could call the *nonsanctification of the executioner*. The immensity, the horror of the crime lent no greatness to the person who perpetrated it. He did not acquire any sacred aura and, given the contradiction produced by his psychology and manners, it gave him no extraordinary, evil features that would be in line with his actions.[22]

His unusual destiny of having committed an unimaginable crime failed to make him someone special. The banality of evil is that atrocious deeds can be committed by ordinary individuals to whom nothing in particular draws attention or assigns the role of performing the unspeakable villainy. The banality of evil reduces the executioner to the level of his or her anonymous, faceless victims: numberless unknowns with no marks designating them for their terrible fate. The insignificancy of the torturers means that over six million deaths were insufficient to transform the committers of the crime into heroes of evil, masters of violence. This shows the murderers' failure to establish the absolute difference that, they thought, would justify their actions.

The scapegoat mechanism makes the victim sacred, but the violence also renders those who commit the violence sacred because violence is the sacred. Executioners, sacrificers, are also "sacred" beings. The violence that they commit sometimes raises them almost to the rank of the gods. Girard lingers over the sanctification of the victim because it is the source from which all of the sacred emerges. The sanctification of executioners and murderers is only indirect and secondary, but it nonetheless is a central theme in many myths and a number of classical texts. Thus, it is Cain and Romulus, rather than their victims, who are the founders of cities. While many foundation myths describe all of culture as emerging from the body of the victim, others, which we could describe as "political," take the hero, the master of violence, to be the founder—Romulus rather than Remus. They do not choose the victim. These myths can be called "political" insofar as they do not tell the story of the creation of the world or the ordering of the universe, but the establishment of a leader, king, dynasty, holder of supreme authority. The way that Girard analyzes sacred royalty suggests there is a close link between politics and the sanctification of the executioner or, more specifically, the *sacrificer*. Girard suggests that the first sacred kings must have been victims waiting to be sacrificed, but already made divine in anticipation, who were able to take advantage of the wait to delay as long as possible the time of their sacrifice, or to shift the violence onto other victims, and transform themselves into sacrificers.[23]

According to Marcel Granet, in ancient China the first lords were both sacrificers and victims par excellence.[24] Between the sacrificer and the sacrificed, the distance is never very great since the god who demands victims is himself or herself the first sacrificial victim. It is thus not surprising that in "political" myths, the sacrificer often becomes the sacrificed, and the hero or executioner transforms into the victim. Livy told two versions of the death of Romulus. According to the first, a storm broke out while Romulus was inspecting the army, and he was raised directly to heaven, where he became Quirinus, god of war. According to the second, during the course of the same storm, he was the victim of a collective murder: he was assassinated by the assembly of senators. Already modern, Livy was surprised by the naïveté of his fellow Romans, who so easily accepted the blatant lie invented by the senators in order to hide their crime. According to him, the former version of the death of Romulus was simple ideology, an artifice designed to dissimulate the truth in order to strengthen the power of the Senate. A Girardian reading does not necessarily reject the entire "ideological" analysis, but it profoundly changes the meaning. First, it is from the eyes of those who assassinated the victim that the myth dissimulates the truth of their crime. The fact that misrecognition is universal, that it includes the Senate, rather than be reserved for those whom it is intended to trick, the populace, does not make it impossible, and in fact makes it more likely, that some will exploit it to their own advantage.

Once he or she has become a victim, the hero becomes a god. Even though he or she often manages to delay the time, the sacrificer, master of violence, rarely escapes a violent death. The sanctification of the hero already results, however, from the heroic violence itself, from the superior position that the hero has forcefully taken in mimetic rivalries. Violence rewards the winners with sacred prestige. It makes them the masters of the game in which divinity remains the absolute sovereign. It is no accident that the deified victim is so often a hero who has finally failed rather than just any random individual. The hero's own violence, which is seen as a model to be imitated, makes it more probable that violence will converge on him or her, and then be more consistent with his or her transformation into a god.[25] The sanctification of the hero, executioner, or sacrificer ensures proportionality between the individual and his or her violent actions. It is an essential, ontological accord. The proportionality, the measure between the person and the violent action, is precisely what defines him or her as a hero.

However, in the modern world, there are no longer really any heroes in this sense. There are certainly still "masters of violence," but increasingly they are nothing more than that: violent people. Glory escapes them; all who remain are their victims. In the end, this is what the thesis of the banality of evil means: between the violent and their actions, balance has disappeared. There is no longer any fit between the actor and the action. There is only disproportion between unimaginable crimes and the insignificant individuals who commit them, all ordinary people. In Arendt's eyes, Eichmann embodied this discrepancy, this disproportion. He was proof that, in the world we live in, the most terrible evil has become banal since it is within the reach of anyone.[26]

The disproportion between mediocre actors and horrible actions can be seen first in the form of a mismatch between the action and the intent behind it. The bad consequences of the action are not the actor's goal; they are not what incite him or her to act. It is not that the actor is unaware of them, much to the contrary, but they are only secondary, incidental to the goal. During his trial, Eichmann repeated a number of times that he was not motivated by atavistic hatred of Jews.[27] His personal goal was not their physical destruction. He was motivated only by the desire to do his work well and to please his superiors. Arendt was struck by the insane discrepancy between the action, namely, organization of the systematic extermination of millions of persons, and the intent, the reasons that led Eichmann to become the chief operating officer of the industry of death: the desire to have a successful career and be a good civil servant. Eichmann wished his victims no evil; for him, six million deaths were never more than a means of advancing his career! This monstrosity is what stupefied Arendt because, while a desire to have a career is the most normal thing in the world, the destruction of millions of human lives is an incommensurable crime. Eichmann remained unaware of this abyss right to the end. This failure to *think about what one is doing* is, according to Arendt, precisely what makes the evil banal, what makes anyone able to accomplish the most monstrous crime.

Just like those who unflinchingly witnessed the murder of Alain de Monéys, Eichmann never imagined having to give up what he desired in order to come to the aid of strangers, people with whom he had no shared history, outsiders to whom he was linked in no special way. However, it might be said that between "those who had done nothing," and Eichmann, who was a main player, a party to a monstrous undertaking, there is an enormous difference. Of course! However, there is also continuity, for what made Eichmann's participation so easy, what underlay his inability to think about what he was doing, is the very same thing that authorized the inertia of the "spectators" at the Hautefaye crime. Neither had any special "reason" to protect the victims that *others* were murdering—this is also something that Eichmann constantly repeated.[28] On Eichmann's part, the argument was clearly a lie because he was actively engaged in the crime and could not exonerate himself by invoking the outsider status that he was trying to claim. However, it is also revealing. The reason Eichmann used it was because he took it for granted, as normally shared by those to whom he was speaking, that one should feel indifferent toward those to whom one owes nothing. He expected that all would acknowledge that no one has any obligations to strangers, and he gave as "evidence" to prove he was not a monster the fact that in 1943, when the Final Solution was under way, he had helped the daughter of his former Jewish employer to emigrate to Switzerland.[29]

Violence and Action

Proportion between the agent and the action, balance between the intent and the act are not self-evident truths. Even though the theme of the banality of evil expresses Arendt's amazement with the disproportion between the crime and the criminal, a balance between the actor and the action is not a natural, spontaneous phenomenon. On the contrary, it is socially constructed by a process of interactions among agents. According to Arendt, actors create themselves by acting in public. Their actions and the words that accompany them say who they are.[30] By revealing me to others, the action reveals me to myself because the intent is always, at the origin, inadequate in relation to the action, at least if we have to understand by "intent" that which precedes and motivates the action, for every action inaugurates a series of unpredictable events and therefore its meaning cannot be given in advance. This is why, for Arendt, action is inseparable from speech. Acting is first claiming authorship of one's actions. It is accepting oneself as one discovers oneself in action, constructing oneself at the instant when one's action becomes visible. Acting is choosing oneself when promising, asking for forgiveness, challenging opponents, or giving in to them. Thinking about what we do, weighing the consequences, succeeding in putting ourselves in the place of others are, according to Arendt, skills indissolubly linked to our capacity to speak, state, and contradict, to recognize ourselves and to agree to be recognized as the authors of our actions.

These attitudes suppose that there is a public space where the action can manifest itself in contradiction. Acting in the proper sense is possible only within such a space, and corresponds to the dimension of the human condition that we call political. According to Arendt, action is the fundamental means of lucidity. Politics enables us to discover the nature of our actions and whether we are ready to accept their consequences. Understood in this way, politics is the institutionalization of the public process by which equilibrium is established between our intentions and our actions. It is a rational space for public discussion.

Thus, we can ask whether Eichmann's failure to "think about what he was doing," whether the discrepancy between his action and the intention that motivated it, was not due to a public speech failure in Nazi Germany, to the absence of a common space where agents could have claimed their actions publicly and argued about their meaning. A bureaucrat in a repressive regime where all opposition was muzzled, Eichmann never climbed onto the stage where actions could be presented, interpreted, and judged. This would explain his "absence of thought," his inability to put himself in the shoes of others. In Hitler's Germany, it was not possible to debate or challenge the worth of the Final Solution. It was not a possible topic of discussion. Those who knew and whose daily work was the administration of death, certainly had to be able to communicate among themselves in order to achieve the undertaking, but the objective itself was never exposed to contradiction or challenged. While it was permissible to refuse to participate in mass murders by invoking one's weakness or lack of courage, the murderous policy itself could not be disavowed. Eichmann's incapacity to "think about what he was doing," and that of the other participants, collaborators, and executioners, their inability to imagine the moral horror of their actions, would also go hand in hand with the inability to speak, the lack of public space for discussion. The banality of evil would be both the reflection and the consequence of this disappearance of public speech.

However, it is not certain that the existence of a public space for discussion is sufficient to protect us from the temptation to engage in violence. There is no assurance that it can guarantee that our decisions will be good and our actions just. "Thinking about what we are doing" prohibits neither violence nor atrocious political actions. Greek cities, Athens in particular, were for Arendt examples par excellence of public spaces where actions and intentions could be expressed publicly and be weighed. The public discussions that we can read, for example, in Thucydides, confirm this assessment. Even though the debates reported by the Greek historian are not, properly speaking, "historical" and do not reflect the exact words that were spoken on those occasions, they show that Athens's decisions during the Peloponnesian War were taken with full awareness of the reasons, after public discussion, by actors aware of the consequences.

Thus, Mytilene, a member city of the Delian League, revolted and joined Sparta. When it was reconquered by Athens, the public assembly decided to condemn to death all the men of military age rather than to punish only the members of the aristocratic party who had stirred up the revolt. The next day, the assembly, having thought things over, opened the debate again. After a discussion that Thucydides reports in detail, clemency just barely won. In contrast, when the Athenians took Melos, a Lacedae-monian colony that they had attacked because it had refused to join their league, even though it had wanted to remain neutral in the conflict between Sparta and Athens, they exterminated all the men, reduced the women and children to slavery, and repeopled the city with Athenian settlers.[31] It was genocide by the book, in the precise sense given to it by Raphael Lemkin, who invented the term.[32]

In both cases, the action was chosen publicly and all of its consequences were accepted. As Bernard Eck shows, the massacres committed by the Athe-nians during the Peloponnesian War, the extermination of the entire male populations of a number of conquered cities, were not decided upon in the heat of the moment. They resulted from considered decisions, voted upon by the assembly of citizens after public discussions, and were often executed once the military action was already finished.[33] Exterminating the men, reducing the women and children to slavery, repeopling the conquered city with Athenian settlers: mutatis mutandis, it is what Hitler proposed to do in Poland and the Ukraine. All of the Athenian "final solutions" were decided publicly, after free, democratic debate.

The banality of evil thus does not reflect a lack of politics. The most terrible political crimes can be reconciled perfectly well with deliberative democracy and the existence of a public space for discussion. The banality of evil goes hand in hand with the establishment of modern political systems, whether they are democratic or not, in which executioners and victims are no longer made sacred. The prohibition against speaking openly or publicly dis-cussing the well-foundedness of extermination policy suggests, in fact, that a residue of the aura of sacredness is still attached to the murderous action. The evil does not really become banal until the destruction of entire popula-tions becomes official state policy. When nuclear annihilation of millions of individuals becomes a topic of public debate, of reasoned arguments among free, responsible citizens, then evil truly has become banal.

In fact, what the lack of proportionality between the action and the actor shows is not that there is no public space for discussion. The fact that the authors of monstrous crimes were ordinary men means the executioners were not made sacred. It means that their actions, their crimes, their violence did not succeed in transforming them into monsters or heroes. Why? The same mechanism that explains the indifference to the fate of Alain de Monéys on the part of those who had come to the Hautefaye Fair explains the little interest that they took in his murderers. Why did Eichmann's incredible actions, enormous, outrageous crimes not suffice to turn him into a hero of violence or a monster? Because most people were just as uninterested in him as they were in the fate of his victims. Both the nonsacralization of the victims and the nonsacralization of the executioners flow from the mimetic phenomenon that prevents the convergence of the group against a single victim and abandons us each to our own fate.

From "Peacetime Crimes" to Genocide

As we have seen above, Nancy Scheper-Hughes has advanced the idea of a "genocidal continuum."[34] According to her, there are everyday, ordinary violent practices that are accepted by all and that, in a sense, anticipate genocidal actions. They facilitate the general acceptance of atrocious crimes, as if they were normal, "banal" actions. Genocides seem to us to be extraordinary events, with nothing in common with the normal life that preceded them. This rupture is perhaps more apparent than real. It is not always easy to determine where, between genocides and certain usual practices of everyday life, the discontinuity occurs. In line with Franco Basaglia, Scheper-Hughes calls these practices "peacetime crimes."[35] The notion of "peacetime crimes" is in symmetry with that of war crimes. It refers to "the legitimate, organized, and (above all) routinized violence that is implicit in particular social and political-economic formations."[36] However, in contrast with the structural injustices related to socioeconomic conditions and concerning the state of the society, for example, the distribution of disadvantages and advantages, peacetime crimes resemble crimes properly speaking. They are actions committed by identifiable people that violate the rights or the physical or moral integrity of other people.

What makes them different from crimes in the proper sense, and in this they resemble many crimes against humanity, is that, in general, peacetime crimes are perfectly legal actions. Similarly, violence committed by states against their citizens, atrocities perpetrated by their representatives, are very often committed on behalf of a publicly recognized public authority. This is why judicial proceedings concerning crimes against humanity are generally the jurisdiction of international tribunals: in the places and at the times they are committed, they are often not "crimes" at all, but authorized actions and sometimes even prescribed by law. When they are finally dragged before the courts, the authors of crimes against humanity often seek shelter under such legality. Generally, we refuse to give them this right, but perhaps we are jumping the gun in such cases.[37] Authors of peacetime crimes can also claim that their actions are legal because the authority under which they act not only does not punish, but is sometimes responsible for institutionalizing the actions for which they are blamed.

Scheper-Hughes thus suggests that peacetime crimes are used up to a certain point to make "peace" possible; in other words, they are part of the way order is maintained within society. She gives two examples of this: the penitentiary industry in the United States and the way elderly people are treated in many institutions responsible for caring for them. The population of the United States accounts for around 5 percent of the world's population, but people incarcerated in the United States account for 25 percent of the prison population worldwide. There are almost twice as many people in prison in the United States as in China, even though China's population is five times greater! The greatest superpower in the world is the one with the highest rate of incarceration in the world. Of the people in prison, 75 percent have been sentenced for nonviolent crimes, nearly half suffer from mental illness, and more than 50 percent are black, even though the latter account for only 14 percent of the total population of the United States. Finally, 70 percent of prisoners belong to a racial minority. In short, most of the prisoners belong to minorities and underprivileged social groups.[38]

Two main factors explain the rapid continuous growth of the American prison population since the 1980s. The first is the establishment of a veritable carceral-industrial complex with annual revenue of over $5 billion. Prisoners work. They provide cheap labor. Increasingly, American states, municipalities, and even the federal government use private penitentiaries to deal with prison overpopulation and to reduce the cost of building new detention centres. Private prisons are commercial enterprises with a normal, legitimate objective of making a profit. The result is that such companies often have an interest in keeping their captive, cheap workers behind bars. In fact, in private institutions, it is eight times more frequent for sentences to be extended for poor behavior than in federal prisons! The second factor is the security culture and development of an increasingly punitive mentality, which is growing stronger at the cost of prisoners' social reintegration and rehabilitation. It is conducive to heavy sentences, even for minor offenses, and preventive detention for repeat offenders.

The American penitentiary industry is a classic example of injustice and exploitation of underprivileged groups. In this sense, it is a political problem par excellence. However, the rights of some persons are violated in a perfectly legal manner. Those people are mentally ill, immigrants (whether illegal or legal), petty criminals who are given disproportionate sentences, or individuals with income or a level of education that makes it difficult for them to procure a good defense. Overall, the vast majority of the American population accepts such violence. Americans think that such punishment is justified, that those who are in prison deserve to be there. They never wonder whether the sentences are in fact just. This is precisely what defines peacetime crimes: they are normal, legitimate forms of violence that are accepted by all. They are forms of banal, ordinary evil that do not concern us and befall people to whom we owe nothing.

The second example, namely, that of elderly people, is even more troubling because it is not immediately political. When they are no longer able to take care of themselves, we relegate elderly people to homes where specialized staff are assigned to provide them with care and services. Often, over time, in the eyes of employees who are generally overworked, underpaid, and poorly trained, the residents cease to be people and become objects, bodies that have to be washed, fed, cared for, shifted, and moved back to where they will be as little trouble as possible. They become entities to whom one does not respond when they speak, and whose requests are not heard. To the physical and often mental weakness owing to age is thus added the moral indignity of no longer being an individual, or even a person at all. Such violence, such exclusion of all those old people whom we allow to quietly die as if they had nothing else to do, is legal. It is structural and institutional. It occurs in places we visit only rarely, and about which we know very little and do not want to know more. We all accept this state of affairs, which we certainly consider unfortunate, but inevitable.[39]

Peacetime crime: this evil is properly banal, perhaps too banal, some will say, for the thesis of the continuity between peacetime crimes and genocides to be really convincing. Here, we have gone from refusal to help a person in danger to murders on the industrial scale, to the incarceration practices of a democratic state, to the abandonment of elderly people relegated to homes where, rejected by society, they await death. Are these phenomena not too different? Is it not simply false to claim that Eichmann's criminal indifference is the same as our indifference to the fate of elderly people and American prisoners? Indeed, it would be inaccurate to claim so. The thesis I am defending is different. I am not suggesting that the murderous disregard of the administrator of death toward his victims is *the same thing* as our failure to imagine, or to want to know, the consequences of our actions.[40] Eichmann had no cognitive failure with respect to the consequences of his actions. He was perfectly aware of the ultimate purpose of the transportation he was organizing and the conditions in which his "clients" were traveling.

What links these different forms of indifference is the social mechanism that makes them possible. What allows us to be indifferent to the fate of another is that we are neither obliged to intervene in that person's favor nor to hate that person. In other words, the important factor here is not the physical distance or the difficulty in knowing or imagining what is happening to the other; it is not even the social distance, in the sense in which this term is generally understood. It is what we can call the *moral distance* between the agents. The moral distance between two people diminishes as reciprocal obligations between them increase, whether the obligations are of hatred or of aid, and increases as the number of such obligations drops. However, this distance does not depend on obligations that individuals believe they have or that they feel they are supposed to have with respect to one another. The question is not cognitive; it does not depend on what people think or believe. The obligations of reciprocal solidarity that unite the agents are public and objective. Failures to discharge them are punished by the other members of the group, and these obligations also make individuals vulnerable to members of other groups. Moral proximity corresponds to solidarity groups.

In societies like ours, where more or less all intermediary groups have disappeared, the moral distance between all individuals is generally the same: it is maximal. We have no reciprocal obligations with respect to one another, except perhaps with respect to family members and close friends. We are free with respect to one another. This is why we can be indifferent to the fate of others, and this is what leads us to ask *in psychological terms* the question about the attention that an agent pays to the unhappiness of the other and the help he or she is willing to give. Eichmann's indifference is a social phenomenon, as is that of the peasants gathered at the Hautefaye Fair and ours with respect to "peacetime crimes." The psychological aspect of the question is a reflection of the moral distance that separates individuals. It means that the question of solidarity with those to whom one owes nothing is now an issue that each of us has to deal with individually. What makes the most atrocious evil banal is not the indifference itself, but the social arrangement that authorizes it and leaves us to our individual responsibility.

Political Denunciations in Nazi Germany

Moral distance is therefore the cause neither of genocidal violence nor of criminal abandonment of persons in danger. The cause, the driving principle, is rather whatever it was that incited people to exploit to their own advantage the fact that they had no obligations toward Alain de Monéys as he was being murdered. It is whatever leads people to take advantage of having no duties to all those other strangers whom other people murder. What encourages people to be indifferent and leads them to consider monstrous policies as ordinary? Analyzing political denunciations can help us to understand this.

Secret denunciation can be considered one of the forms of political participation that was encouraged by the Nazis (and by many other repressive regimes). Denouncing political and racial enemies was a way for ordinary citizens to contribute to the Nazi's political power and establishment of the new order. It was a way to be politically active and committed in a nondemocratic, totalitarian state. The work by Robert Gellately, in particular, has shown that without active help from many citizens, the Gestapo, given its reduced staff, would have been unable to control the German population effectively, apply the racial laws, or repress undesirable political activities. The great majority of investigations that led to individual arrests, in comparison with group raids, began with a denunciation.[41] The Nazi authorities encouraged "good Germans" to deliver hidden "enemies": those who claimed to be faithful but were in reality traitors, communists, the regime's opponents of all kinds, or Jews who were trying to pass as Aryans. Without the denunciations, without the voluntary, spontaneous support of many anonymous people, the Nazi authorities would never have been able to penetrate so deeply into the daily life of German citizens, or discover and destroy so many "enemies."

Secret denunciation is a very special political practice in that it encourages political participation by all but simultaneously institutionalizes the disappearance of the public space. Contrary to exchanging words in a shared space for discussion, denunciation is a form of nondemocratic political participation. Denunciation is not open to challenge or disagreement; it is done in secret and results in a police investigation that determines the "truth." Whereas public political debates take place in a space distinct from private life, denunciation gives a political dimension to what is private: an action, something said in private, the radio that one listens to at home. This political dimension is nonetheless not public. The "misconduct" very often remains hidden from the eyes of most. It is known only by a few and by those who determine the punishment. Denunciation consists in reporting (often anonymously) to others, who were not there when the "misconduct" occurred, something that was said, done or, more generally, unknown to the authorities. In contrast with political players who expose themselves to risk on the public scene, denouncers do not "act" in Arendt's sense. Indeed, they are the first to acknowledge that they do almost nothing. They limit themselves to informing those who are "responsible," to drawing their attention to "suspicious" behavior or speech, and then they allow events to take their course. This is why denouncers can, like Pilate, wash their hands of any responsibility. They have done only their duty. They are not the cause of the misfortunes of those whose behavior alone has drawn down upon them the wrath of public power. They set into motion a series of events that escapes them. What will happen to the person who was denounced? The denouncer cannot really know. However, as Gellately notes, from the beginning of the war, no one could be unaware of the brutality of the Gestapo's methods, or of the potentially dramatic consequences that informing could have on those who were denounced.

Now, throughout the entire regime, from the time the Nazis took power to the very end of the war, so-called instrumental denunciations were more numerous than racial or properly political denunciations. In other words, there were always many more malicious denunciations with no real political foundation than those with racial or political motivation.[42] Denunciations to the Gestapo most often sought to eliminate or drive away a private enemy, take revenge, or obtain an advantage over a third party. For example, people denounced next-door neighbors with coveted apartments, rivals in love, and commercial competitors.[43] Denunciation functioned like a solution to business and marital disputes. It was a handy replacement for long, costly divorce proceedings.[44] Individuals employed the state's power to resolve disputes among one another. They exploited its violence to their own advantage, indifferent to the consequences that their actions could have on others, but also on themselves, for the denouncers legitimized Nazi violence by using it. According to Gellately, the denunciations facilitated the normalization of the Nazi regime: by denouncing their neighbors, individuals recognized the legitimacy of the power that they were using. In this sense, manipulation of political terror for private ends constructed the legitimacy of Nazi power through people's eagerness to collaborate with it.[45]

The Nazis themselves considered the instrumental, false denunciations as a problem. The Gestapo warned agents about such interested denunciations because instead of making it possible to arrest "public enemies," they endangered the community's harmony. With distance, we can, however, wonder whether, rather than being malfunctions, the "false" denunciations were not in reality an essential component of the system. The regime's stability and the enthusiastic support it received right to the end came perhaps partly from this manner of institutionalizing the "public enemy," which made it possible for each to be violent, either directly with respect to his or her own rivals, or indirectly against innumerable "Alain de Monéys" abandoned to their fate, domestic "enemies" who we one day discover were Jewish or listened to English radio.

The phenomenon of political denunciation suggests that the violence that states commit against their own citizens is not unrelated to conflicts and rivalries that pit individuals against one another. The private denunciations were not motivated by political commitments or ideological beliefs, but by hatred, resentment, ambition, and personal interest, by private rivalries and conflicts. As Götz Aly shows, much more than ideology, personal interest and private motives were frequently what led a person to denounce a Jewish neighbor or a coworker with a "suspicious" political past.[46] The ideological language in which all denunciations, whether "true" or "false," were couched, as well as the claims to good Nazi citizenship that accompanied them, were often only clothing intended to hide their essential nature: the private interest that motivated them.

Rather than revealing a population victim of political propaganda and ideological doctrine tricked by the official anti-Semitic discourse, the private denunciations show us actors who exploited state violence to their own advantage. The authors of the denunciations were not so much puppets blinded by Nazi lies as rational individuals aiming to maximize their self-interest and use state violence as a means to achieve their ends. Study of the denunciation phenomenon reveals a fundamental aspect of the articulation between state violence and private violence. The state is supposed to protect citizens from one another: this is the primary function of the holder of the monopoly of violence. However, when the state turns against its citizens, it is not simply political power that attacks isolated, defenseless individuals, but individuals also: having fallen back into the state of nature, they tear one another to pieces. At the same time, as Étienne de La Boétie saw long ago, the reciprocal violence constructs and legitimizes, in part at least, the power that oppresses individuals.

We can see political denunciations as examples of the "banality of evil" that is located in between peacetime crimes and the explicit violence that states exercise against their citizens. We can see them as phenomena situated halfway between properly political violence and private violence, halfway also between crimes and legal, institutionalized, state-sanctioned violence. This gives us a glimpse of the complexity of the links between political violence and the private violence that individuals commit against one another and from which it is the primary function of the political order to protect them.

CHAPTER 2

The State, Violence, and Groups

The author of *The Discourse of Voluntary Servitude*[1] was the first to recognize the theoretical problem of power turning against those subject to it. This phenomenon is so frequent that we do not see that it is paradoxical, unexpected. Yet if, as political philosophy teaches, power flows from those who are subject to it, if it is from them that the state gathers its strength, how can the state turn its power against those from whom it draws its power? If the source of the state's power is nothing other than the strength of those on whom it is exercised, why do people not break free of chains that they can shake off so effortlessly? This is the problem that struck Étienne de La Boétie.

> Poor, wretched, and stupid peoples, nations determined on your own misfortune and blind to your own good! You let yourselves be deprived before your own eyes of the best part of your revenues; your fields are plundered, your homes robbed. . . . All this havoc, this misfortune, this ruin, descends upon you not from alien foes, but from the one enemy whom you yourselves render as powerful as he is, for whom you go bravely to war, for whose greatness you do not refuse to offer your own bodies unto death. He who thus domineers over you has only two eyes, only two hands, only one

body, no more than is possessed by the least man among the infinite numbers dwelling in your cities; he has indeed nothing more than the power that you confer upon him to destroy you. Where has he acquired enough eyes to spy upon you, if you do not provide them yourselves? How can he have so many arms to beat you with, if he does not borrow them from you? The feet that trample down your cities, where does he get them if they are not your own? How does he have any power over you except through you?[2]

The paradox of voluntary servitude is the paradox of political power itself. The state's coercive ability comes from those over whom it exercises it. If they did not "lend" their power, if they did not agree to serve it, the sovereign power would not exist; it would be nothing. Yet the state very often does violence to those whose voluntary agreement brings it into being. How is this possible? Political power as described by La Boétie is a paradoxical institution: a form of association that, though it results from the agreement of all, can nonetheless manage to, without destroying itself, turn against those who produce its power. The paradox is quite similar to the one framed by Rousseau at the beginning of the *Social Contract*: "'The problem is to find a form of association which will defend and protect with the whole common force the person and goods of each associate, and in which each, while uniting himself with all, may still obey himself alone, and remain as free as before.' This is the fundamental problem of which the *Social Contract* provides the solution."[3]

However, the very way Rousseau stated the problem suggests a solution: "each, while uniting himself with all, may still obey himself alone, and remain as free as before." Rousseau thought that it was possible to find a form of association such that the power would never be able to exercise its violence against those who were subject to it because, owing to their agreement, the strength that power uses against citizens is, by definition, not violence. It is simply a question of "forcing them to be free." This solution, which consists in making the difficulty disappear by redefining it, by transforming bad violence into legitimate force, nonetheless does not solve the problem. How can such power be stable? Why do not society members reject shackles that could not exist without their consent? Why would they ever agree to be "forced to be free"?

Understood in this manner, this problem is the one that, according to many of his contemporaries, was the flaw in Hobbes's political system. If it is from the accord of those who are subject to him that the sovereign draws power, rather than through divine right, how can the sovereign exercise it without losing their support? Yet is it not inevitable that the sovereign will have to use force against them in order to protect them from one another and from their outside enemies?

We have here, in fact, three approaches to the same problem: that of the stability of political power. Hobbes and his critics wondered how a sovereign power could be stable if it was based on the agreement of those subject to it. Rousseau, and a whole political tradition following him, proposed the following answer to this question: it is sufficient to ensure that "each, while uniting himself with all, may still obey himself alone" for each to "remain as free as before." They believe that there is an institutional solution to the difficulty, and that the legitimacy of the power suffices to protect us from abuses. La Boétie was, on the contrary, surprised by the stability of political power. What amazed him was that a power that exercises its might against those who give it its power does not collapse! Why do people continue to support a tyrant who oppresses them when the latter cannot do anything, is nothing, without their agreement? For La Boétie, the question of the stability of political power was not whether a power that comes from the agreement of those who are subject to it can be stable: its stability is far too obvious. The difficulty was rather to understand how this irrational miracle is possible: that people submit themselves to oppression by a power that is nothing without their submission.

La Boétie took it for granted that power is nothing without the support of those on whom it is exercised, that all power comes from the agreement of those who are subject to it, but he never looked directly at that issue. He spent virtually no time on the theoretical problem of the constitution of political power that he was the first to identify because he was most of all scandalized by the myopia of those oppressed by the power. The focus of his reflection was that people are the artisans of their own misfortune. He wanted to explain why and how we inflict so much evil upon ourselves. What La Boétie saw clearly, and what most of those who have come after him have forgotten, is not only that the state can turn against those who bring it into existence through their agreement, but the degree to which this frequent phenomenon is in fact paradoxical and rationally improbable.

Blind passion, vanity, and greed lead individuals to enslave themselves by enslaving others. This is what he thought explained power's capacity to oppress us and our eagerness to support it. Each finds interest in hijacking public power and turning it to his or her own interest. We each pay the authority the tribute of our submission in the hope of being able to exploit the power to our own advantage.[4] The *Discourse of Voluntary Servitude* thus provides a moral answer to the question that it poses: it is the moral weaknesses of agents, their passions and their vices, that are at the origin of political violence and that give the state the capacity to attack those whom it should protect. Modern political thought, taking Rousseau as the model, has preferred to renounce such moralism and provide an institutional answer to the question.

Rationality and Unanimity

In fact, the problem of state violence, understood as illegitimate use of force by the power that has the monopoly of legitimate violence, plays a central role in modern political traditions. Liberal, republican, and Marxist political thought all place fundamental importance on the questions of freedom and oppression, and on the danger of the state turning against those whom its role is to protect. All three traditions try to counter this danger either by an institutional arrangement that protects individuals or by a revolution that breaks the chains that oppress them.[5] In the liberal democratic tradition, flowing from thinkers such as Hobbes, Locke, and Rousseau, subjects' consent to the laws to which they are subject is the foundation of political power. The solution that this tradition offers rests on agents' rationality, individual rights, and the concept of political legitimacy. More precisely, this tradition thinks it has found the solution to the problem precisely where La Boétie saw the heart of the paradox: the fact that citizens consent to the power to which they are subject.

Why do people give up their original liberty and their right to defend themselves? It is in order to establish lasting peace among one another that individuals renounce free exercise of vengeance and abandon the right to decide between good and bad violence themselves. By the action of renouncing and through reciprocal agreement, they raise a power able to protect them from themselves and from outside dangers. People receive freedom by giving it up, though the freedom they receive is not quite the same as the one they gave up. By abandoning their right to everything, they gain freedom of action, which was prevented owing to conflicts flowing from opposing claims and the care that each had to give to his or her own defense. The rational agreement to submit is the founding link, the source from which the state's legitimacy springs. Moreover, it not only protects members of society from one another and from their outside enemies: the agreement that precedes the advent of the state also prevents the state from becoming tyrannical. It protects members of society from abuses of the power that they have thus created, or at least it gives them a remedy against such abuses. Indeed, if the state exists thanks to the consent of those subject to it, it is clear that they will abandon it if it turns against them, at least if they are rational.[6]

It is the rationality of the link between submission and protection that protects subjects against abuses of power. Agents trade their submission for the protection that the sovereign offers, and as Hobbes had already said, when that protection fails, people return to their original freedom. They are freed of their subjection and can, without acting incorrectly, repudiate their commitment. To act rationally is to act in function of a good that one seeks, whether it is egotistical or altruistic. In contrast, an irrational person is someone who behaves in a way contrary to the goal that he or she pursues. Is it not evident that rational individuals who, in order to be protected, submit to a power that they erect through their agreement will, if the power tyrannizes them, withdraw the support that made it strong? If, moreover, the sovereign is rational also, is it not just as obvious that he or she has no advantage in oppressing subjects? As soon as he or she grasps that all state power comes from citizens' agreement, the sovereign becomes their hostage: he or she can do nothing against them.

As soon as we take it for granted that people are rational, abuses of power become almost conceptual impossibilities, logical contradictions. Only an irrational sovereign would be tempted to oppress subjects because to do so would be to take the road to ruin. The social contract thus looks like an institution that is almost perfect, protected by its very institution from power possibly going adrift, at least in theory. However, in reality, things are quite different. Sovereigns often abuse their power. They violate the rights of their citizens, whose freedom they reduce far more than necessary for public peace. As much as possible, they target their own advantage rather than that of those who are, in fact, their principals. Yet their power does not crumble. Do they still enjoy the support of those whom they "govern" in this way? Should we consider that neither the sovereign nor subjects are perfectly rational?

However, the theory is not so easily cornered. These counterexamples, these "anomalies," as they will be called, do not force us to abandon the hypothesis of the agents' rationality because we should not think of the link between citizens' protection and their consent to the power to which they give birth in a causal manner, but in a normative way. Citizens' agreement is not *what explains* the emergence of political power in history, but *what defines its legitimacy.* By consenting to the laws that govern them, people become the authors of those laws. They are thus subject to laws that they have given themselves. A logical fiction, the social contract is the measure by which we gauge the legitimacy of power, but it is not a mechanism that explains its emergence in history. Understood in this way, citizens' agreement defines a norm the respect of which ensures their protection. It establishes the legitimacy of the power, but does not create it.[7]

Thus, for anyone who wants to really protect citizens against abuses of power, the solution is clear: reality has to be made as consistent as possible with the norm defined by the ideal theory. Democratic institutions have to be established that will make the sovereign depend on the people's agreement and thus provide a foundation for the legitimacy of sovereign decrees. It is also important to state explicitly, in the form of unalienable rights, the fundamental interests that individuals can never renounce: physical integrity, and freedom of thought, speech, and movement, in short, the minimum necessary for their survival. Democratic change of government and basic rights do not make abuses of political power impossible, but they give individuals forms of recourse, means of protecting themselves, and limit the degree to which power can be used against citizens.

There is thus no paradox of voluntary servitude. Rational individuals may submit because they are forced to do so, but they will not vote for or consent to a power that oppresses them. This is precisely what is expressed by the distinction between the legitimacy of power and the mechanism by which it is constituted. All power is not legitimate. A state that oppresses its citizens exercises its power without their agreement, so from the beginning it is illegitimate. Rationality suffices to solve both the theoretical and the practical problems of abuses of power. It shows where the difficulty lies and what the solution is. La Boétie was unjust when he accused his fellow citizens of myopia and immorality. The cause of their servitude was different. They were living under an illegitimate regime that did not allow them to assert their rights or to express their political will other than by violence.

However, when we take a closer look, it nonetheless seems that the difficulty cannot be solved so simply, by an appeal to individual rationality and its democratic institutionalization, because those who exploit to their own advantage the violence of power that they legitimize by participating in it are not acting irrationally. For their behavior to be judged irrational, or for it to be considered necessarily myopic and imprudent, the unanimity of members of society also has to be supposed. It has to be supposed that by acting in that way, they go against their own self-interest, but that is far from evident. From the theoretical point of view, a very special form of rational unanimity has to be supposed, which is what modern social contract theories generally do. It is only when *the reasoning of a given agent is supposed to apply identically to all the others* that it is irrational to consent to the political power that oppresses us. If there is no unanimity, then it is manifestly not irrational to support political power that *oppresses certain people*, even if, officially, its function is to *protect all*.

The unanimity of members of society is thus indispensable to the legitimacy of power. The agreement of a few, or even of many, cannot make the subjection of all legitimate. The social contract, the consent given by subjects to the power that governs them, has to be unanimous. The rationality of the agreement alone does not suffice to make the power legitimate: we have to suppose in addition that the rational agreement is unanimous. The unanimity is likewise implicit in the notion of universal fundamental rights, for while such rights are supposed to correspond to individuals' vital interests and engender correlating duties among others, their universality supposes a unanimous agreement on the interests in question since, by definition, they cannot be privileges reserved for a few.[8] The unanimity of the agreement creates a situation in which we each find ourselves facing a power to which, with the others, we have given birth, for we each choose by and for ourselves to consent to the sovereign, even though, by hypothesis, our reasoning is identical to that of all the others. Fundamental rights, because they are based on this unanimous agreement, give each the protection that flows from the agreement of all.

Descriptions that give a central role to unanimity in the relations between the governing power and subjects involve an opposition between isolated individuals on one hand, and the state on the other. They seek in individual universal rights a means to protect individuals from the state apparatus. However, the violence, in particular crimes against humanity, that states exercise against their own citizens suggests a different configuration of the relations between the state and those facing it.

Group Crimes

In *Crimes against Humanity: A Normative Account*,[9] Larry May defines crimes against humanity as "group crimes." According to him, a crime against humanity is a group crime in one of the following two senses: "To determine if harm against humanity has occurred, there will have to be one of two (and ideally both) of the following conditions met: either the individual is harmed because of the person's group membership or other non-individualized characteristic, or the harm occurs due to the involvement of a group such as the State."[10]

This is to say that there is a crime against humanity either when the victims of the harm have been targeted because they belong to a specific group, for example, a religious, ethnic, or social group, or when the perpetrators belong to an organized group, such as the state, or when both of these conditions have been met. May draws his readers' attention to the fact that in his definition the notion of group has two distinct meanings. Unfortunately, he does not analyze this difference further.[11]

Indeed, according to this definition, the group to which the victims belong is conceived of as a collection, a set of individuals. The members of the set may share one or more characteristics, such as language, gender, religion, cultural habits, place of residence, and so on, but in the end they may have nothing in common aside from the fact of belonging to the group in question. Their unique shared characteristic is then what identifies them as belonging to the group, for example, being chess players, or "enemies of the people," or "enemies of the revolution." A group of this type thus does not always correspond to what could be called a "natural division" of the population, as are, for example, ethnic or religious minorities, or even certain trades, the presence of which is obvious to all. It may very well be that the group exists uniquely as the result of an administrative operation. Thus, when people are assigned to a specific socioeconomic category because their income is below a certain threshold, they form a group. The unique necessary characteristic for them to be members is to have an income beneath the threshold; all of the other characteristics of the member individuals can be different. We can call groups of this type *statistical groups*. In order to belong to such a group, it is not necessary to know the other members or to have any ties with them at all. The group exists only through the outside operation that designates it. It resembles a mathematical set that need only be postulated to exist. Thus, the numerals in my telephone number form a set. So do all the books with green covers that are in the bookshelf in my office. It suffices to postulate such a set to be able to perform various operations on it, for example, to count its members, order elements according to size, arrange them into various subcategories, such as even and odd numbers, or books written in French, English, or Italian, and so on. The same goes for the set of all those who have at least one Jewish grandparent, or Cambodians who wear glasses.[12] Such groups do not exist "naturally." They have no reality other than the one that results from the fact that they have been postulated. The components of the set exist independently, but only the capacity to define the set gives it being and makes it possible to perform various operations on it, such as count its members, imprison them, or exterminate them. Such a group has no autonomy; it has no existence independent of the action that designates it.

In contrast, groups that commit crimes against humanity are, according to May, organized entities, such as associations, leagues, militias, or even states. Logically, an organized group is a set of individuals with a specific structure. It follows that, if the victims of a group crime are themselves members of an organized group, they meet May's first condition, according to which the victims of crimes against humanity belong to a group in the sense of a set or collection of individuals. Unlike members of a *statistical group* or, for the most part, those who belong to a "natural division" of the population, members of an organized group necessarily maintain specific relationships with one another. There are more or less clearly defined hierarchical relationships among them. They do not necessarily all know one another, but they can generally recognize one another as members of the group in question. Above all, the members of an organized group are actors who act together. This is why it makes sense to say that groups, rather than isolated individuals, commit crimes against humanity. The members of an organized group are not disparate individuals brought together by a law that determines the group's composition, as are, for example, all residents not born within the borders of the country. Instead, they form a body social, a group of people who can say "we" when speaking of themselves. Such a group is autonomous; it is not necessary to postulate it in order to make it appear. It performs, on its own, the operation that distinguishes it from the environment from which it emerges.

International courts adopt a definition of crimes against humanity similar to Larry May's. They also conceive of them as group crimes. They consider that there is a crime against humanity when two conditions are satisfied. First, the violent acts have to have been systematic and on a grand scale. Second, for there to have been a crime against humanity, the criminal must not have acted alone, in other words, as an individual, but as a member of a group or organization.[13] In relation to the accused, international courts define crimes against humanity in the same way as May. These crimes are committed by individuals who are members of organized groups. Insofar as they consider only violent acts that have been "systematic and on a grand scale," the courts acknowledge, implicitly at least, that the victims form a group in the sense of a collection or a statistical set. Saying that the violent acts have been "systematic and on a grand scale" implies that the victims were not chosen randomly. The two conditions required by international courts to determine whether there has been a crime against humanity closely resemble those stated by May, but, unlike him, international courts require both conditions be met, not just "one or the other, and ideally both."[14]

As Antoine Garapon says: "A crime against humanity implies a twofold imbalance. First, with respect to the nature of the individuals involved . . . : on one hand, a political organization that increases the strength of individuals tenfold, and on the other hand, isolated persons."[15] Crimes against humanity are group crimes. They are perpetrated by organized groups against "isolated" individuals. The systematic nature of the attacks reveals that the victims are members of a group. They are isolated, but in the sense that Alain de Monéys was isolated: they lack the protection of a group. They are alone, but they also have the misfortune to belong to a group, be it the "Prussians," and it is because they belong to the group that they become victims. In crimes against humanity, behind the apparent face-to-face between an isolated individual and the state, there looms a different configuration: that of a confrontation between groups. It is precisely this structure that defines them as crimes against humanity.

Larry May sometimes uses the expression "non-individualized characteristic" to draw attention to the fact that the victims of crimes against humanity are targeted because of characteristics that are not specific to them as individuals. However, this expression hides an important difference. It can mean, first, universal characteristics that an individual shares with all, for example, membership in the human species. If a crime targeted such a universal characteristic, we would be able to see that it was indeed a crime against humanity. The offense would indeed be an attack on what is common to all humanity. "Non-individualized characteristics" can also refer to characteristics that, while not universal, are, as May says, features that an individual "shares with many others," for example, the fact of speaking French or being a Shiite Muslim, in other words, group characteristics. Victims of group crimes in May's sense, in other words, victims of crimes against humanity, do not become victims because of characteristics that they share with all other members of humanity.[16]

What makes their persecutors pick them out are the characteristics that they share—or that they are considered to share—with certain others exclusively. It is not simply because they are human that women, Jews, bourgeois intellectuals, Armenians, Tutsis, Kurds, and Kosovars are attacked and beaten, their villages burned, and bombs exploded in the markets where they shop! It is because they belong to specific groups. It is because they are thought to have in common certain characteristics that their persecutors do not share—or think they do not share—that the victims of group crimes become victims. The assassins do not target universal humanity, but specific groups. Crimes against humanity do not target humanity, but groups of human beings.

The three issues, namely, the unanimity that places individuals in opposition to the state, the idea of universally shared basic rights, and the notion of crimes against humanity, form a whole that tends to hide the special structure of confrontations between groups that underlies the worst forms of political violence. The idea of fundamental rights that protect individuals against state abuses of power is part of the issue of unanimous agreement. Rights give each individual the protection provided by the unanimous agreement that is the source of the state's power. Their ability to protect individuals against the state supposes this unanimity. However, the reality of political violence suggests that what is at stake is precisely the loss of unanimity, the reappearance of separate, opposing groups within the body politic. The consequence of this break in unanimity is that some are excluded from the agreement that protects those who are parties to it. They thus lose "the right to have rights." Such individuals always belong to specific groups, whether statistical or natural. Membership in a group is always the reason given to justify the violence inflicted on them.

We thus need to understand how unanimity is established within a community and why its disappearance leads to violence.

Hobbes: Unanimity, in Other Words, the Disappearance of Groups

Contrary to the majority of modern political thinkers, Hobbes rejected the distinction between legitimate and illegitimate power. Yet he did not reject the distinction between what is legitimate and what is not. He simply considered that the only criterion for power to be legitimate is its existence. All power is legitimate, not because it comes from God, but because, by definition, all power necessarily flows from the consent of those who are subject to it. Hobbes's argument is close to the modern conception in that Hobbes also thought that the legitimacy of power comes from the consent of those subject to it. His conception is different insofar as, according to him, power's legitimacy is inseparable from the process by which domination of some over others becomes established.

Hobbes did not see subjects' consent to the sovereign's rule as a normative requirement that is sometimes met and sometimes not, but as a necessary condition for the appearance of political power, a condition that flows from the nature of power in general.[17] According to him, an individual's power corresponds to his or her ability to lead others, more specifically, to the individual's ability to use for his or her own ends the power, strength, know-how, intelligence, and knowledge of other people. To have power is precisely to *have the power to* bring together the abilities of other individuals in order to accomplish a purpose, and that power is all the greater when the number of individuals is larger. There is power as soon as it is a question of taking common action.[18] However, bringing the strength of many people together is possible only if they "consent" in some way to the use to which their strength will be put. According to Hobbes, it does not matter whether the "consent" is free or forced, implicit or explicit. There can be power only if those subject to it accept it in some way. It is thus by definition, owing to the nature of what power is, that political sovereignty rests on the consent of those who are subject to it. The agreement of those who are subject to the power that controls them is not a characteristic reserved for certain types of political systems, for example, for representative regimes, because it is precisely what constitutes power as power. This is why, according to Hobbes, all political sovereignty is legitimate simply by existing, for those subject to it necessarily "consent" to its exercise.

The Hobbesian approach *naturalizes* power. Hobbes considered it as a phenomenon that appears naturally in relations among individuals. Power supposes submission. Why do people submit and give up the right to govern themselves? According to Hobbes, protection is the reason for submission: "The obligation of subjects to the sovereign is understood to last as long, and no longer, than the power lasteth by which he is able to protect them."[19] Protection is what gives meaning and value to submission because individuals submit in order to obtain it. "The end of obedience is protection; which, wheresoever a man seeth it, either in his own or in another's sword, nature applieth his obedience to it, and his endeavour to maintain it."[20] Naturally, people surrender to him, her, or them who can protect them. The subjection of people to people is a natural phenomenon; it emerges spontaneously in relationships among individuals. Thus, a child, Hobbes explained, has a duty of obedience to his or her mother that is both immediate and natural because *she could have exposed him or her* at birth, but she chose to provide protection instead. On the contrary, the obligation that a child has to his or her father is only mediate and conventional. It is derived from the wife's submission to her husband.[21] In his analysis of the notion of *subjugation*, we find the same equivalency between protecting and abstaining from destroying what one protects. It is not, Hobbes said, the one who loses in combat who is subjugated, but the one who *receives life in exchange for a promise of obedience*, and who thus becomes a *subject*.[22] The power that protects us is first that which spares us. The gift of life is always given by the person who could have taken it away. Protection is the flip side of the possibility of extermination, and the duty to obey is part of the fundamental ambiguity of the action that establishes power, which is both a promise of protection and a threat of death. However, the natural tie of submission is not yet sufficient to establish a stable political order or to give birth to a legitimate sovereign whom subjects would be morally required to obey. Left to themselves, natural relationships of submission do not provide a way out of the state of nature in which each is always free to repudiate the relationship of submission depending on the danger and self-interest.

Hobbes's philosophy is supposed to imitate nature, which Hobbes considered as the *art* by which God created the world, and to thus produce an artificial man: the republic or the state, "of greater stature and strength than the natural."[23] All existing states have been established spontaneously, in ignorance of the nature of power and the conditions that make it possible. *Leviathan or the Matter, Forme and Power of a Common Wealth Ecclesiasticall and Civil* was intended to render conscious and explicit the causes and principles of the emergence of the state and to describe the institutions that ensure its strength and stability. While Hobbes's approach to politics is naturalistic, his ambition was rationalist and artificialist. The purpose was to correct Nature, to do consciously what it accomplishes blindly, and to thereby create an artificial object that is more perfect than that which nature can produce spontaneously.

So, how does the state emerge? What is the process by which it is generated? Hobbes postulated that there was originally a state of nature, which was a state of universal war preceding the birth of societies. He portrayed it as a struggle of every individual against every other in a situation where there may have been natural, spontaneous ties between people, but they were not stable. The violence of the state of war drives people apart. It condemns them to radical solitude. Alliances, pacts, and promises in the state of nature are simply opportunistic. They do not make it possible to establish sustainable groups that would constitute true associations. Such alliances are thus simply expedient actions that are wise to take or abandon depending on the circumstances, the urgency of the moment, or anticipated gain. They are therefore completely unstable and are constantly challenged by the search for individual advantage or safety.

In the "Review and Conclusion" of *Leviathan*, Hobbes said that what motivated him to write that treatise on political philosophy, the purpose of which is to teach his fellow citizens about the link between submission and protection, were the upheavals and violence of the civil war that was tearing England apart. This is probably also why he said that the portrait of the presocial state of nature resembles, in fact, what occurs during a civil war. "Howsoever, it may be perceived what manner of life there would be, where there were no common power to fear, by the manner of life which men that have formerly lived under a peaceful government use to degenerate into a civil war."[24]

However, Hobbes's conception of the state of war is at first sight different in an important way from the English Civil War, the violence of which he claimed was to a certain degree his theoretical model. *Leviathan* defines the state of war as a situation in which radically individualistic conflicts oppose each individual to every other individual. In contrast, the English Civil War was a war of parties. Royalists, Parliamentarians, Scots, the English, Presbyterians, Anglicans, and Independents clashed. It was not a struggle of all against all, but a conflict between established groups. Hobbes's analysis does not take this into account at all. It occurs entirely at the level of isolated individuals whose rationality drains away as they pursue their own advantage. Why?

The individualism of the Hobbesian state of war is neither an accident nor an error. There is a philosophical reason consistent with the intention to make people aware of what nature does spontaneously that explains Hobbes's theoretical choice, even though he never discussed it explicitly. Hobbes described the conflicts that erupt in the state of war as if they took place between isolated individuals because, according to him, if we assume agents are rational, division into groups is not essential. Opposition between individuals corresponds to the *logical grammar of conflict*.

The reason for this is that the agents who adhere to a party, faction, or league do not know the source of the authority that they obey. They are ignorant of the power generation mechanism to which they submit. If they were aware of it, they would not join the group because they would understand the inanity of their submission to such an association. The source of the group's power is in fact only themselves, the consent that constitutes their faithfulness to the party. It is suffrage that they exchange for the protection of a power that they create by subjecting themselves to it. However, the factions, groups, and leagues cannot provide that protection. According to Hobbes, all groups smaller than the state are powerless to protect their members. This is not an empirical assertion but, as we will soon see, a partial definition of the state. Consequently, groups simply reproduce, on a smaller scale, the inequality and insecurity that generate the state of war. Their conflicts express *grosso modo* what the war of all against all says in detail. The oppositions among groups reproduce on a larger scale the oppositions among individuals. Neither situation is more secure than the other. The truth of conflict is revealed by the struggle among individuals, which is the simplest form of confrontation.

In accordance with the two hypotheses, namely, that agents are rational and that power exists only through the consent of those subject to it, groups and parties are unstable, fragile institutions, as are all promises in the state of nature, where the slightest fear suffices to create uncertainty. We have no moral obligation toward such groups because they are unable to protect us. The state, which emerges from the submission of all to a single power,[25] defines the level of association where there are political obligations, in other words, the level where the ability to protect becomes such that it engenders the moral obligation to fulfill the promise of submission from which it arose. This obligation exists inasmuch and as long as the sovereign is able to protect his or her subjects. For Hobbes, the word "state" meant an association large enough to provide its members with *sufficient* protection. It is only at this level that there is *sovereignty*, legitimate power that members of society have a moral obligation to obey.

Thus, for Hobbes, there was a logical reason for excluding groups from the state of nature, and from the social contract that follows. By definition, the state corresponds to the level of association that creates power adequate to protect members of society from themselves and others. It appears at the point when rational individuals become aware of groups' inability to defend them or, and this amounts to the same thing, at the point when one group is powerful enough to eliminate all the others. First, it seems natural to interpret this condition as relative to the size of the group able to become a state.

However, according to Hobbes, it is impossible to determine, in an independent manner, the size sufficient for us to be able to say that a group is a state. What size does a group need to be to offer sufficient protection to constitute a state? According to Hobbes, the answer to this question depends on the size of the opposing enemy group located outside the state. "The multitude sufficient to confide in for our security is not determined by any certain number, but by comparison with the enemy we fear; and is then sufficient when the odds of the enemy is not of so visible and conspicuous moment to determine the event of war, as to move him to attempt."[26]

What determines whether a group is sufficiently large to provide those who submit to it with adequate protection is not the number of members, but the size of the adversary group. The metamorphosis of an unstable group, in which each can change allegiance according to whim, into a legitimate state that citizens have an obligation to obey depends on the presence on its borders of an enemy group of more or less equivalent size. In other words, within a population of enemy groups, states correspond to the minimum size that ensures that the members of the group are reasonably safe from attacks by other groups. This definition implies that any form of association (smaller than a state) that aims to provide protection for those it brings together will be prohibited within the state. To put it another way, this supposes that the state holds the monopoly of legitimate violence. Politically, expelling groups from the state is equivalent to unanimity because it frames members of society as isolated individuals in relation to the state, insofar as there is no group within the state that can defend them. All are identically subject to the same power to which they give their consent in exchange for protection.

Logically, however, unanimity is a requirement stronger than simple exclusion of groups. Expelling groups from the state does not mean that there is unanimity: individuals may disagree. Unanimity involves the exclusion of groups, their disappearance in the universal agreement. However, if, as Hobbes thinks, it is through opposition to a common enemy that groups come to be excluded, this is equivalent to unanimous agreement on who is the enemy. For Hobbes, the political means of satisfying the logical condition of unanimity within a real society is not a universal feature of the human mind, according to which the reasoning of only one would suffice for all, but the disappearance of groups within the state, in other words, the end of internal divisions under pressure from "the enemy we fear."

The expulsion of groups from the Hobbesian state nonetheless does not mean that they disappear entirely from Hobbesian theoretical problems. Indeed, their exclusion from the state and the presence of an enemy outside the state are simply two sides of the same coin. The groups are still there, but in a different form: that of states, and their reciprocal opposition is what, according to Hobbes, in the end establishes the peace that members of society enjoy in the shadow of their sovereign.

"Friends" and "Foes"

According to Carl Schmitt: "The concept of the state presupposes the concept of the political."[27] In other words, what is political is broader than that which we call the state, which, since Hobbes, has been at the center of political thought. Politics is not only broader, but prior to and more fundamental than the state because it explains the conditions of the state's birth and disappearance. The state as we know it, in the form of the holder of the monopoly of legitimate violence, is only one possible expression of the political. According to Schmitt, the distinctive feature of all political relationships is the "friends-foes" dichotomy.

Just as the opposition between good and evil is fundamental to morals and that between beautiful and ugly is essential to aesthetics, the opposition between "friends" and "foes" determines the field of political relations. All political phenomena—wars, partisan conflicts, the state, international relations, even prestate forms of political relations—flow from the conflictual dynamic between "friends" and "foes." This was Carl Schmitt's fundamental thesis in *The Concept of the Political*, an essay he described as an attempt to "provide a theoretical framework for an immeasurable problem."[28] The boundaries of what is political cannot be clearly demarcated because we cannot reduce political phenomena to a set of specific institutions and relationships. Anything that can be an opportunity for a "friends-foes" opposition can become a political problem. "The political . . . does not refer to a specific domain, but only to the intensity of association or dissociation of human beings whose motives can be religious, national (in the ethnic or cultural sense), economic, or of another kind and can effect at different times different coalitions and separations."[29]

This is why the "friends-foes" dichotomy is not a definition of the political, but a distinctive criterion for recognizing all political phenomena, no matter what they are. The word "political" designates conflict phenomena that, Schmitt argued, depending on the time and place, lead to different divisions and *groupings*. What characterizes the political is thus not only conflict, but also association. The political is the field of conflicts between *enemy groups*.[30] As we have just seen, no matter what it is, the origin is not what determines whether the conflict is political or not. What makes a confrontation political is the fact that groups are opposed and not simply isolated individuals. "An enemy exists only when, at least potentially, one fighting collectivity of people confronts a similar collectivity."[31]

Political friendship is simply the other side of enmity relations between groups. A "friend" is a member of the same "set of grouped individuals" as oneself. Friends in the political sense are those who see themselves (or are seen) as members of the same group. Political friendship and enmity are in no way properly personal. Such relationships are based on what Larry May calls "non-individualized characteristics": characteristics that are shared by several individuals. The flip side of the opposition between "foe" groups is the assembly of each group into "friends," and the scope of the political is determined by these two relationships of opposition and association, which are interdependent.

Schmitt also said that a political enemy is the Other, the stranger, in other words, he or she who is such that with him or her extreme conflicts "can neither be decided by a previously determined general norm nor by the judgment of a disinterested and therefore neutral third party."[32] Strangers and "foes" are thus those who do not share the same dispute resolution rules and who, in their conflicts, do not acknowledge the same "neutral third party" as arbitrator. This clarification concerning the nature of the enemy may seem watered down compared with the original criterion, namely, the "friends-foes" dichotomy. That criterion made the opposition itself the essential characteristic of the political, while Schmitt now seems to want to find the cause of the conflict in the absence of shared norms: "foes" are strangers to the group. In fact, however, the two formulations are equivalent. The absence of shared norms refers to the other side of the political relationship, to the fact that the opposition between two groups is also, at the same time, the associative link that creates the unity of each group. "The endeavor of a normal state consists above all in assuring total peace within the state and its territory. To create tranquility, security, and order and thereby establish the normal situation is the prerequisite for legal norms to be valid."[33]

The state gives "friends" shared rules for resolving disputes so that they can live in peace. It establishes law and the "neutral third party" to whom they can appeal and whose decision they must obey. It ensures order and the rule of law everywhere within its borders, and excludes hostility, in other words, private wars, as means of resolving disputes among its subjects. In other words, by seizing the monopoly of legitimate violence, the sovereign excludes groups within the state. According to Schmitt, the essential characteristic of the modern state (in this respect he proves to be a faithful disciple of Hobbes) is the internal pacification that makes the "friends-foes" division coincide with the inside and outside of the state. In consequence, only states now have properly political "friends-foes" relationships with one another. Within each state, there are now only "friends." Politics has disappeared. There remains only the police and the administration of justice.

However, this civil friendship reigns only in "normal" situations, in other words, when the system of norms established by the state functions and is generally accepted. This is not always the case: the necessary task of intrastate pacification, said Schmitt, sometimes requires the sovereign to take the initiative to designate the enemy within, the public enemy.[34] There then emerges a new form of "foes": enemies within. They are different from the "foes" outside in that their emergence corresponds to exceptional circumstances, a critical situation in which the state's very survival is at stake. Such exceptional situations correspond to points when the state is founded or reestablished. "The exception appears in its absolute form when a situation in which legal prescriptions can be valid must first be brought about. . . . For a legal order to make sense, a normal situation must exist, and he is sovereign who definitely decides whether this normal situation actually exists."[35]

Schmitt said that the sovereign is the one who decides "on his own initiative" who is the enemy within, the public enemy, and by doing so creates (or reestablishes) the order thanks to which legal norms can apply. In contrast, the external "foe" is by definition part of the normal situation, in which there are several internally pacified states that have expelled "foes" outside their borders and where the relationship of hostility coincides with the separations among states. The outside enemy is the normal foe. The outside foe is characteristic of the state system, in which states have political relationships with one another and recourse to force as a means of resolving disputes is not constant, but always possible.

Schmitt did not differentiate clearly between these two types of foes. He simply said that the "friends-foes" dichotomy is the criterion for the political, but did not make a clear distinction between the public enemy and the outside foe. However, the enemy within is different from the enemy outside in at least three ways. First, it seems that it is more the relationship of opposition to the enemy within, than to the external foe, that is the foundation of the political order. Second, this founding role defines the enemy within as an extraordinary enemy, rather than a normal one. Finally, third, the normal "friends-foes" political relation supposes two groups that mutually define themselves as foes, whereas it is "on his own initiative" that the sovereign decides who shall be the enemy within. Is there a link between these different characteristics of the enemy within?

Behind these two enmity relationships, there are two different narratives of the creation of the state. According to the first, which looks almost exactly the same as Hobbes's, the enmity relationship that occurs between groups is the other side of the associative links that hold each group together. According to the second narrative, which Schmitt never clearly formulated, it is from the opposition to the enemy within the group that the state emerges. While foe groups are involved only in a struggle that is "at least potential," protecting the state, according to Schmitt, requires, on the contrary, the definitive expulsion or extermination of the enemy within.

The Traditional Space of Hostility and Solidarity

In societies where the political has not yet emerged as an autonomous domain, we find a dual relationship of hostility and solidarity between groups. The research brought together by Raymond Verdier on vengeance and vindicative systems suggests a space of conflict divided into three concentric circles, with the center occupied by the ego, the individual subject.[36] In a number of classical works in anthropology, we find the same principle of organization of relations of hostility and solidarity, even though the shape of the relations to which it leads is not always described in terms of concentric circles.[37] The principle is that of the primacy of individual-to-individual links, family ties, and subservience over more general relationships that an individual has with the rest of the populace to which he or she belongs. This is why the image of a space divided into concentric circles is useful. It employs distance from the center, which the agent, ego, occupies, to show the greater or lesser strength of the ties that bind the individual to others. As one gets further from the center, the use of violence to resolve disputes becomes freer, and the strength of solidarity obligations diminishes.

The circle closest to the center is that of kinship or clan *identity*. It is where the more or less extended family is located.[38] In this space, recourse to violence is in principle forbidden. Transgression of rules and prohibitions results in quasi-legal sanctions and/or requires ritual purification. The punishment can be terrible: a father may sacrifice his child or the family may condemn one of its members to death, but these are legitimate sanctions, not acts of violence. In return there is also unlimited solidarity in this circle. Food is given freely to those who need it and, if applicable, we expect them to provide equally generous assistance. We tolerate breaking of the rules of exchange and equity by those near to us, even though we would demand compensation from others. Very close to the ego, even stealing is not a crime.[39] The reciprocity requirement is not absent from such relationships, but it is not strictly enforced. It is not calculated, or at least not too much. An individual has to have greatly wronged those close to him or her for them to refuse to provide that individual with help because the wrong they would thereby commit would inevitably reflect upon them.

As Marshall Sahlins has seen clearly, solidarity and hostility are closely linked.[40] The obligation of unlimited solidarity implies duties of violence, namely, those to revenge and protect members of the solidarity group. While in the inner circle good has to be returned for good, and wrongs and offenses must not be taken into account (too much), unless they are transgressions in the proper sense that require punishment, outside that circle, wrong has to be rendered for wrong, and compensation has to be demanded for offenses suffered by oneself and one's family members, kin, and clan. This revengeful solidarity is simply the other side of the prohibition against violence within the world of *identity*. Hostility toward outside others is simply another expression of shared solidarity. In *Eumenides*, Aeschylus said that having "friends" means facing the same "foes" together. The violence that *must* be exercised against others is inseparable from the help that *must* be given to those close to us.

The first circle is surrounded by a second, which is dominated by *adversarial* relations. Relationships of measured reciprocity replace the unlimited solidarity characteristic of the circle of *identity*. They structure both conflictual relations, and ceremonial and matrimonial exchanges. Here, reciprocity is always the rule. A wrong provokes a response in kind, and a gift demands an equivalent countergift. Ideally at least, vengeance and compensation remain balanced. Either they are sustained through a vendetta cycle that, while it maintains the violence, also imposes on it a degree of measure; or, when sufficient balance between rights and wrongs is reached, a sacrifice or matrimonial alliance seals the reconciliation. The same logic reigns in ceremonial exchange, gift and countergift, the *potlatch* and the *kula* cycle described by Bronislaw Malinowski in *The Argonauts of the Western Pacific*.[41] While there are free gifts in the first circle, in the second every gift requires a countergift. However, this reciprocity does not prohibit antagonism or challenge. What is required is to do better than the other, but not "too much" better. In exchange as in fighting, keeping things "in proportion" does not mean not testing the other. The agonic dimension of these relationships encourages each to ensure that the other's contribution, or wrong, is sufficient, and the rule of reciprocity becomes all the more finicky as the degree of conflict in the relationship rises.

Sahlins uses "balanced reciprocity"[42] to refer to the principle that regulates relationships in the second circle, and balance is indeed what is in question. For each individual, each group and each social player, what is important is to not lose. It is fine to win, perhaps, but without inspiring too much envy or jealousy. All players seek to maximize their own advantage under the constraint of interests that sometimes diverge from but sometimes converge on those of others, who are trying to do the same. Sahlins thus has good reason to compare the relationships that we find in the adversarial circle with those that Hobbes postulated in the state of nature.[43] In both cases, relations among agents are characterized by rationality, the fear of being ousted, and the danger of unrestrained, escalating violence. However, in this case, unlike what Hobbes imagined in the state of nature, agonic conflicts and exchanges play roles in social cohesion.[44] They create ties that limit violence among groups and individuals.

Yet further out there is a third circle or, perhaps more precisely, there is a space beyond the second, for the ultimate border of the last space remains undetermined. This is the place of all those with whom ego does not have recurring relations, with respect to whom ego has no duty of vengeance, no alliance, no hospitable relations, no kinship, not even distant. In other words, it is the realm of "Others," strangers, those who may not even be people,[45] those with whom we have no ties of reciprocal obligation, those to whom we owe nothing and who owe us nothing either. Verdier defines it as the circle of *warlike hostility*, in other words, the place where we can exercise unrestrained violence, where we can exterminate Others, or reduce them to objects of trade or consumption. In this more distant space, trade sometimes occurs. According to Sahlins, this, more than any other form of primitive exchange, most closely resembles modern market exchange.[46]

The prohibition against violence inside the *identity* circle is immediately the obligation to take violent revenge against violence that comes from outside. This is an obligation that encompasses and protects all those who cannot employ force against one another, and it divides individuals into distinct groupings of solidarity that have the potential to be in opposition with one another. Here, as in Carl Schmitt's thought, the associative link that brings "friends" together is the reverse side of the relationship of opposition to "foes." Solidarity and hostility are two faces of the same reciprocal ties, and these two sides of reciprocity are inseparable. This is especially obvious in the circle of adversity, where the same groups are sometimes foes and sometimes allies. The families with which matrimonial alliances are made are also the same with which we are in rivalry, and rejecting a marriage proposal means unleashing a vendetta.

The borders that separate these three circles are fuzzy and more or less porous. Individuals and groups can sometimes move from one to the other, from being *adversaries* to being part of the circle of *identity*, from being an *adversary* to belonging to the circle of *warlike hostility*, or vice versa. We should not think of these circles as perfectly sealed off from one another. The threefold division of the space of solidarity and hostility can accommodate individuals with multiple identities. It does not correspond to three impenetrable enclosures determined once and for all. Concerning conflicts in kinship societies, Simon Simonse writes: "Which identity is relevant in a particular encounter and which level of consensus an individual social actor should comply with depends on the situation of the moment."[47]

The space of conflict is a plural space where individuals have to negotiate among several identities. What is essential is the threefold structure. The division of solidarity/hostility space into three can be considered the expression of a recursive function that divides relational space. It can be applied to every new area encountered, and applied again to any space to break it down into smaller pieces. However, it is always the case that as the social distance separating the agent from those with whom he or she is in conflict grows, violence that was initially prohibited becomes permitted, and is gradually authorized to reach ever higher levels. Inversely, solidarity grows as distance decreases.

At the center of these concentric circles, we find the ego, the actor, the subject. Yet the solidarity/hostility space has no real extension. It does not correspond to a physical space, but is a model of interactions. It is true that sometimes we find this model embodied in the structure of physical space. The (threefold) division of solidarity/hostility space is then reflected in the spatial organization of the place where members of society are located. The first circle, for example, then covers more or less the place where the agent lives, the second the village or neighboring villages of the same tribe, and finally the third the outside world. In a number of societies, the divisions characteristic of the solidarity/hostility space can be identified in the physical space occupied by the tribe or clan, in the organization of the village and in the distribution of places within living spaces. However, even when this is the case, the divisions of the spaces of conflict and solidarity remain indissolubly attached to the self and the self's social relationships, independent of any anchoring in a territory or physical space.[48] In a way, the agent carries with himself or herself the structure of the solidarity/hostility space wherever he or she goes. It is distance in the space of social relationships, rather than shifts in physical space, that authorizes greater violence and weakens solidarity obligations. The distance in the traditional space of hostility reflects first the person-to-person relations in question, which have always been partly determined by the groups to which people belong, and the position that they have within those groups.

These reciprocal ties not only define groups of friends and enemies, but also distinguish legitimate from illegitimate violence in societies where no one has the monopoly to make that distinction. The division between good and bad violence does not refer to a specific authority, to a body with moral authority. It is part of the space of solidarity/hostility relations. The threefold division of the solidarity/hostility space reflects the structure of political relations in traditional societies.[49] It determines the form taken by political phenomena in such societies. We can even see in it an outline of the distinction between the private and the public.

The conflicts and transgressions that occur within the circle of lineage and clan identity are not political because they do not involve opposing groups, but individuals belonging to a single group. The deadly violence that sometimes occurs in this circle is a crime as such, but it is neither a political action nor political violence. Such conflicts are private rather than public, and they are resolved by appealing to rules that are recognized and accepted by all: sacrificial expiation, ritual purification, or even a fine. In contrast, the confrontations that occur in the adversarial circle are political phenomena. Even when they involve only two individuals, those two confront each other as members of separate groups. Such confrontations between adversaries are conflicts between groups, public disputes. The same goes for the war that we bring to those to whom we owe nothing. Their extermination, reduction to slavery, and consumption during ritual meals are political phenomena. No matter what the reasons for such conflicts, whether religious, economic, or flowing from atavistic hatred, these confrontations are political and public. They are clashes between "friends" and "foes."

The (minimally) threefold division of the traditional solidarity/hostility space entails that there are complex, differentiated relations of hostility and solidarity. Those who belong to the circle of identity are "friends." Linked by solidarity obligations and the inseparable duty of violence, they form a group confronted with other groups. However, all these groups do not have the same type of enmity relations with one another. Their relations are adversarial in some cases, but of warlike hostility in others. In segmented societies,[50] political relationships, "friends-foes" relationships encompass two distinct types of oppositions: limited confrontations between adversaries and unlimited conflicts between enemies with nothing in common, that nothing can reconcile. Between adversaries, hostile relations sometimes ineluctably turn into alliances. This is why in such cases we can imagine that recourse to violence is something like a shared rule of dispute resolution. In warlike hostility, the "friends-foes" relationship goes all the way to extermination: there is strictly no shared rule for dispute resolution, aside from destruction, pure and simple, of the "Other."

Thus, in societies where the political has not yet become autonomous, the "friends-foes" relation also proves to be twofold. The solidarity/hostility space is structured by two forms of conflict. However, in this case the extraordinary enemy, whom one is allowed to exterminate, is not the enemy within, but the most distant. This is in contrast with the normal enemy with whom we have a relationship of "at least potential" confrontation. Social and cultural distance is the principle that governs the shift from low to more extreme animosity.

War and Sacrifice

According to Girard, opportunities for violence, conflict, and rivalry occur more often among those who are close. Mimetic desire first affects those who are in contact with one another; more than any others, they influence one another and are liable to become obstacles for one another. The many myths about enemy brothers reflect this danger, and testify to the great degree of violence among people who are close within a society. It is thus not surprising that reciprocal solidarity relations strictly forbid violence among those who are close and make it more acceptable as the social distance between those in conflict increases. This structuring of the solidarity/hostility space is designed to protect the group from violence. It imposes rules on agents' spontaneous violence. The purpose of the prohibition of violence within the circle of lineage identity is to prevent conflicts between spouses, parents and children, brothers and sisters from exceeding a certain threshold of intensity, and so to avoid an explosion of violence within the family and its immediate allies, for this is not only where it risks being the most ferocious and uncontrollable, but also where it is most dangerous for social order. This structure of the solidarity/hostility space is in fact a response to the fact that it is of highest importance to distance violence from the mythological birthplace of the crisis: conflicts between those who are close.[51]

From the Girardian point of view, the meaning and the function of the threefold division of the solidarity/hostility space are clear. Since it is composed of three concentric circles, this structure determines the objects of legitimate violence in accordance with the social distance from the subject. This structure, like sacrifice, shifts violence onto acceptable victims. First, there are those who are close, against whom all violence is forbidden, next there are adversaries, rivals whom we respect up to a certain point and with whom we maintain relations of exchange and measured violence, and then there are enemies, "Others" against whom everything is permitted. Violence grows as solidarity gradually disappears. This is a question of distancing violence from where it is most threatening to the community and finding substitute victims for it. The solidarity/hostility relations that both link and place people in opposition are part of the sacred, the system that protects individuals from their violence while allowing rivalries to be expressed by offering sacrificable victims in tribute to violence.

This is what is suggested by an Arab proverb: "I against my brother, my brothers and I against my cousins, my brothers, my cousins and I against strangers." The division of the relational space into three (or into n, where n is equal to or greater than three) spaces is simply the same as the sacrificial principle. Conflict with my cousins reconciles me with my brothers, conflict with more distant others reconciles me with my cousins, and so on. The third term operates as a substitute victim against whom rivals find reconciliation. From this point of view, the adversarial relation of measured violence is made possible by the relation of warlike hostility. There cannot be one without the other. The consequence of the unlimited hostility that we carry to distant others is that it permits rivalries between those who are close, the violence of which, without this release, would rapidly destroy the community.

This link between war and sacrifice can be seen more or less clearly in many institutions. An interesting example can be found in the ritual anthropophagy of the Tupinamba. The victims of the Tupinambas' ritual feasts were prisoners of war, and the primary purpose of war among the Tupinamba was to capture prisoners so that they could be eaten. Once the prisoner was brought back to the tribe, he was treated more or less like any other member of the group, except that he did not participate in war. Sometimes, a prisoner would even marry and have children with a woman who was a member of the tribe in which he was a captive. She was sometimes the widow of a warrior who had died during the expedition in which the prisoner had been captured.

In fact, a number of years could go by before it was decided to sacrifice him.[52] However, that day would inevitably come.

Prisoners destined to be eaten during Tupinamba ritual meals were both adversaries and enemies. They were adversaries because war was a ritualized activity the purpose of which was not to exterminate the group that one attacked, but to take prisoners who would become ritual victims. They were enemies because they were inevitably killed. Nothing could save them from total destruction. They were also illustrations of the enemy who was both closest and furthest. They were not killed until after a long period of assimilation that literally "domesticated" them, in other words, made them similar to those who were going to destroy them. They were both "members of the community" and marked by an otherness that nothing could erase.

◆ ◆ ◆

As we have seen, the unanimity postulated by social contract theories cannot be reduced to an insipid agreement of opinions. It is not based on those highly vaunted common values. It corresponds to the disappearance of groups, to the fact that individuals find themselves alone, isolated, facing the whole power of the state. We have seen this disequilibrium as a danger, a source of oppression (and sometimes a cause of alienation) from which the individual has to be protected. In truth, the atomization of members of society is equivalent to individuals' legal independence. Thanks to it, each is protected by the agreement of all. The "systematic, large scale" violence of states against their citizens and others rejects the legal independence of individuals. Crimes against humanity are group crimes. They are committed by organized groups against individuals who are members of other groups, which hatred, or indifference, designates as victims.

Hobbes and a whole tradition of political philosophy that came after him rightly see in the exclusion of groups within the state, in the state monopoly of legitimate violence, the condition for domestic peace. However, they do not see, or if they do glimpse it they immediately forget it, that this unanimous reconciliation requires an enemy group external to the state. Carl Schmitt, who, on the contrary, makes the "friends-foes" dichotomy the distinguishing sign of political relations, is led to posit a twofold relationship of enmity. In addition to the "foe," in other words, the opposing group with which we have a relationship of limited conflict, he also mentions, though without distinguishing it clearly from the former, an enemy within, a deadly enemy who has to be exterminated in order to ensure the survival of the state. The "friends-foes" opposition then divides into two and ceases corresponding to the separation between the inside and the outside of the state.

Now, in societies where politics has not yet emerged as an autonomous domain, we also find a twofold relation of enmity between groups that is inseparable from a relationship of friendship internal to each group. Here also there is a normal enemy and an extraordinary enemy, an enemy with whom we have a relationship of measured opposition, and an enemy whom we can annihilate. However, in these societies the extraordinary enemy is the furthest and most different, the most outside, while in states that have the monopoly of legitimate violence, it seems that it is the enemy within, the closest and most similar, who is the object of the most extreme violence.

CHAPTER 3

Territory and War

New countries are a wide field open to violent individual activities that, in long-established states, would come up against certain prejudices, against a wise, regulated conception of life. In colonies, these activities can develop more freely and then better assert their value. Thus, colonies can, to a certain point, be used as a safety valve for modern society. This usefulness, even if it were the only one, is immense.

—Carl Sigler, *Essai sur la colonisation*

According to the Hobbesian fiction, the state is born when members of society cease being enemies of one another. In truth, as we have seen, the unanimous social contract that puts an end to the state of war occurs when the sovereign seizes the monopoly of legitimate violence and excludes clashes between "friend" and "foe" groups. When this is successful, social actors are broken apart from one another. It is the necessary condition for agents' legal independence. The state sets the rules to be shared by those who live together. It gives its citizens laws, shared norms for resolving the disputes that can arise among them. There is not, or at least there should not be, any disagreement among the citizens of a modern state such that "in the extreme case" conflicts cannot be "decided by a previously determined general norm," and the sovereign is the "disinterested and therefore neutral third party" to whom it is always possible to appeal. Because the sovereign has a monopoly over legitimate violence, his or her word is by definition final.

However, the domestic pacification, the "friendship" among citizens, is inseparable from the presence, on the borders of the city, of an enemy that everyone fears. It is just as much in order to protect themselves from the enemy as it is to protect themselves from each other that individuals abandon their original freedom. There is thus no modern state that can exist in an isolated manner. Although political philosophy has had in the past and still has today a tendency to think of the sovereign state as if it were alone and perfectly autonomous, every modern state is a member of a community of states, political entities of the same type. This inattentiveness, this forgetting of the fact that states exist with others and that there is an indispensable presence of "foes," has been essential for thinking of rights and equality as universal, though they are, in fact, always limited to members of a closed community.

Carl Schmitt considered that Hobbes was the most brilliant theoretician of classical European states, absolutist states resulting from wars of religion.[1] Schmitt wrote: "The classical European state had managed to achieve the entirely incredible thing, which was to establish domestic peace and exclude hostility as a concept in law." In other words, it prohibited dukes and barons from engaging in war, and thus established "peace, security and order within the borders of its own territory."[2] Absolute monarchies eliminated the private wars characteristic of feudalism. By taking control of the monopoly of legitimate violence, the state became veritably sovereign. The hostility between "friend" and "foe" groups was no longer legitimate except in relations between states. Within each state, properly political relations disappeared, and from then on what was called "political life" was no longer anything more than policing and administrative management. The classical European state confined politics to relations between nations, and made the "friends-foes" dichotomy coincide with the borders between states.

The absolutist state was born out of the centralization of power in the hands of absolute sovereigns toward the end of the wars of religion. It was from real wars, veritable violent exclusions, that the modern state was born. The modern state was created by pacifying the land over which it exercised its authority and confining the relation of enmity to relationships between states. In 1648, the Treaty of Westphalia, which authorized sovereigns to impose their religion on their subjects, both instituted a principle of noninterference and made it possible to align religious divisions, which had been the main source of conflicts between groups, along borders between lands. By codifying rules for relations between sovereign states that were in principle equal, despite the huge difference that there could be between a country like France and a little principality of the German Empire, this international agreement, which put an end to the Thirty Years' War, gave birth to the modern state and a new conception of sovereignty.

The delegitimization of groups in Hobbes's political thought, their exclusion as political players, is the theoretical translation of what Carl Schmitt considered to be the incredible dual achievement of the classical European state: the establishment of domestic peace and the exclusion of hostility as a concept in law. This theoretical banishment made politics "the Other" of violence. Hobbes transformed into logical truth the elimination of groups from political life. Not only are "foes" now to be found only outside of national borders, but Hobbes confined violence to the chaos of the state of nature, outside of which political order is established. The presence of the enemy at the borders of the state, which is in fact necessary, tends to disappear from political reflection. The role of enmity in political relations disappears at the same time as that of groups. Politics thus became identified with law, which is the contrary of force. The indispensable coercion designed to enforce compliance with shared rules is seen uniquely as a means of turning us away from violence. Legitimate violence is not considered violence.

Exclusion of groups is equivalent to simplification of the space of solidarity and hostility. It replaces the threefold division by a twofold one. Once the "friends-foes" division is identified with the difference between the inside and outside of the state, the multiple, complex relations of enmity and aid that used to both divide groups apart and bind them together are replaced by a simple dichotomy that both links and isolates individuals. As we have seen, the threefold division of the solidarity/hostility space reflects the sacrificial dimension of the rules that structure that space. It shows the shift of the violence toward acceptable targets. Rules that proscribe the use of violence among those who are close do not eliminate conflict. They forbid its expression. This "repression" is precisely what makes it necessary to have recourse to sacrifice and other means that allow violence to be expressed by redirecting it onto sacrificable third parties. The threefold division of the solidarity/hostility space indicates how fragile the rules of protection against violence are. Like sacrifice itself, it shows that violence can never be wholly prevented and that we always have to offer it substitute victims if we want to distance it from the community.

The modern state's simplification of the underlying hostility corresponds, on the contrary, to *an attempt to renounce the sacrificial principle.* It is an effort to establish a purely rational political order in order to institute a principle of coexistence in which violence never occurs without reason, is never a pressure valve, never targets anyone but those who "deserve" being violently attacked. The modern state wants both to entirely exclude violence from relations between "friends," and to limit its uses to enmity relationships that justify it. The transformation of members of society into "citizen-friends" through the social contract is thought of as the result of a rational renunciation of violence and a pact to ensure reciprocal security.

The Classical State and Simplification of the Space of Hostility

The institution of peace within the absolutist state is the first phase of an attempt to simplify the solidarity/hostility space that led to the establishment of *territory* as a principle and foundation of the modern political order. Territory is not simply a geographical space, the physical expanse over which a state exerts its influence. Properly speaking, there is no territory unless the borders of the state coincide with the "friends-foes" dichotomy, in other words, unless groups have been excluded as political players. This action expels from the state the "friends-foes" relationship in both of its forms: adversarial relations and warlike hostility. Both of these are dissolved in the opposition between the inside and the outside. This blurring of categories nonetheless does not entirely eliminate the difference between the two forms of animosity. On the contrary, as we have seen above, it tends to reappear in the distinction between the *enemy on the outside, with whom one has limited relations of enmity, and the enemy within, who has to be exterminated.* In truth, the action that expels groups from the state is never completely successful. Despite what Schmitt implies, groups and the conflicts between them reemerge, but in a new form, inside the absolutist state.

In stateless societies, hostile relationships between different groups cannot be dissociated from the ties of solidarity that unite the individuals and families who are members of the groups. Not only are there no "friends" without "foes," but different types of solidarity obligations correspond to different types of enmity relationships. Solidarity and hostility are two versions of the same relationship. However, while the absolutist state transforms the enmity relationship by forcing it out of the area where it exercises its authority, it does not simplify solidarity ties in the same manner. The new political structure that it imposes comes with deep social changes that destroy or weaken traditional solidarity relationships, but the holder of the monopoly of legitimate violence does not manage to create new, sufficiently strong ties of solidarity at the level where the new hostile relations arise, in other words, in the state as a whole. To put it in different terms, while the absolutist power may expel "foes" from the state, it does not turn everyone living in the state into "friends." Since it maintains the hierarchical differences inherited from feudal times and consecrates the threefold ancien régime division, the absolutist state retains a structural principle based on person-to-person relationships between people belonging to separate groups. It maintains the divisions that were meaningful only in the "friends-foes" opposition that was eliminated by the domestic peace it imposed. At the same time, the absolutist state establishes centralized government, where what should be a new principle of solidarity is expressed: the unification of all citizens under a single authority holding the monopoly of legitimate violence. However, this principle of solidarity is radically different from the one that motivated the conflicts that have just been prohibited and that used to structure the groups of which the state still maintains traces, for it isolates individuals from their groups so as to link them to a single source of authority.

In a traditional society, solidarity ties are generally inseparable from relationships of superiority and subordination, but the reciprocity that characterizes them gives meaning to the inequality that marks them. In a society that has a central government, these unequal relations tend to rapidly transform into privileges with nothing given in return, especially when they are not directly related to the exercise of power. The more sovereign the power, the more the capacity to identify the "foe," moves toward the center and escapes traditional groups, the more the center proves able to ensure protection for all—for example, by substituting royal for local justice—the less privileges, which used to go hand in hand with protection that has now disappeared, seem justified. The establishment of a central government consequently increases the probability of disputes inherent to divisions between groups, and shifts the location of those conflicts.[3] The "friends-foes" dichotomy in which they express themselves is different from those the state has just prohibited. The groups involved are not the same as those that the state has just stripped of their political power. The conflicts between feudal lords were replaced with the opposition between the third estate and the two others, the nobility and the clergy. Moreover, this new dichotomy proved to be, properly speaking, orthogonal to territorial enmity. As is shown by the "universal" goal of the French Revolution, which was to bring freedom to all people, the "friends-foes" dichotomy that was at its core did not coincide with the division of Europe into distinct territories, but divided each state on the inside.

The tensions pervading the absolutist state were the cause of the French Revolution, and gradually led to transformation of the system everywhere in Europe. In modern terms, what was lacking in the absolutist state was citizens' equality. Inequality, the difference between the orders, was the legacy of a relationship of hostility for which there was no longer a place once internal peace had been established and "foes" had been expelled from the state. Thus, in *Qu'est-ce que le tiers état?*[4] Sieyès suggested sending the nobles back into the forests of Franconia, from which, according to him, they had come. This famous recommendation shows that, for him, any group that enjoyed special privileges within the state could come only from the outside. Anyone who breaks the equality that has to reign between "friends" is by definition a "foe" and thus a "foreigner." Inside the pacified state, all must be "friends," equal, and know no divisions other than between them and the outside foe.[5] Within the pacified state, there must be the reign of unlimited solidarity, characteristic of the circle of identity. The territorial state cannot accommodate a difference between orders that reveals hostility between groups since such hostility has, in principle, ended. The 1789 Revolution reduced these tensions by instituting a principle of solidarity and identity designed to be in harmony with internal pacification and expulsion of "foes" from the state: the equality and brotherhood of all citizens.

Transformation of the Bonds of Solidarity

As Lucien Scubla has noted, "by giving itself the monopoly of legitimate violence, the state establishes what will become the nation by combining the middle circle into the innermost circle, which it thus expands."[6] The nation requires not only that foes be expelled from the state—this requirement was already one of those of the absolutist state; what characterizes the *nation* is the extension of solidarity, characteristic of the circle of identity, to all citizens. This expansion of the first circle of identity so as to include all citizens, and finally even all members of society, leads to a deep transformation in solidarity relations.

In segmentary societies, solidarity relations among members of a group are reciprocal relations in the same sense as are, for example, neighborly and household relations. Of course, kinship ties and clan and lineage solidarity entail obligations that go beyond the immediate neighborhood and bind agents to others whom they do not know. However, these more distant ties are also reciprocal. They take the form of what Marcel Hénaff calls "ceremonial exchange."[7] Each obligation that is fulfilled can in this sense be considered a gift, which in turn creates an obligation for the person who has benefited. It creates an obligation toward the person who was initially obligated. In this way, the conflicts and alliances that are created and undone within the circle of adversaries take the form of negative or positive reciprocity. It might be said that all these ties of solidarity are reciprocal in a "nominal" manner. They occur between people we can identify by proper names. Within the traditional threefold organization, reciprocity does not imply that there is symmetry between the giver and receiver, or that the gifts and countergifts are equal. Generally, they are not. It simply requires that each obligation honored engender an obligation in return. Within the threefold space of hostility, solidarity relations both map onto and model the network of agents' social relations. However, these obligations in no way exclude the existence of hierarchical relations or inequality among the agents that they bring together.

In contrast, the fusion of the circles of identity and adversarial relations that is accomplished by the modern state separates obligations from the fabric of social relations. The unification of the two circles into one entails a simplification of the web of solidarity relations. In the traditional space, this had the form of a network with many different nodes, the overall structure of which was the same for all, but in which agents, depending on their different membership or the interplay of alliances, were linked mainly to distinct nodes. Moreover, since the reciprocity of solidarity relations does not require that there be symmetry between the giver and the receiver, it follows that the distance separating A from B is not necessarily the same as that separating B from A. The former's obligations to the latter are not mirror images of those of the latter to the former. In contrast, unification of the fields of adversarial relations and identity under the sign of the *universality of law* replaces this asymmetrical multinode interlacing with an arrangement that has a unique center. In this arrangement, ideally, all are at equal distance from everyone else and from the center. All citizens are united together by their identical membership in the nation and uniquely by that. The destruction of intermediary groups accomplished by the French Revolution in the name of equality had the (intentional) consequence of ensuring that no one would have any special allegiance that could turn him or her from equal commitment to all members of the state. Reducing the two spaces of adversarial relations and lineage identity into a single one forces solidarity relations to take the form of a homogenous, isotropic net in the sense that all are equally close and distant from one another, and similarly attached to the nation.

All are also equally separated from one another. Replacing the former threefold organization with a single division between inside "friends" and outside "foes" leads, on one hand, as we have seen, to relative lack of distinction between the two forms of the relation of hostility; on the other hand, it also leads to partial confusion of solidarity and hostility relations. For, while combining the two circles of identity and adversity into a single one extends solidarity to the entire nation, it also detaches it from its anchoring in personal relations. It separates solidarity relations from immediate loyalties to the family, clan, or village.[8] It replaces these ties, which we now often call communitarian, with a more abstract obligation to others with whom we have no strict link: an obligation to all the others that is independent of the affective relations that bind us to some. Establishing solidarity at the national level not only weakens local ties, but requires that relationships with more distant others, who are included in the circle that it delimits, be constructed on bases other than reciprocal, individual-to-individual, group-to-group allegiances. The result is a gradual weakening of traditional solidarity ties.

First, they lose their importance, for the new solidarity is now called upon to be exercised outside of the framework that these relations used to determine. Second, the area where solidarity is exercised wastes away. Indeed, as the distance between those who used to feel obligated to one another grows, the less those ties are justified since they become socially redundant when their function is taken over by new solidarity ties.[9] Consequently, affective bonds become internalized and private. They are abandoned to subjects' free choice.

Freed of the traditional solidarity obligations that used to gather them into distinct groups, agents are transformed into individuals. Their actions influence others in unequal ways, but there is also a sense in which they affect everyone in the same way because individuals no longer have any (or almost any) specific obligations to anyone in particular, aside from those that are voluntary. Thus, the forms of competition typical of adversarial relations withdraw out of what used to be the domain of lineage identity and invade the new, broader circle of solidarity. The world where we used to give without keeping accounts, or at least without keeping precise accounts, it now subject to cost-benefits analysis. Within the space pacified by the monopoly of legitimate violence, more and more social relations tend to become purely mercantile and utilitarian. "Universal" solidarity detaches agents from their specific bonds of solidarity, and brings into contact individuals who, a priori, nothing but the prohibition of violence unites into a community. It leaves them free to choose, in their relationships with one another, between indifference and optional affinities. The principle that brings these individuals together is that each owes nothing to anyone except what he or she owes to all the others. The egoism typical of adversary groups, which was inseparable from the solidarity among the members of each group, has been replaced by individual selfishness, which produces no solidarity in return.

Territory

Territory is the form taken by the domain of "friends" when the transformation of solidarity ties has been accomplished, in other words, not only when "foes" are expelled from the state, but when the two circles of identity and adversarial relations, merged and folded into one, are united under the sign of citizens' equality. This simplification of the space of hostility separates political relationships of enmity and friendship from agents' social relations. This is a separation that, in segmentary societies, used to exist only in the case of warlike hostile relations because it used to be exercised only between strangers who had no other relationship. In modern societies, the relationships of political association and dissociation are no longer related simply to the social distance or an opposition between different groups; they have been transposed onto a completely different level, that of the nation—where, in principle, everyone is a "friend"—and the nation's relationship with other nations, which alone can be "foes." Among citizens, community reigns. All the other groupings, whether they are less extensive than the nation or the same size as it, as can be unions and professional and sports associations, or larger than it, such as religions, are "authorized to exist" only if they renounce their political dimension, their capacity to form groups of "friends" and "foes."

By proclaiming friendship (community) among all members of the nation, in other words, among all those living in the space pacified by its monopoly of legitimate violence, the modern state immediately makes the territory that it controls a principle of solidarity. It transforms a physical space into a concrete expression of belonging that identifies "friends" and distinguishes them from outside "foes." Yet a territory is not a simple physical space. Like the threefold space of solidarity/hostility in segmentary societies, a national *territory* corresponds to a certain way of thinking about our political relationships with others ("foes") and our relationships among ourselves ("friends"). Consequently, it constitutes a strange mixture, a hybrid synthesis of physical space and moral predispositions. A territory means the establishment of moral relationships, relationships of political hostility and friendship, not in function of kinship, lineage, membership in a given order or social status, in other words, not by person-to-person ties, but by borders set in physical space.[10]

The transformation of bonds of solidarity and hostility that detaches them from the fabric of social relations is inseparable from the emergence of *history* and *culture* as political themes that the state has to maintain and promote as legitimate objects of sovereign concern.[11] Relationships of membership in a lineage or clan, of kinship or even of feudal allegiance, which in traditional societies determine agents' identities, are immediately given in proximity. They are obvious to everyone, at least over one or two generations, and they are likewise transparent to close neighbors. Their representation beyond this everyday obviousness forms a major part of the accumulated culture and knowledge of traditional societies. However, this culture, even when it is special knowledge reserved for a select few, remains in continuity with the social relations of the agents for whom it is memory and provides a reason for being. The gradual destruction or, if one prefers, "disarming" of these bonds and their replacement with a form of solidarity that no longer matches the framework of the relationships among agents requires that a new form of identity be established. In territorialized societies, it is history and culture, culture that is conceived of essentially as national heritage and the legacy of a shared history, that provide this identity.

As Benedict Anderson has shown so well, shared history is a way to anchor people in a territory, in a physical space that they share, and give them an "imagined" identity that is independent of the specific ties that they have with one another.[12] Centered around territory, national history links individuals with those who preceded them, independent of any kinship relationship. Under the pretext that the events that it describes occurred in a physical space, which later becomes, for example, France or Japan, it retrospectively brings together enemies of yesteryear into the unity of the nation. For, while Bordeaux and Dijon are indeed now part of France, there was a time when the Aquitaine and Burgundy were foreign powers and foes. History casts onto the past the ties that it aims to create in the present.

Blood, race, and ethnic identity are also ways of ensuring group solidarity, even in the absence, it seems, of shared territory, but not without reference to a shared history. Ethnic relationships, like the relationship to territory, supplement with a bond that is supposed to have existed in the past the lack of a present link between all those whom the monopoly of legitimate violence both assembles, or aims to assemble, and breaks into discrete units. In fact, territory and ethnic identity are mutually complementary. Either territory is conceived of as the source of the "ethnic" link that ties individuals together in the present, or the ethnic link is seen as an eternal relationship that legitimizes in the present the exclusive occupation of a territory or the unification of a set of territories under a single authority. Territory, culture, and race—in the sense that it was understood in the nineteenth century when people spoke of the French or English "race"—form an inseparable threesome, but in it territory plays a fundamental role. It has a closer relationship to the monopoly of legitimate violence than the ideas of race and shared culture. Because it corresponds to a physical space, it embodies a more abstract requirement of the monopoly of legitimate violence: the homogenization of members of society. People can be homogenous in different ways, including shared ethnic and cultural identity, which are only two among many; for example, the same language or shared religion, or even origin in the same social class. In all cases, the state is built by purifying its territory, by expelling the "others" and thereby ensuring that the "friends-foes" dichotomy coincides with the interior and exterior of the territory.[13]

The Democratic Paradox

As we have seen, the action of expelling "foes" from the state never works perfectly. Groups and conflicts always tend to resurface. While the absolutist state may be constructed by rejecting them and banishing political conflict, we can consider that modern democracy has chosen the opposite solution: to accept political *dissent*. Democracies have also succeeded in a way, different from that of the absolutist state, in achieving something completely "incredible." They have reintroduced the "friends-foes" dichotomy into the state, yet without dividing it violently. Modern liberal democracies have, in fact, kept the essential of the features of classical European states: sovereignty, monopoly of legitimate violence, pacification of the entire territory, and exclusion of private wars as a means of solving disputes.

According to Schmitt, in consequence they also exclude any veritable political activity from occurring within them. We can nonetheless point out to him that, contrary to the absolutist state that represses any form of expression of the "friends-foes" dichotomy within the state, democracies encourage at least some forms of political opposition; they have even been entirely constructed to give such opposition free rein. What makes possible the exercise of the antagonistic "friends-foes" relationship within a state structured by the monopoly of legitimate violence is the type of conflicts that democracies authorize and the nature of the groups that confront each other.

Note that, for Schmitt, a conflict is political when it is such that "in the extreme case" it can be resolved neither "by a previously determined general norm nor by the judgment of a disinterested and therefore neutral third party."[14] However, democracy institutionalizes a procedure that gives the dispute resolution process a means of reworking its own rules. In other words, it allows the rules themselves to become what is at stake in the conflict. Democracy makes it possible for already agreed-upon rules for resolving conflicts to be challenged and changed by the very process that resolves the conflicts. Democratic debate is a means of modifying shared norms and accepted rules. In this sense, the conflicts that occur within it are indeed such that they cannot "be decided by a previously determined general norm." They are political conflicts because the rules for resolving them, in other words, laws, are precisely what in this case are in dispute. From this follows what we can call the "democratic paradox." In a democracy, laws, rules for resolving conflicts, have to simultaneously appear as neutral, external to the conflicts that they make it possible to resolve, and nonetheless be able to be changed by the resolution of those very conflicts.[15] Constitutional rules in democracy can be seen both as an expression of this paradox and as a way to circumvent it. The constitutional rule that requires a majority of 70 percent in order to amend the constitution can itself be amended by a 70 percent majority.

We could say that democracy has domesticated, in both senses of the word, the "friends-foes" opposition. First it transformed this opposition into a domestic conflict. It reintroduced into the heart of the democratic home the dichotomy that the classical state had thrust outside of its borders. However, democracy has also domesticated opposition in the sense that it has tamed it. It has made it more peaceful, less violent and wild. Modern democracy offers a special solution to the political question. It is a fragile, paradoxical solution because the political animal constantly threatens to return to the wild state. This paradox and the always imperfect control of political antagonism are what explain the fragility of democracies and the fact that they can self-destruct through democratic means. The "metarules" that authorize the transformation of dispute resolution rules can themselves be changed following a conflict, and cease being democratic rules. This is how an elected democratic majority voted in favor of laws authorizing Hitler to muzzle the opposition and prohibit political parties other than the Nazis.

Domestication of the "friends-foes" opposition is based on a transformation of the composition and status of groups authorized to participate in political debate, in other words, groups that can challenge, within the confrontations opposing them, the accepted dispute resolution rules. What makes democracy as we know it possible is that political opponents *do not form social groups.* This is linked, in part but not exclusively, to the idea of political representation. Those who confront each other in a democratic manner are elected: they are representatives whose power and authority come from the electoral support they have received. In consequence, conflict passes through a buffer: it occurs through intermediaries. However, as the classical work by Donald Horowitz on ethnic conflict has shown,[16] political representation is insufficient. When the various political parties coincide with ethnic divisions, the outcome of elections quickly becomes predictable because it reflects the ethnic composition of the population. Moreover, since each representative can stand for only the members of his or her own community, not only are some in consequence deprived of representation, but above all the clashes between political parties become confrontations between sociological groups. In other words, they become conflicts that oppose groups to which individuals are assigned when they are born, independent of their will.

Democratic debates cannot occur between communities that transcend the individuals confronting each other, in other words, between groups to which people belong from birth to death. Only "voluntary associations" may be pitted against each other. Membership in a political party, or more simply the right to vote, must not reflect a contingent origin, but the rational interests of individual agents. This limitation on the nature of opposing groups is what makes it possible for democratic debate to escape violence, for it restates in its own way the Hobbesian exclusion of groups from the state. Reducing "friend" and "foe" groups to voluntary associations is what makes it possible for political opposition to return inside the state because it implies that individuals form only temporary alliances and are always ready to abandon them if greater benefit can be had by doing so. Agents' political commitments are thus subject to the vagaries of individual choices independent of any membership in a group. This is the only way that accepted dispute resolution rules can be challenged. The metamorphosis of "friends" and "foes" into voluntary associations is a sign of the dissolution of groups into rational self-interest.

If this explanation is correct, then why do rational conflicts between individuals remain peaceful in democratic societies while in the state of nature they lead to the war of all against all? To ask this question is to provide an answer at the same time: because the conflicts occur in the shadow of a sovereign power that authorizes them but holds the monopoly of legitimate violence. What allows rationality to be the Other of violence is not a property intrinsic to reason, but the presence of a master of violence, a presence that is equivalent to the expulsion of groups from the land the state controls.

In consequence, democracy is something like an attractor for modern states. It is a form of political organization toward which they spontaneously tend to evolve. The homogeneity that is demanded by solidarity among all the members of the state, the equality that it implies, and the free rein given to individual rationality through abandonment of traditional obligations make it an ideal means of collective management of private interests. This point toward which modern states naturally gravitate nonetheless does not correspond to the "end of history."[17] Democracies, just as much as absolutist states and nation-states, can exist only as members of an international community of states that are potential mutual enemies, since each is the absolute master of its own *territory*. Even though democracies allow the political dichotomy to occur within them and the rules for resolving disputes to be challenged, they are possible only if each one manages to expel "enemy" groups from the state and make the "friends-foes" distinction map onto the borders that separate the state from the international community. A modern state, even if it is democratic, inevitably has "foes" and sometimes also internal enemies. Even if there were a universal community of democracies in which there was rule of law and global justice that could establish the transborder equality of all individuals,[18] the problem linked to the distinction between the inside and the outside of the state would not be solved; the possibility of war would remain.

Groups and Conflicts

Schmitt says: "The friend, enemy, and combat concepts receive their real meaning precisely because they refer to the real possibility of physical killing."[19] He adds that it is impossible, and dishonest, to try to find a rational justification for political conflicts. He says that no rational end can justify people killing one another.[20] Political enmity is legitimate and makes sense only insofar as it is situated at an existential level and brings different forms of existence into opposition: "If such physical destruction of human life is not motivated by an existential threat to one's own way of life, then it cannot be justified."[21] In his eyes, only this existential dimension can justify recourse to violence.

However, this existential dimension corresponds to the fact that, like membership in a group, most often political conflict is imposed on the individual from the outside: it is not a choice. It is imposed on individual agents as a destiny that they have to take on, and while engaging in the struggle may sometimes be a personal decision—for example, to be or not to be a member of the resistance—the conflict itself is never a simple option among others. This "existential justification" for political violence is for Schmitt an empirical description just as much as it is a normative recommendation. It is clear that, for the majority of individuals, the intergroup violence in which they are caught more closely resembles a vicious cycle in which they are prisoners than a freely chosen action. For those, for example, who are living in Iraq, Afghanistan, Palestine, or Israel today, political conflicts are external factors that limit their choices. To say that the justification for political conflicts can only be existential is first and foremost to recognize this fact. For each, the conflict is rooted in his or her membership in one or the other opposing group, and this fact is itself normative in the sense that it has consequences on the normative level. Membership in a group imposes duties that constitute the individual as a moral being. To say that the justification for conflicts among groups is existential and that they impose themselves on individuals is to say that, in relation to those conflicts, individuals are bound by moral obligations to help and support those who are their "friends."[22] Thus, the existential justification corresponds to a "metanorm": that of fulfilling set obligations.

The reason Schmitt considers that there is no reason that can justify the death of a person is because there is no reason able to justify the "friends-foes" opposition, provide the foundation for political conflicts, and legitimize recourse to violence between groups. This apparent "irrationality" simply repeats in a different manner what, according to him, constitutes the essence of political opposition: *a conflict such that it can be resolved neither "by a previously determined general norm nor by the judgment of a disinterested and therefore neutral third party."* Political conflict cannot be explained rationally. Otherwise, there would be at least one shared norm, namely, rationality, that would be able to resolve it, and it would be in principle possible to appeal to a neutral third party, namely, rationality itself. To refuse to give a rational justification for political violence is to reject the idea that rationality is a norm external to the conflict and able to draw the line between good and bad violence.

The "existential" need to maintain "one's own way of life" that Schmitt thus situates beyond all reason indicates that "friends-foes" groups are not simple voluntary associations. They are not groups that anyone can join or leave freely. Here, membership in the group justifies giving one's life or killing for it. It also justifies declaring as "foes" those who want to break away from it and refuse to fight for the group's survival.[23] This justification of political confrontation by a moral relationship of membership in distinct groups confirms our analysis of democracy: the "friends-foes" dichotomy cannot be reintroduced into a state without risk unless the groups underlying it are voluntary associations, groups that individuals can join or abandon for personal interest reasons. Rational interest provides moral groups with no protection from violence. It protects only those who remain individually subject to the sovereign power of the one who determines the distinction between good and bad violence.

The Two Clausewitzian Wars

In Clausewitz, we find the distinction between two types of warlike confrontation: "wars of armed observation" and "wars of extermination." The former are military undertakings with limited goals. They are consistent with the famous saying, "War is a continuation of politics by other means." The latter, wars of extermination or annihilation, aim to destroy the enemy political entity. Their goal is unlimited in the sense that no partial success, no specific advantage, can put an end to the conflict: the only thing that can is total defeat of one of the parties. In a war of extermination, each group struggles for its own survival, rather than for a limited objective. This is what explains the "escalation to extremes" that is characteristic of it. In contrast, a war of armed observation, because it is motivated by specific reasons, political reasons, can be ended when a limited advantage is achieved.

For the author of *On War*, this conceptual distinction corresponds historically to the difference between the European wars of the seventeenth and eighteenth centuries, which were wars of armed observation, and the revolutionary and Napoleonic wars, which were wars of extermination. Clausewitz explained that the reason for the transformation was because the French Revolution replaced mercenary armies, which were largely composed of people who were foreign to the nation they were serving, with *the people in arms.* Consequently, it was no longer simply a question of confrontations between armed men in service to different political authorities, but nations and peoples who were in opposition. From then on the fight mobilized entire populations.

According to him, the French Revolution profoundly changed the goals and nature of war. The objective of revolutionary wars is not simply to obtain a limited material or political advantage, such as a treaty amendment or annexation of a province, but to eradicate tyranny and despotism. Such wars have goals that are properly moral: the purpose is to export a way of being and living together that one judges to be the only good and just one. The Revolution also changed the nature of wars. Owing to its capacity to call upon the entire nation, the Republic succeeded in mobilizing ever larger armies. Maintaining and equipping them required the participation of a greater proportion of citizens in the war effort and led to increased exploitation of occupied peoples. However, according to Clausewitz, the latter feature remains less important than the former because what motivated and made possible the most complete mobilization of France in the revolutionary and Napoleonic wars was their objective: to free the peoples of Europe. This was a moral, or rather, in his eyes, immoral, objective.

Wars of extermination are in fact *moral wars* from Clausewitz's point of view. Wars of liberation, struggles against tyranny: these are wars that those involved consider to be just wars. They are violent conflicts in which two distinct forms of existence come face to face with each other for survival. This is why no specific reason, no local advantage, no benefit, no matter how large it may be, can put an end to them. The only thing that can is total defeat of the adversary. According to Clausewitz, this "moralization" removes war from the political arena, which is characterized by rational negotiation for limited objectives. It makes war a clash of ideas, an ideological conflict. In fact, wars of extermination escape politics in yet another way. They tend to become independent of the political objectives that were at the origin of the conflict, and in the end the conflict becomes its own end. A war of extermination quickly stops being the "continuation of politics by other means" and becomes only pure violence freed of all constraint. It then transforms into an unlimited conflict, a confrontation that is no longer anything but destruction, relentlessness, and the "escalation to extremes," driven by the infinite will to conquer.[24]

The revolutionary and Napoleonic wars also rejected the territorial order of absolute monarchies. They were conflicts that refused to identify the "friends-foes" dichotomy simply with the borders between nations. The Revolution substituted for or added to the opposition between separate countries the struggle between peoples and tyrants. In the same stroke, it introduced within the states to which it was opposed a dichotomy between "friend" and "foe" groups—the opposition between the people and the great—that threatened the sovereign's monopoly of legitimate violence. The hostility that moved the Revolution against its enemies was located, in the proper sense, on a different level in relation to the "friends-foes" dichotomies that were structuring Europe at the time. A feature of wars of extermination, or at least of the revolutionary and Napoleonic wars, is that they reintroduce and legitimize the relationship of enmity within the space pacified by the sovereign. In contrast, wars of armed observation are consistent with mapping states' borders onto the "friends-foes" distinction. Even though such wars often aim to change the borders in question, they do not challenge the principle of enmity that underlies the division between the nations.

About one century later, Carl Schmitt, who was working on Clausewitz, established a fairly similar distinction between political wars and moral wars. Political wars are limited wars, framed by the shared rules of the law of war, *jus in bello*. According to him, they illustrate the "friends-foes" relationship as it was thought of in classical Europe. In contrast, in moral wars, the enemy is no longer considered as simply a "political enemy" that, according to Schmitt, "must be compelled to retreat to his border only,"[25] but as an embodiment of evil that one has the right to eliminate, exterminate. Moral wars give central importance to *jus ad bellum*, to the question of the just war. The law of war imposes on both the aggressor and the victim identical rules that are designed to limit the intensity of the violence. It supposes a form of moral equality among all combatants. On the contrary, the idea of a just war imposes a radical moral difference between the two parties: an unjust aggressor and an innocent victim. Once the enemy has been defined as morally bad, as the "great Satan" or the "axis of evil," as an Other with whom one shares no common norms, there is no longer any "law" or "right" that could limit the violence of the confrontation. While a political conflict is impersonal and without hatred, according to Schmitt,[26] moral wars express hatred of the enemy considered as a moral monster, which must be destroyed at all price.

Contrary to *political wars*, which are limited, *moral wars* are total: they can come to an end only through complete destruction of the enemy. They are wars of annihilation. Whereas, for Clausewitz, the revolutionary and Napoleonic wars were moral and of extermination, according to Schmitt, the two world wars in the twentieth century were moral and total. Both World War I and World War II were fought in the name of ideological principles, and it is clear that both were wars of extermination that targeted the total destruction of an enemy considered morally reprehensible.

This distinction between two types of wars, political and moral wars, bears a striking resemblance to the difference between the circles of adversarial relations and warlike hostility in segmentary societies. The distinction is first moral, and concerns permitted use of violence. Between political and moral wars, as between *adversarial relations* and *warlike hostility*, the greater intensity of the violence is related to the absence of rules to provide a framework for and limit the confrontation. In the case of political and *adversarial* wars, the violence itself is considered as a shared rule for resolving conflict: as an acceptable means for resolving the dispute. In contrast, the unlimited violence of moral wars and wars of *warlike hostility* goes hand in hand with a lack of shared norms. However, a difference remains. The violence of *hostility* is unlimited because it is amoral. The absence of moral bonds between members of different groups is what authorizes recourse to extreme violence. However, it is the justification that a moral war receives from condemnation of the enemy as morally bad that authorizes the greatest violence. This is why Schmitt condemns moral wars, which he considers immoral because they provide a moral legitimization for their violence.

As we have seen, passage between the different circles of hostility and solidarity depends on the social distance in relation to the agent. This distance is also embodied in real space. The moral distancing of those against whom one can exercise unbridled violence also most often corresponds to greater distance in physical and cultural space. Insofar as it is a question of distancing the violence from the heart of the community, it is not surprising that social and physical distance vary in the same manner. However, in the case of political and moral wars, this spatial transposition of the principle of hostility apparently does not take place. The revolutionary and Napoleonic wars, like the two world wars in the twentieth century, were essentially conflicts between neighboring states belonging to the same general culture. Here we find a disjunction of moral distance and physical distance in that, in the case of the enemy within as in that of moral wars, the moral deformity of the adversary no longer corresponds to distance in physical space. In both cases, we are dealing with a relation of hostility toward those closest to us.

The Return of the Sacrificial Principle

According to Schmitt, the *purely moral conception* of the distinction between limited and unlimited wars is a recent innovation that has taken the place of another way of thinking about the difference and legitimizing violence. Indeed, contrary to Clausewitz, Schmitt does not think of the two forms of warlike opposition as two successive moments in a history of military combat, but as lasting components of an evolving system. Initially, the principle of the distinction was not moral, but territorial or spatial. It categorized conflicts in terms of their distance in geographical and cultural space, and made the distance itself the foundation for the moral distinction between different types of armed conflict.

It is in *The Nomos of the Earth*, written during World War II, that Schmitt rediscovered and proposed an explicit theory on the threefold division of the space of hostility (and solidarity) that the "friends-foes" dichotomy seemed to divide into only two orbits when he introduced it in the 1920s. Schmitt insisted on the spatial dimension of this form of violence management. In effect, it is because the principle of the distinction between two forms of conflict is spatial that it is possible to go beyond the simple "friends-foes" dichotomy, and recognize a threefold distinction in international space: a division of types of violent conflict into three distinct areas. Like the threefold division in segmentary social systems, the threefold division of the space of international relations consists in once again performing the operation that originally divided "friends" from "foes" by situating them inside or outside the state. The area where the most extreme violence is permitted, where the laws of war do not apply, is now located furthest to the outside. It is the area beyond the community of sovereign states that are "enemies" but share equal rights.

According to Schmitt, between the birth of the modern state and 1914, the wars in Europe did not generally resort to extreme forms of violence. This limitation would have been possible because there was a "free" space outside Europe, where the rules designed to limit the intensity of combat did not apply: the colonies. In that space, European powers could give free rein to violence that was encumbered neither by the rules of war, nor by respect for international law.[27] The removal of prohibitions applied not only to relationships between Europeans and "Others" living in that space, but also to the conflicts over control of that space that could arise between Europeans.

The fundamental thesis of *The Nomos of the Earth* is that the disappearance of this space—a result, according to Schmitt, of a rather unwise attempt to extend to Others the European Law of Nations—has led to a return of unlimited wars in Europe.[28] *Moral wars* are thus the form that extreme confrontations take when they no longer occur in a land inhabited by "Others" to whom we owe nothing, in other words, when the moral difference between the adversaries no longer corresponds to a spatial difference. The threefold division of the modern space of hostility is stable only if it is embodied in both geographical and cultural distance. When the moral difference between permitted and prohibited violence takes physical form in territory, in a space where distance goes hand in hand with foreignness, it is possible to unambiguously situate "Others" on the scale of enmity and to distance from us the most violent forms of warlike confrontation.

The institution, outside of the European space, of this free space, open to the most violent conflicts, was more or less contemporaneous with the appearance of the modern state holding the monopoly of legitimate violence. It is indeed a question of institution, not simply "discovery," because, as Schmitt shows, international law and explicit treaties enshrined this difference in use of violence between that occurring on European soil and that in the new worlds the states were discovering. This embodiment of the threefold division of the hostility/solidarity space in the spatial and cultural space established by modern states extended the principle of *territory* to worldwide international relations. Moreover, in the domestic space, this principle gradually replaced the traditional structure of interpersonal enmity and solidarity relations. The difference between legitimate and illegitimate use of violence and the legitimacy of recourse to greater or lesser violence no longer depended on relationships between agents and the groups to which they belonged, but on the place where they were born and where they lived: on the national territory and the moral space of cultural identity.

Like the anthropological space of conflict in segmentary social systems, the territorial system of the modern global community is divided into three distinct areas: the nation's territory; the Concert of Nations, in other words, a political community of equal collective subjects whose relationships are governed by international law the development of which all in principle participate; and finally the free space where we find what Rabindranath Tagore called "non-nations."[29] This meant colonies, "new lands," "frontiers," protectorates, in short all territories and political entities that are not modern states. This system is "territorial," and its division into three reflects the distance from the center that is the nation's territory, a homogenous space, every part of which is equal to the whole. Distance from it is measured along two dimensions that, in principle, should evolve in parallel: physical distance and cultural separation. "Non-nations" are ideally both the most distant in physical space and the most foreign culturally.

The reappearance of *warlike hostility*, insofar as it remains confined to the most distant spaces, is in conformity with the territorial order. It does not threaten the simplification of the relationship of enmity, the reduction of the space of hostility to the "friends-foes" dichotomy. On the contrary, because it restates the original principle, namely, the exclusion, distancing, and foreignness of "foes," it reasserts the legitimacy of territory.

Schmitt's thesis thus does more than simply rediscover the threefold division of the space of hostility. It also glimpses its sacrificial dimension, as well as the principles of its functioning and malfunctioning. Extreme conflicts and conflicts "to extremes" are the condition of possibility for more limited wars. They allow us to control violence, to keep it among us within certain limits. However, they can play this role only if *adversariality* and *warlike hostility* remain clearly separated, only if the latter does not contaminate the former. Moral wars, unlike colonial atrocities that shift unbounded violence into the distance, reveal, beginning with the Napoleonic Wars, a confusion between the two forms of enmity, which destroys violence's capacity to protect us from itself. In fact, Schmitt is certainly right to think that the normal solution is to expel extreme forms of violence as far from the community as possible, and to consider that the return of such forms of violence among us corresponds to a crisis situation. However, at least two reasons suggest that this crisis in the international order is not, unlike what Schmitt thinks, the result of the unwise decision to extend the protection of our law to "Others," but indeed the consequence of a fundamental instability in this way of managing violence.

Territory and Its Other

The primary cause of this instability is, as Kant saw so long ago, the spherical shape of the earth. It entails that the exterior to which we want to expel extreme violence will inevitably disappear, sooner or later.[30] The spatial distinction between the two forms of enmity can last only a certain time: in the end it is doomed. The failure to export unrestrained violence is necessary rather than accidental. There is no doubt that the most extreme conflicts will return to European soil. It is only a question of time.

The connection between the two concepts of war allows us to glimpse the other reason for this instability. It suggests that the revolutionary and Napoleonic wars were, in relation to Schmitt's thesis, anomalies. Given the explanation in *The Nomos of the Earth*, they in fact occurred too early. They had all the characteristics of moral wars. Yet it was not until the end of the nineteenth century and the beginning of the twentieth century that, according to him, the threefold organization of international space, which made it possible to limit conflicts in Europe, was dismantled. However, from our point of view, far from being an anomaly, the French Revolution and the ensuing conflicts targeting the establishment of equality were fundamental stages in the institution of the territorial order of nations. By making equal citizens out of all those who shared the territory of the state, and ensuring they were identically united in their opposition to outside enemies, the Revolution and the wars that followed brought to completion the exclusion of groups outside of the space pacified by the monopoly of violence, even though for that it was first necessary to challenge the territorial system in which European monarchies were mutual adversaries.

However, abolition of privileges for some also led to the establishment of new groups generating new conflicts: the people, the proletariat; the fight for freedom and the class struggle. These were new groups and conflicts that, as we will see below, came from the internal dynamics of the territorial order and quickly threatened its stability. *Moral wars* are not, as Schmitt thinks, the result of the *failure* of the violence exportation mechanism: they are direct results of the attempt to expel violence to extremities, an attempt that was a response to the unbridled conflicts that brought Europeans into opposition with one another. The appearance of extreme forms of violence on European soil during the two major conflicts of the twentieth century is, properly speaking, the *return* of practices that had not been eliminated or abandoned by Europeans but, as Hannah Arendt saw so clearly, had simply been distanced, put to work elsewhere, against others.[31]

The fundamental rule of the territorial order entails that physical distance, cultural foreignness, and moral deformity evolve in parallel and consequently that the use of extreme violence is shifted into the distance. Moral wars break this rule. They also bring new groups into play. Already during the revolutionary and Napoleonic wars, and even more so during the two world wars in the twentieth century, behind the confrontations between nations, we glimpse the profile of a struggle between social groups that is not consistent with the ancient "friends-foes" division. The relationship of enmity then breaks into two relationships of opposition, of which one coincides with borders between nations, while the other is transversal. Moral wars, wars of extermination, are thus also characterized by the emergence of the enemy within, in other words, by the return of new groups to the interior of the space pacified by the monopoly of legitimate violence. They are the enemy within that is also the extraordinary enemy, against whom the greatest violence is permitted.

CHAPTER 4

The Traitor and Reason

The torture of Alain de Monéys was above all an affirmation of identity. Smallholding peasants, dispersed throughout a region whose rural hamlets appear to have lacked cohesion, saw the fair as an opportunity to celebrate the life they shared. . . . The people who gathered for a short while on and around the fairground of Hautefaye found it easier to talk politics there than anywhere else. They could openly voice their political views and even translate them into political acts. And they could celebrate their loyalty to the sovereign and his dynasty without fear of ridicule. . . . If we look beyond the august personage of the emperor, we see that the torture of Alain de Monéys is one sign of a sudden intensification of nationalist sentiment earlier in the month. As rancor over the republican opposition's rhetoric turned to outright enmity, peasants dreamed that the entire nation would suddenly coalesce in opposition to the invader.

—Alain Corbin, *The Village of Cannibals*

The unanimity is in this case an illusion, as can be seen from the indifference of those who abandoned Alain de Monéys to the atrocious fate to which he was destined by the frenzied attackers.[1] The latter wanted everyone to participate in his torture. According to Corbin, the Dordognian peasants had the impression they were engaging in a highly patriotic action by sacrificing the "Prussian," and that this shared undertaking would revive the unity that they generally lacked. However, what is surprising from this point of view, just as surprising as the indifference of those who let them do it, is the murderers' indifference to this indifference. In fact, Alain de Monéys's murderers had no special reason to require anyone to participate in their action. The "fanatics" may not really have wanted *everyone* to participate in the murder as much as they wanted everyone who participated to participate *equally*. In relation to the others, to those who were indifferent, they were satisfied with feeling, in this sense, "delegated" to perform a task to which no one was opposed, and the lack of opposition was sufficient for them to feel "delegated." As true patriots, they were working for the emperor, and they considered the friends of Alain de Monéys, who accused them of mistakenly attacking the wrong person, to themselves be making the mistake, period. The sought-after unanimity did indeed remain a dream. It did not become embodied in the "unanimity less one" that brings together all members of society against a single victim. Unanimity was simply sketched out, glimpsed in the action that was intended to create it by expelling the enemy within, the traitor, the "Prussian," the one who, voluntarily or not, played the "enemy." The indifference of those who let things happen prevented the configuration of unanimity from being achieved. Diverging desires lead to indifference; they do not produce the fruit of the convergence of the hatred of all onto a single victim.

Alain de Monéys played the role of two kinds of victim simultaneously: located at the focal point of converging hatred, he was the sacrificial victim; abandoned to his fate by all those who did not want to get involved in the conflict, he was the victim of indifference and the banality of evil. The collective murder of Alain de Monéys is at first sight an example of the scapegoat mechanism. He became the common target of the accumulated resentment of his torturers, who saw in him the prime "foe" against whom it was permitted, even recommended, that they as a group commit violence in order to merge into the rediscovered unity of the nation. However, the mechanism remained local, in the strong sense, because the violence left indifferent three-quarters of those who were present that day. The contagion remained contained. The violence was nothing more than an especially atrocious crime, and became neither the beginning of a crisis nor the unanimous action that brings a crisis to an end.

The action by the fanatics in Hautefaye was "political" in the sense that it was intended to destroy a "foe," an individual marked by his membership in a group. The group was not organized, but a collection of individuals of whom the distinctive sign of their collusion with the "foe" was their (supposed) attachment to the Republic. Destroying this "foe" was licit in the eyes of those who did it. Their violence was not a crime, but legitimate. They were certain they had served the emperor well, and a number of them were even hoping for a reward.[2]

The political dimension of the action was twofold, as can be seen from the apparent inconsistency between the accusation that Alain de Monéys was a "Prussian" and the crime of which he was accused: to have shouted "Vive la République." This twofold accusation superimposes two "friends-foes" dichotomies. The former coincides with the borders of the state, while the latter divides it on the inside. The sacrifice of Alain de Monéys destroyed an external "foe" and was also supposed to unite the nation by exterminating an enemy within. It testified to the persistency of the threefold division within the attempt to reduce it and simplify the relationship of enmity. Moreover, it confirmed the sacrificial dimension of the reiteration of the "friends-foes" division. "Enemies within" are not "compelled to retreat into their borders only." They are exterminated. Finally, it illustrated how true sacrificial violence and the banality of evil are interlinked, how collective violence and disseminated laissez-faire indifference are bound together. The killing of Alain de Monéys was like a condensed portrait of the fundamental features of modern political violence.

His death and all the labour to reestablish the nation in peril were nonetheless in vain for those involved: it led them only to the gallows. De Monéys was a bad victim for his torturers. He not only failed to generate unanimity against him and led to the conviction of his persecutors, but the reaction to his death did not manage to transform the crime into a real political action. Arrested, tried, and convicted, Alain de Monéys' murderers were nothing more than that: murderers. They never gained the dignity of political players. The severity of the punishment: five death sentences and three life sentences, and the reactions to which they gave rise nonetheless provide a glimpse of an important aspect of the dynamics of political violence in modern societies.

As Alain Corbin notes, the verdict aroused indignation in the region, where people saw it as the expression of revenge by the new republican power against the countryside, which had always supported the emperor. Despite the many appeals for clemency from elected officials and local prefects, the sentences were maintained and the convicted were executed on the very site of the crime: the Hautefaye fairground. According to an anecdote, the evening before the execution, the village barman refused to serve the executioners, and according to Corbin, in the elections that soon followed, the "magnitude of the republican defeat in the Hautefaye area would have been astonishing if one knew nothing of the trauma that people had just been through."[3] Nonetheless, the sacrifice of Alain de Monéys failed as a political action because no one identified with the violence aside from the torturers in a moment of collective enthusiasm, which was soon forgotten. The punishment for the crime did awaken some sympathy for the murderers transformed into victims of republican power, but not enough for the crime to cease being a crime and become a true political action.

This failure reveals, *a contrario*, what political violence is: it is violence that legitimizes itself. It is violence with which those other than those who commit it identify. It is violence they find good, justified, legitimate. This is precisely what did not happen at Hautefaye, where no one laid claim to the crime, praised those who had committed it, took their defense, proclaimed that the action was good and just. Political violence is violence in which people other than those who originally commit it see themselves and are ready to participate. The political dimension of violence does not depend on any specific feature of the action, but is based on the transfer to those who commit the violent action of the violence of (some among) those who do not commit it. If this transfer does not occur, the violence is only a crime that requires redress. *All political violence is an exercise in shifting the violence of some onto acceptable targets, sacrificable victims.*

This structure of political violence is in fact implicit in the theory of the modern state. In it, the foundation for the monopoly of legitimate violence is the unanimous transfer to the sovereign of the right that all members of society have to defend themselves: the transfer to the sovereign of their right to vengeance, the transfer of their violence. The mechanism of the unanimous shift of violence to other acceptable targets is what establishes the monopoly of violence and gives it its legitimacy. The acceptable targets may be external "foes," against whom one can exercise controlled violence. In such cases, they are adversaries. They may also be "Others," which is to say internal enemies, whose excessive otherness authorizes us to destroy them. In these cases we are dealing with hostility.

The same applies to all political violence, whether it is in opposition to the monopoly of legitimate violence or flows from it. The more people identify with the violence, the greater its political worth will be, and the more it becomes legitimate. The transfer of violence may be direct and immediate, as in the case of those who spontaneously joined in the murder of Alain de Monéys. However, as we have seen, so long as the contagion remains at this level, the properly political value of the action remains limited. For an act of violence to acquire a truly political dimension, the transfer also has to be indirect and mediate. Others, who did not participate in the violence, have to identify with it. This phenomenon of indirect identification often occurs when an initial act of violence gives rise to an indiscriminate reaction by the authorities. If excessive oppression links uninvolved people to the original violence, it can lead them to consider the initial violence justified and to see themselves in it. Political violence is violence that structures and brings people together. It establishes groups. It unites and divides at the same time.

For the unanimous transfer of violence to the holder of its monopoly to protect those subject to him or her, it is required by definition that the sovereign exercise his or her violence against targets that are "external," foreign, other than his or her subjects. However, since the monopoly of legitimate violence turns all those living in the physical space of the territory into the sovereign's subjects, it is impossible for the sovereign to resort to a nonspatial definition of the externality of his or her victims—for example, membership in a minority ethnic group or a body in political opposition to the sovereign—without being inevitably led to shift the border that separates "friends" from "foes."

The Traitor: Theory

Furthermore, this fraternity is *the right of all* through everyone and over everyone. It is not enough to recall that it is also violence, or that it originated in violence: it is violence itself affirming itself as a bond of immanence through positive reciprocities. This means that the practical power of the bond of fraternity is simply (in immanence)[4] the free transformation of the fused group by everyone . . . into a group of constraint. This lack of distinction is particularly evident when the sworn group proceeds to the summary execution or lynching of one of its members (suspected rightly or wrongly of betraying the group). The traitor is not excluded from the group; indeed, he cannot extricate himself from it. He remains a member of the group insofar as the group—threatened by betrayal—reconstitutes itself by discharging *all its violence* onto him. . . . lynching is a praxis of common violence for the lynchers insofar as its objective is the annihilation of the traitor. It is a bond of fraternity aroused and accentuated amongst the lynchers, insofar as it is a brutal reactualization of the pledge itself and insofar as every stone that is thrown, every blow delivered, is a new affirmation of the pledge: whoever participates in the execution of the traitor reaffirms the untranscendability of group-being as a limit of his freedom and as his new birth, and he reaffirms it in a bloody sacrifice which, moreover, constitutes an explicit recognition of the coercive right of all over every individual and everyone's threat to all.[5]

This remarkable text by Jean-Paul Sartre has to be read in light of the collective murder of Alain de Monéys. The existence of a traitor, whether he or she has really betrayed or is simply supposed to have done so (Sartre does not make a distinction between the two) implies that there is an opposing group, as the author said in the footnote on the page quoted. In fact, the presence of another "foe" group is fundamental to the transformation of the "fused group" into a "group of constraint," and Sartre had already said earlier that "a collective derives its possibilities of self-determination into a group from its *antagonistic* relations with an already constituted group."[6] This presence, at the moment when the "traitor" is executed, of another group on the horizon of the group that kills the traitor, is a central difference with the phenomenon that Girard describes in the sacrificial crisis. It does not matter whether the plague that strikes Thebes is truly an illness or simply a metaphor for war. Oedipus is not guilty of being a traitor, but of incest and patricide. The violence that tears the Greek city apart has its source in the city itself rather than in a relationship with an outside group. This difference is perhaps what explains, at least in part, why, according to Sartre, the traitor, despite his or her betrayal, is not cut out of the group, but continues to belong to it. Indeed, it may seem surprising to say, as Sartre does, that the one who is put to death by the members of his or her own group is not expelled from it.

In fact, we can also see in this statement a remnant of the positive value of the victim. This is what Sartre explicitly suggested when he said that the reason the victim does not *manage to remove himself or herself from the group* by the action of betrayal is precisely because the group, threatened by the betrayal, reconstitutes itself by annihilating the traitor. In other words, whether innocent or guilty, the "traitor" plays a vital role in constituting the group, or at least in reaffirming its essential bonds, and so he or she is not really expelled. The "traitor" is indispensable to the group, and he or she has to be a member of the group: otherwise he or she would not be a traitor. Sartre wrote, "this exterminating violence is still a link of fraternity between the lynchers and the lynched in that the liquidation of the traitor is grounded on the positive affirmation that he is *one of the group*; right up to the end, he is abused in the name of his own pledge and the right over him which he acknowledged in the Others."[7] This persistence of the positive value of the victim is however of a special type since it rests on rational recognition of the functional role of the victim. This recognition is indifferent to the question of the victim's guilt or innocence. The positive value of the victim is not, as in the case of the resolution of the mimetic crisis, *experienced* after the fact by the lynchers, discovered in the experience of the incomprehensible rediscovered peace. On the contrary, it is *conceptualized* by the philosopher with respect to its rational efficiency independent of any experience.

Sartre saw a bond of fraternity in the annihilation of the "traitor" because he thought that "the exterminating violence is still a link of fraternity." He saw that solidarity and hostility are simply two sides of the same relationship. This cruel rationality, imperfect knowledge of the scapegoat mechanism, is inseparable from a situation that prohibits the divinization of the victim and makes it impossible to transform him or her into a sacred, transcendent being. The "traitor," whether "Prussian," "collaborator," or "objective enemy of the working class," is only a human being. No matter how contemptible and despised, he or she remains an "ordinary member of the community." Contrary to when the scapegoat victim is put to death, when the "traitor" is killed, the animosity of which he or she is the expression is not brought to an end. The reason it does not terminate the conflict is not only because the antagonism is supposed to spring from outside the community. It is mainly because executing the "traitor" reaffirms and replenishes the substance of the power relationships in the confrontation of which he or she is the victim. The death of the "traitor" does not bring back peace. It reestablishes the validity of the "friends-foes" opposition of which it is an example.

The cathartic effect of the "sacrifice" of the "traitor" is not based on unanimous convergence of violence onto him or her, but on the diversion of each individual's violence against an external "foe" represented by the "traitor." It is a diversion in which the killing of the "traitor" is both an instance of putting into practice and a justification. The annihilation of the "traitor" does not put an end to the violence: it restates the difference between legitimate and illegitimate violence by renewing the animosity that founds it. It brutally renews the "pledge" that, as Sartre says, embodies the "untranscendability of group-being," and establishes its coercive power by reminding each individual of the animosity that justifies the power of the one who holds the monopoly of legitimate violence. Moreover, in this case, the holder of that monopoly can be only the fused group itself proceeding to "the summary execution of . . . one of its members."

While the sacrificial victim is transformed into a transcendent being by being killed, the "traitor," whose murder reaffirms both the community's existence and the fact that its existence is threatened, nonetheless does not become external to the community. Consequently, the "traitor" cannot play his or her role and embody the "practical power of the bond of fraternity" by transforming the "fused group" into a "group of constraint" unless two conditions are met. The first is the tangible presence of the adversary under the eyes of which, so to speak, the execution of the "traitor" must occur. The second is that the "foe," with which the "traitor" is identified, has to be immediately perceived as external to the group that will be reunited through the killing. While the execution of the "traitor" may not remove him or her from the group, it nonetheless expels the evil from the community. At the end of the operation, the "foe" who was temporarily incarnated in the "traitor" turns back into an external reality. The "foe" is a threat that is both universal and external, a danger that is shared and visible.

Political violence, the extermination of the "traitor," is both different from and similar to the original violence that brings an end to the mimetic crisis. It is similar insofar as it also flows from a shift in violence. It is different because it brings people together by identifying a common enemy rather than by pacifying the community by freeing it of its violence. In other words, political violence fails to bring the scapegoat mechanism to its final culmination. The "traitor," political victim par excellence, is never more than a "representative" taking the place of another "enemy" who is inaccessible for now, and his or her murder does not put an end to the conflict. On the contrary, it increases its imminence. Consequently, just as the "traitor" is not removed from the group that eliminates him or her, he or she also does not become sacred. The "transcendence" of the "foe," in which he or she plays a role, is reduced to the foe's spatial exteriority, to *being elsewhere* in physical space. The "foe" is a real adversary, another similar group; it is not, by definition, a transcendent being of irresistible power. Sartre clearly felt that this limitation of the "foe," the "foe's" distance in physical space rather than on another level of existence, is precisely what creates the problem because it makes it possible to measure the distance and the danger that it represents.

Sartre told us that the capacity that each thus has to judge the imminence of the "foe's" danger is what threatens the group with dissolution. He argued that the *pledge* and *terror* are means of preventing this possible dissolution. These two terms in fact refer to two aspects of a single reality that one can, without being unfaithful to his thought, reduce to *terror* alone. "The fundamental re-creation, within the pledge, is the project of substituting a real fear, produced by the group itself, for the retreating external fear, whose very distance is deceptive. And we have already encountered this fear as a free product of the group, . . . and it is called Terror."[8] For Sartre, terror is the *material form* of the pledge, which has in itself only an *ideal* reality. Terror is what, finally, makes the pledge real.[9] In fact, Sartre said, the pledge is not necessarily a veritable operation: "it is enough that violence, both in its negative forms (the liquidation of the uncommitted, and the suspect) and in its positive forms (fraternisations) manifests itself in such a way that the state of permanence becomes an immediate certainty."[10] Terror, violence in its negative forms, and fraternity are necessary for the "fused group" to be able to survive over the long term and not fall apart, as was the case of the crazed group in Hautefaye. Terror is what makes the pledge real, gives it body and existence, even if it has never been spoken.

Cambodia: Putting Theory into Practice

Alexander L. Hinton suggests an anthropological analysis of the genocide in
Cambodia.[11] He reminds us that the Khmer Rouge took power in 1975, after
five years of civil war in which the Americans, for reasons related to their
involvement in Vietnam, had rained upon Cambodia nearly three times
more bombs, in gross tonnage, than those that fell on Japan during all of
World War II. At the end of the civil war, Cambodia had around 2 million
internal refugees, accounting for nearly a quarter of the total population.
Most of them were in the Phnom Penh area; during the period, the city's
population had grown from 600,000 to 2 million inhabitants. In addition
to the major upheaval in normal social relations owing to the civil war and
the refugees' more or less broken local and family ties, the Khmer Rouge
added a new trauma as soon as they took power by ordering the populace to
leave the cities. They made a conscious political effort to further increase the
breakdown in the fundamental bonds of the preceding society.

The Khmer Rouge ordered the evacuation of the cities both to ensure
their control over power and to institute a radically new social order. They
wanted not only to transform city dwellers into peasants, but also to destroy
certain institutions central to traditional Cambodian society, in particular,
religion and family. All religious practices were forbidden, and thousands of
Buddhist monks were executed. Families were not abolished or prohibited
properly speaking, but the relationships that constituted and maintained
them were devalued and became difficult to maintain. Thus, men and women
were assigned to different work groups and very often spouses did not see
each other for days or even weeks. Meals were taken in common rather than
in individual houses, and children were separated from their parents from a
young age. They were taught that their first duty was to the state, or Angkar.[12]
Likewise, adults, including spouses, were encouraged to report each other's
"bad actions," and children were commended for denouncing their parents.

According to Hinton, this attack on the family had special meaning in
traditional Cambodian society. In Cambodia, normal social relations are
structured by patronage systems that partially overlap family relationships
and are thought of and represented in terms of kinship. Thus, the word that
designates the patron in a patronage relationship means "grandfather," and
clients are called "grandchildren." Patronage relationships reproduce the

structure of family relationships, and extend them beyond the scope of what is properly speaking genealogical. The networks of patronage and families organized Cambodians into distinct groups and prevented them from facing political power as individuals. The groups were governed by unequal power relations, which were examples of the very "feudal" relations that the Khmer Rouge wanted to replace with equality for all citizens, in other words, with a modern state.

Moreover, the Khmer Rouge were ferocious nationalists. One of their principal objectives was to make Cambodia completely autonomous on the economic level (autarchy), and, as soon as it took power, the regime decided to refuse any international aide. The expulsion of city dwellers from the cities was part of this program. They were supposed to become peasants, and their work was supposed to increase the production of rice in order to make the country self-sufficient in food.

Despite their communist ideology and the equality they were trying to establish, the Khmer Rouge instituted new social distinctions and re-created a hierarchical society. A new social division distinguished the *new people*, former city dwellers who had been expelled and now lived in the countryside, from the *old people*, in other words, those who had always been peasants, and who were considered more in favor of the new regime. However, very often the only thing that distinguished *new people* from *old people* socially was their place of residence at the time the Khmer Rouge had taken power. Of course, there were some merchants, bourgeois, and intellectuals among the city dwellers who had been expelled, but relatively few people fell into those social categories in Cambodia, even before its transformation into "Democratic Kampuchea," and many of them had been executed as soon as the Khmer Rouge had taken power. In reality, most of the surviving "city dwellers" were peasants who had been chased to Phnom Penh by the war or who had recently come to the city in the hope of improving their prospects. In other words, the distinction between the *new* and the *old people* had virtually no social foundation. In that respect, it was perfectly arbitrary. It corresponded only to a political difference—support for the new regime—which was more imaginary than real. Above the two ordinary "peoples," there was the Party and the army, which formed a single organization. At the very bottom of the national hierarchy, there were Cambodians of Vietnamese origin and members of the Cham minority.

It was nonetheless easy for the Khmer Rouge to persuade themselves that this hierarchical arrangement was in fact a perfectly egalitarian society, or at least on the way to soon becoming one. The distinction between the Party and the people corresponded to the division between the state and citizens since all members of the Party were also ordinary citizens from another point of view, as could be seen from the successive purges of the Party. The distinction between the *new* and *old people* was political and administrative. Its purpose was to achieve equality, to hasten the assimilation of city dwellers into peasant communities. Finally, Vietnamese Cambodians and Chams were foreigners. They were not Khmer. In short, all citizens, or at least all Khmers, were equal and if they were not, they soon would be.

Despite all the Khmer Rouge's efforts to reduce the social importance of the family and the patronage relationships within the Party itself, as soon as an individual became the head of a village or district, or the commander of a region, he or she gave all the important positions under his or her jurisdiction to relatives and friends. While at the national and social level the Party preached equality, it was itself organized into cliques and clans, and each region tended to turn into the personal fief of the local commander. The problem was in part cultural. As we have seen, family and patronage relationships were the framework of Cambodian society and the model for "normal" relations. It was also a consequence of the strategy employed by the Khmer Rouge during the civil war, which had been to leave the local commander total freedom with respect to military operations and recruitment. Thus, the power of each commander rested on the foundations that he or she had built by bestowing positions and benefits on "indebted" clients. In order to create a modern, egalitarian state that held the monopoly of legitimate violence, all of these small powers had to be subject to a single center.

Observers generally consider that there were three distinct stages in the massacres committed by the Khmer Rouge. First, there was the destruction of Lon Nol's regime, which meant not only killing Khmer Republic army officers, but also many privates, and very often extermination of their entire families, along with elimination of the former intellectual and economic elite. For the Khmer Rouge, this was a way to bring the civil war to completion, to make the adversary's defeat definitive and irreversible. The second stage in the massacres is seen as the consolidation of power. It corresponded to attempts to get rid of local commanders who were too powerful and, as much as possible, to replace them with more reliable individuals who were more obedient to the central power. This supposed destroying the social foundation of the local authorities, the patronage networks that the commanders had established and that supported them. Very often this led to eliminating all those who owed their advancement or position, no matter how modest, to the commander who had been condemned to death. The violence of the third stage was motivated by the desire to eliminate traitors to the revolution. Historically, the second and third stages tend to merge. This is not surprising since the difference between them, both in terms of objectives and rationalization for the violence, was in fact illusory.

If we are to believe Sartre, the attempt to consolidate a group's power has to go through the summary execution of some of its members, who are traitors or presumed to be so. This violence, which "constitutes an explicit recognition of the coercive right of all over every individual and everyone's threat to all" is what ensures the "untranscendability of group-being." The violence gives concrete form to the pledge that unites the group and anchors the community over the long term. The reason there was no veritable break between the second and third stages was because, first, there is no better way than an accusation of treason to cut down a local commander who is too powerful.

There is a second, more empirical, reason why the two political goals (to centralize power and to eliminate traitors to the revolution) quickly became impossible to tell apart. The Khmer Rouge's two political objectives, namely, complete economic self-sufficiency and the creation of a perfectly egalitarian society, rapidly proved impossible to achieve. Rice production very quickly collapsed, famine struck in a number of regions, and the Khmer Rouge military front fighting communist Vietnam was losing every battle. However, since these objectives defined the very meaning of their political undertaking, they could not be challenged. According to the leaders of the Khmer Rouge, these failures could not flow from political mistakes on their part. They had to be due to actions by traitors, internal enemies on the payroll of the Americans or other imperialist powers.

What importance and what meaning should we give to the Khmer Rouge's explanation and justification for the violence—that there were traitors who were paid agents of foreign powers and who were sabotaging the revolution? Did the authors of the genocide really believe it, or did they think, like Sartre, that the traitor's guilt is not necessary for his or her death to rebuild the community, that it is sufficient for him or her to be "presumed guilty" so that the group can discharge "all its violence" upon him or her? Thinking that the Khmer Rouge believed that their victims were guilty may be a little too generous to them. What they certainly did believe was that the "traitors" had to be *presumed guilty.* This is why it was fundamental for them to admit and confess their "crimes." The question is thus not what Pol Pot and his associates truly thought deep down. Did they really believe that all the "traitors" were really guilty, or did they think that there were simply a few "eggs" that had to be broken in order to create the revolutionary omelette? The Party, which had made self-criticism a veritable "religion" in the villages, never accepted the slightest challenge to its policies, and any criticism was immediately considered to be treason. This was institutionalization of willful blindness, which eliminated the moral difference between one who is considered to be a traitor and one who has truly committed treason. This blindness was later to play an important role in the development of the genocide, for execution of "traitors" never managed to fulfill the fundamental condition of unanimity: the convergence of all violence against a single enemy. Moreover, this repeated failure to bring back domestic harmony and reestablish the group could be explained only by the fact that there were still "traitors," and this gave reason for new executions.

Groups and the Monopoly of Violence

Toward the end of his book, Hinton speculates about the violent practices in the sadly famous Tuol Sleng Prison, also known as S-21. The issue he is interested in is why the interrogators tortured and performed atrocities on defenseless victims when they could have, so to speak, limited themselves to killing them quickly and cleanly. Those who entered Tuol Sleng were in effect already condemned, and while it may have been necessary to "encourage" the "traitors" a little so that they would sign confessions and denounce their accomplices, it was not necessary to torture them ceaselessly for weeks or months, cause them to die slowly in atrocious suffering, rape their wives, or kill their children before their eyes. Why all the useless barbarous violence? More generally, what Hinton wants to know is why massive violence always leads to monstrous practices, baroque torture, and incredible atrocities? I am not sure whether he provides a satisfactory answer to this question, but his analysis sheds interesting light on another fundamental issue: no genocide can take place without the participation of a large part of the population. Participation may be passive—people may simply let the assassins do as they wish—or active—in which case the assassins are helped and other people may even take part in the killing. How is such involvement by the community obtained?

According to Hinton, the living conditions of the S-21 interrogators reproduced, in a very intense way, some features common to life in Democratic Kampuchea. The first was uncertainty. No one knew whether he or she was not suddenly going to become a suspect, and immediately guilty—since the Angkar never made a mistake—of crimes of which he or she was unaware, but to which he or she would nonetheless have to confess before being executed. Indeed, to become a suspect, it sufficed for your name to appear in the confession of someone, for it to be mentioned during the interrogation of a suspect, or for you to be linked in one way or another to a local leader who had been arrested. According to Hinton, the interrogators' excessive violence was a way for them to discharge against powerless victims their frustration, fear, and hatred, which they could not express directly against those or that which truly threatened them; the fear that each interrogator had of every other, for each could "obtain" a denunciation that could endanger any other colleague.

It is also important to note that the violence of the Tuol Sleng interrogators was *excessive* in relation to a level of violence that was already very high. This excessiveness manifested itself in torture, atrocities, and horrible torment when it would have been possible to engage in only a few beatings and rapid executions. Thus, the question we are really asking is not why the S-21 interrogators tortured their prisoners for no apparent reason, but rather why they were more violent than average. Why did their violence go beyond that which had become normal behavior in Democratic Kampuchea, where internal political enemies were killed without hesitation?

As we have just seen, the answer that Hinton suggests is that there is a "psychological mechanism" not much different from that of a man who kicks his car or beats his wife and children because he cannot attack his boss directly. Girard also appeals to this mechanism at the beginning of *Violence and the Sacred.*[13] Hinton postulates that the excessive violence of the Tuol Sleng interrogators was the result of a shift of their violence toward sacrificable victims. The victims were "sacrificable," first, because they were powerless, defenseless, and, second, because they had no one to protect them: no one could take revenge for them. Moreover, Hinton suggests that much of the violence that occurred in Democratic Kampuchea could be explained in the same manner. From the top to the bottom of the political and social hierarchy, each individual's violence was a way of compensating for the violence to which he or she was subject or with which he or she was threatened by his or her superiors. The violence of the S-21 interrogators was in response to their fear of one another, and their frustration and desire to secure a place in the power structure. Everyone did more or less the same thing until they finally came to the *new people* and the Cham and Vietnamese minorities. They were the last groups of victims, below which there was no longer anyone to be persecuted.

There was another source of violence more directly and paradoxically related to the Khmer Rouge plan for social transformation and the difficulties it faced. While the Khmer Rouge wanted to destroy the family and "feudal" patronage systems typical of traditional Cambodian society, the social foundations of the power of individuals within the Party were, as we have seen, nonetheless based on networks of precisely this type. This went from the village chief who made his brother responsible for water distribution to the regional commander who appointed close allies as prison directors and troop transport commanders. The latter proceeded in the same manner to recruit guards and truck drivers. Within the Party, at every hierarchical level, each reproduced the form or organization and networking that it was the official Khmer Rouge policy to eradicate. Moreover, there was constant rivalry between the various patronage networks to take control of this or that village, district, or region. The rivalries translated into purges of traitors and enemies of the revolution. Just as in the case of S-21, where each interrogator was in conflict with every other one, since each could at any moment become the holder of information that incriminated another interrogator, each network had interest in portraying itself as faithful to the official policy and in denouncing its rival as a clique of traitors, with the simple fact that it was organized into a network as the best proof of guilt. These murderous rivalries, which took place within the Party, were the driving forces behind the successive purges that finally destroyed the Khmer Rouge and made it easy prey for the Vietnamese army.

The new order instituted by the Khmer Rouge also allowed many people to "settle old scores." For example, it allowed the new village chief to take revenge on the old one who used to humiliate him, or who had found against him when resolving a dispute between villagers. The new order gave power to those who had been oppressed and victims of all sorts of annoyances, and had many reasons to want revenge or to feel resentment. Finally, by abolishing money and individual property, the Pol Pot regime reduced to a single dimension the domain where rivalries between agents could be expressed: political power. In Democratic Kampuchea, nothing else had any value. There was no way to resolve a dispute or to obtain an advantage other than to become a member of a patronage network, but such membership was also by definition dangerous.

If Hinton's anthropological analysis is correct, this means that the "political violence" of the Khmer Rouge can be explained essentially by two typically nonpolitical phenomena. First, there was resentment, frustration, and fear with respect to people against whom one was powerless. It was shifted and transformed into violence against others who were defenseless. Second, there were petty rivalries, hatreds, and conflicts between neighbors; inheritance disputes that had been simmering for years; ordinary jealousy, envy, and rivalry: in short, mimetic desire. It is true that generally and in normal situations, so long as the monopoly of legitimate violence reigns, rivalries between colleagues and conflicts between relatives and neighbors lead only to middling animosity. However, it would be naive to minimize their importance. As we will now see, as soon as conditions permit, conflicts of this type play a fundamental role in political violence.

Individual Interest: Hijacking Political Violence

In a fascinating book entitled *The Logic of Violence in Civil War*, Stathis Kalyvas analyzes the distribution of occurrences of excessive violence in the context of civil war. Here we understand "excessive violence" to mean large-scale murders and massacres: the burning of villages, killing of all who do not manage to flee in time, extermination of entire families including several

generations, torturing of victims, mutilation of dead bodies, and so on. These
are no longer cases of war, of opposing armies and civilians accounting for
more or less extensive "collateral damage," of combat and bombing, but
of voluntary extermination of certain members of the civilian population.
Kalyvas's point of departure is the following observation: in a given territory where civil war occurs over a long period, the distribution of massacres
and excessive violence is not homogenous. If we take two similar villages,
of almost identical size, that are equally easy (or difficult) to access and are
sometimes separated by only a few kilometres, over ten years of war there
will be six massacres in one village but none in the other. What we need to
understand is why massacres occur in some places but not in others, very
nearby, that seem to have nothing different in particular.[14]

The explanation he suggests involves a number of components, and the
factors that account for the overall extension of excessive violence are not of
the same type as those that explain its local distribution. At the global level,
massacres occur most often, but not exclusively, in disputed areas, in other
words, in places where neither of the adversaries has managed to establish its
supremacy in a sustainable manner. In contrast, at the local level, field studies
and interviews with survivors show that the fundamental factor is the intensity of interpersonal conflicts within a village. Massacres occur in divided
communities. The key to understanding why certain villages are places where
massacres and killing occur, whereas others are spared throughout the war,
is to take into account interpersonal conflicts tearing members of the community apart. The more divided the village, the greater the probability that it
will become a theater of large-scale violence against part of its population.[15]
Kalyvas's inquiry thus complements Hinton's thesis insofar as it not only cor-
roborates the role of interpersonal conflict in the development of political
violence, but also reveals the fact that such conflicts are first and foremost
between friends, neighbors, relatives, members of the same village. It also
makes it possible to understand how interpersonal conflicts influence political violence. Massacres most often occur in communities divided by internal
conflicts because the local players, the villagers, exploit political violence in
order to resolve private disputes: to drive away a rival in love, to punish a
long-standing enemy, to take revenge against a competitor, and so forth.

"Political violence" is always stronger when interpersonal conflicts
merge with political opposition, in other words, when agents exploit political

conflicts to their private advantage. They use violence professionals to resolve their own disputes. They denounce the families of their enemies to the guerillas or soldiers; they accuse their rivals of hiding weapons or of providing the insurgents with food. In short, they seek to maximize their advantage by using the violence of others, which they direct toward their private enemies, to achieve their own ends. The more the exploitation of political violence for private ends increases, the more political violence loses its properly *political* function, which is to bring together and unite the community. Finally, it becomes only destructive chaos, the war of all against all.

Robert Gellately's work on Nazi Germany confirms the importance of these phenomena of private exploitation of political violence.[16] It shows that, throughout Hitler's regime, deliberate false denunciations accounted for over 50 percent of the denunciations sent to the Gestapo. Thus more than half were spurious. The false denunciations were intended to resolve family disputes, replace long, costly divorce proceedings, acquire a neighbor's coveted apartment, get rid of a renter who was too noisy or who didn't pay on time, and so forth. Yet, as Gellately notes, from the beginning of the war, at least, no one could ignore that being summoned by the Gestapo was something that could only finish badly.

Given the findings from Kalyvas's study on civil wars, we could think that if over half of the denunciations were false, a large number of the properly political denunciations were in fact motivated by interpersonal conflicts, rather than strictly ideological reasons. Just as in civil wars, members of society in Nazi Germany exploited political conflict to their own advantage, and by doing so they increased its violence. Indeed, according to Gellately, everywhere that the local archives of the Gestapo survived the war and defeat, they show that all of the people arrested by the Gestapo for political crimes were brought in after a denunciation, and not because of any detective work done by the police officers themselves.[17]

The Khmer Rouge not only permitted—they could not do otherwise—individuals and specific groups to exploit political violence to their own advantage, they institutionalized, properly speaking, the confusion of personal and political conflicts. By abolishing not only private property but also individual property, and especially by "de-issuing" money, by prohibiting the use of money anywhere in Cambodia, which made it almost impossible to engage in any trade relations or to accumulate wealth, they transformed all

Cambodians into servants of the state with no distinguishing features aside from their position within its apparatus. By doing this, they reduced to a single dimension, that of political power, the area in which rivalries between agents could occur. However, to make matters worse, they also refused, from the beginning, any form of transcendence of power or of the state. By abolishing money, of course, but also by emptying the cities, they made nonsense out of all the monuments that make power clear and show that it is above those who exercise it. In the same way, they rejected the court system, the institution of law separate from the individual decisions of those in charge.[18] Consequently, they instituted a crisis of differences, caused all rivalries to converge on the political level alone, made power invisible, and destroyed any possibility of a distinction between private and public violence.

As these examples show, the rational exploitation of political violence by each individual and each group corresponds to a failure to shift the violence of all onto a single adversary. When the number of "traitors" grows, it is a sign of their inability to "rebuild the community" and to "anchor the community over the long term." This inability is a direct result of efforts made by individuals and groups to take advantage of the official violence, and it flows from the violence of each, from which political violence can no longer be distinguished. Violence thus loses its ability to become properly political, to form individuals into distinct groups. It fragments into the individualism of the state of nature. It becomes endless and its power to protect us from itself evaporates.

"Right Reason" and the Reason of Terror

Hobbes rightly considers politics as a way out of the violence of the state of nature. The original conflict is seen by him as a confrontation among isolated individuals: the war of all against all. According to him, its causes are situated on the individual level, more precisely at a level where individual actors are not clearly distinguished from groups of subjects. The causes are self-interest and the uncertainty of each in relation to the relevant intentions of others.[19] Most commentators consider that, for Hobbes, not reason but passions explain the development and exacerbation of the state of war, ever-increasing violence.[20] In fact, the Hobbesian thesis is more subtle. According to Hobbes, in the state of nature, it is impossible to know whether a human action is a rational form of behavior or an emotional reaction. This is because both passions, such as fear, jealousy, and vanity, and rational reflection lead individuals to do exactly the same things. Thus, it becomes difficult to distinguish between what results from the influence of one or the other, as can be seen from the following passage:

> And therefore if any two men desire the same thing, which nevertheless they cannot both enjoy, they become enemies; and in the way to their end (which is principally their own conservation, and sometimes their delectation only) endeavour to destroy or subdue one another. And from hence it comes to pass that where an invader hath no more to fear than another man's single power, if one plant, sow, build, or possess a convenient seat, others may probably be expected to come prepared with forces united to dispossess and deprive him, not only of the fruit of his labour, but also of his life or liberty. And the invader again is in the like danger of another.
>
> And from this diffidence of one another, there is no way for any man to secure himself so reasonable as anticipation; that is, by force, or wiles, to master the persons of all men he can so long till he see no other power great enough to endanger him.[21]

Given this distrust, "there is no way for any man to secure himself so reasonable as anticipation; that is, by force, or wiles, to master the persons of all men he can." This is reason's recommendation. However, from this clearly follows the very thing that it wants to protect us from: that each "may probably expect" that if "one plant, sow, build, or possess a convenient seat, others may probably be expected to come prepared . . . to dispossess and deprive him, not only of the fruit of his labour, but also of his life or liberty" because this recommendation leads us all to take preemptive action to protect ourselves from one another, and thus to produce the result from which our action was intended to protect us. In the state of nature, seeking one's own pleasure, or simply one's own protection, leads to the same generalized distrust that constitutes the rational justification for preemptive violence. This recourse is in turn the principal source of the generalized distrust. Between what people do out of rational prudence and what their emotions lead them to do, there is no significant difference. Both types of motivation lead to the same actions and the same result: the war of all against all, the constant use of violence to expand or secure one's possessions.

Hobbes also made no significant distinction between the behavior of groups and that of individual persons. Indeed, he writes, "where *an invader hath no more to fear than another man's single power, . . . others may probably be expected to come prepared with forces united.*" This strange shifting between the individual and the group in the same sentence indicates that, in the state of nature there is no clear separation between the two because all alliances are only casual. They cannot establish lasting ties that could bring an end to the radical isolation of those whom violence pits against one another.

This twofold lack of distinction, in the state of nature, of reason and the passions, on one hand, and of individual and group behavior, on the other, flows from the fact that, according to Hobbes, there is no "right reason" by nature. In his eyes, individual reason, subjective rationality, does not provide sufficient resources to allow individuals to avoid conflicts or resolve their disputes. Consequently, it is unable to maintain them in peaceful society.

> The ablest, most attentive, and most practised men may deceive themselves, and infer false conclusions; not but that reason itself is always right reason, as well as arithmetic is a certain and infallible art: but no one man's reason, nor the reason of any one number of men, makes the certainty; no more than an account is therefore well cast up because a great many men have unanimously approved it. And therefore, as when there is a controversy in an account, the parties must by their own accord set up for right reason the reason of some arbitrator, or judge, to whose sentence they will both stand, or their controversy must either come to blows, or be undecided, for want of a right reason constituted by Nature; so is it also in all debates of what kind soever.[22]

"Right reason" is not the reason of a given person because everyone, even the most capable and experienced, can sometimes make a mistake. It also does not correspond to the agreement of the greatest number because many are just as likely to make a mistake as one alone. It is "right reason" only if people agree on an arbitrator for the decision that they will obey. The root of the problem is not that agents act irrationally in the state of nature, but that individual, subjective rationality is not normative. It cannot state a conclusion that universally applies. This is why it fails to protect us from violence and why, in the state of nature, the recommendations of individual reason do not differ from those of the passions.

"Right reason" is the result of an artificial institution: that of a sovereign whose strength protects us from our own violence. If there is not this supreme violence, capable of restricting the free exercise of individual reason, violence remains a rational option that often looks like the optimal solution for resolving conflicts between individuals and groups. There is no right reason except in the shadow of the holder of the monopoly of legitimate violence.

Two contemporary authors, Russell Hardin in *One for All*, and Ronald Wintrobe in *Rational Extremism*, have in their manner confirmed this Hobbesian conclusion.[23] The purpose of these two authors is to show that it is possible to provide a rational explanation for the most extreme violent behavior, such as ethnic cleansing, large-scale massacres, terrorism, and suicide attacks. They argue that such violence is not proof of agents' failure to be rational. It is not the case that the only possible explanations for these actions have to appeal to irrational passions or unconscious impulses. On the contrary, Hardin and Wintrobe claim to be able to explain them completely, using either rational decision theory or the public choice paradigm and complying with the essential rules of methodological individualism. From their point of view, the most extreme violence is viewed simply as an option among others that agents may or may not choose depending on the range of available actions, their various interests, and the interactions they have with others. It is thus possible to show that there is nothing irrational about such violence. It is a means to an end, both for leaders of extremist groups who set such policies and for individual members who carry them out, even if the goals of individual militants do not always coincide perfectly with their leaders' objectives. All such violence, including the most terrible, such as massacres and torture, has according to them a rational purpose, for example, to terrify or intimidate the adversary, or to force the adversary to negotiate.

The acknowledged objective of these two authors is to demonstrate that the violent behavior of terrorists and other actors in extreme political conflicts, as well as actions described as unreasonable violence, are explicable in the framework of methodological individualism and are in no way counterexamples to the classical hypothesis of agents' rationality. However, this demonstration implies something that those who suggest it do not generally notice. The very success of rational explanations for extreme violent behavior means that rationality provides no norm that could bring an end to conflict, that it is not an alternative to continuing violence. On the contrary, as in the state of nature as Hobbes sees it, it is the rational pursuit of rational interest that is the reason, the cause for all this "senseless" violence!

As Hobbes saw, if there is no sovereign with the monopoly of legitimate violence, there is no difference between what reason prescribes and what violence recommends. The behavior of those who, during the Cambodian genocide, took the initiative and accused their rivals of being traitors to the revolution was in no way irrational: Hardin and Wintrobe are perfectly right. It was, on the contrary, the most reasonable means of guaranteeing their security. There is no right reason by nature. Only the unanimous transfer of the violence of each, which makes the monopoly of legitimate violence possible, allows "Reason" to emerge as the "other of violence."

Reason and "Others"

The dialectic of reason and violence is not limited to relationships between the state and the state of nature. We also find it on the international level and in particular in relationships between modern states and "non-nations." When the relationship of warlike hostility is pushed far from the national territory, beyond nearby lands where there are "foes" who are nonetheless our equals, recourse to stronger violence is made legitimate because we are dealing over there with beings who have no reason. At the time when, within a state, the monopoly of legitimate violence crumbles and the traitor tears apart the country's pacified space, the moral difference between violence and reason also evaporates, testifying to the fragility of a distinction that only this monopoly makes possible. In contrast, in the threefold space of international relations, reason becomes the principle of a fundamental moral difference that, as in the case of moral wars of extermination, authorizes recourse to greater violence. In our relationships with "Others," as in the case of moral wars, a fundamental moral difference authorizes a more extensive use of violence. In moral wars, it is the first recourse to violence, considered as a fundamental moral failing, that in turn authorizes greater violence. In colonial wars, it is the claimed reason or lack of reason of the "natives" that constitutes the principle of this fundamental moral difference.

According to this thinking, in distant, exotic lands, there are beings whose lack of reason justifies the use of forms of violence that would not be permitted among ourselves. For example, Hegel, in *Lectures on the Philosophy of World History*, considers that Africa has not participated in world history in any way because Africans, according to him, are not beings gifted with reason: "The Negro is an example of animal man in all his savagery and lawlessness, and if we wish to understand him at all, we must put aside all our European attitudes. We must not think of a spiritual God or of moral laws; to comprehend him correctly, we must abstract from all reverence and morality, and from everything which we call feeling. All this is foreign to man in his immediate existence, and nothing consonant with humanity is to be found in his character."[24]

In consequence, even though, according to him, slavery is by definition unjust, Hegel considers that where, as in Africa, there is no rational state, "slavery is still necessary: for it is a moment in the transition towards a higher stage of development."[25] A little further, Hegel says that the reason so many Africans die in confrontations with Europeans is because their stupidity leads them to throw themselves in front of the mouths of cannons![26] The problem is not only that of prejudice, which now seem utterly brutish to us but was at the time common. What is at stake is the justification for violence (and exploitation) based on a lack of rationality. The justification opposes Europeans as a group against "Others" who have only limited access to reason, as is clearly indicated in the structure of *Lectures on the Philosophy of World History*. Violence is in this case indeed the Other of reason, but this does not make it what reason is not. In this context, violence is not seen as an irrational means of resolving conflicts. It is rather the opposite: in colonies, as in the state of nature in the absence of a holder of the monopoly of legitimate violence, violence reappears as the only reasonable way to resolve conflicts with Others who are not reasonable. Their lack of reason justifies recourse to violence in our dealings with them: "Natives understand only the rod!"

This transformation of the value of violence—forbidden and irrational among us, rationally justified in our relationships with "them"—corresponds here also to the absence of a holder of the monopoly of legitimate violence, or at least to the holder's "silence." In their relationships with Europeans, the colonized are also deprived of the ability to protect themselves from offenses that Europeans may commit against them. In other words, they do not have, on an equal footing with the colonizers, the sovereign's protection against the violence that any European could commit against them. This entails that so long as the violence is committed against a native, the state in the colonies abandons to each settler what constitutes in the motherland its essential prerogative: the right to make the distinction between legitimate and illegitimate violence.

In Hegel's attitude we can see the shadow of a fundamental figure of modern moral and political rationality that is based on what can be called "conditional rationality." Subjective rationality, which aims to maximize the agent's advantage, is, as we have seen, unable to dissociate rational action from violence. Reason conceived of an alternative to violence is based, on the contrary, on a specific type of relationship with others: reciprocity. Acting reasonably toward others, seeking peaceful rather than violent solutions to our conflicts, requires that they also be disposed to do the same. The obligation to behave rationally, rationality conceived of as a norm, does not become established unless the others are also ready to accept that norm.

In Hegel's text, the argument is slightly different. It is indeed the absence of reciprocity, in the sense of a lack of rational behavior among Africans, that authorizes the use of greater violence against them. Except that, in this case, the lack is supposed to be congenital. The failure to meet the condition of reciprocity by acting rationally is not voluntary; Africans are naturally incapable of it. In fact, according to Hegel, Africans not only suffer from a lack of rationality. They are also powerless to raise themselves to the reciprocity that constitutes the foundation of all moral relations.[27]

However, leaving aside the prejudice, the rule invoked by Hegel is precisely the one that makes the obligation to comply with certain norms dependent on the willingness of others to comply with them also. This conditional reciprocity, indispensable to rationality conceived of as an alternative to violence, is a kind of generalization of the idea of a social contract. Conditional reciprocity plays a fundamental role in contemporary conceptions of the just society. Yet justice is not possible unless it can rule upon undecidable conditional reciprocity, in other words, determine whether others are willing to act reasonably on the condition that I am also willing to do so. We will find that, as in the case of "right reason" according to Hobbes, only the holder of the monopoly of legitimate violence can reassure each that the other is "also willing."

CHAPTER 5

Indifference and Charity

The example of Cambodia shows that becoming the master of violence is not sufficient to ensure success in excluding groups and achieving a politically efficient transfer of violence. While to hold the monopoly of legitimate violence it suffices to hold the monopoly of violence, the fact is that no one can create a sustainable foundation for a monopoly of violence without holding the monopoly of legitimate violence. These are two sides of the same thing. Holding the monopoly of legitimate violence thus means something other than simply having superior strength and violence at one's disposition. It is also not simply a question of winning hearts and minds to one's cause. It means acquiring the authority that defines the difference between good and bad violence, and making one's violence alone the substitute for the violence of each.

Building such a monopoly is possible only if the traditional institutions that disseminate this authority within the society have been dismantled. However, as the Cambodian example also shows, this "dismantling" cannot take place in just any way if the political metamorphosis of violence is to be achieved. In particular, the disappearance of traditional institutions cannot result from violence alone. The Khmer Rouge tried to abolish traditional ties through pure and simple application of greater violence. On the contrary,

115

the abandonment of traditional ties has to appear to individual agents as a *free choice* they can take or leave. The option has to become established in customs before the state can consider institutionalizing it.

In this chapter, I would like to suggest a hypothesis about the way the dismantling of traditional hostility and solidarity obligations occurred in Europe.[1] This abandonment is the precondition for uniting solidarities and universalizing a single principle of hostility. It preceded the birth of the modern state, although the latter proceeded to play a major role in increasing and accelerating the process of abandoning traditional obligations. Historically, all states, not only modern states, are human groupings that transform the scope and meaning of rules of solidarity based on the family, clan, or social group. What characterizes the modern state, and makes it possible at the same time, is the gradual abandonment of these rules that, though changed, had always retained a role and central importance in political organizations.[2] The modern state is created little by little as those rules become obsolete. This action is partly reciprocal. Beyond a certain threshold, traditional solidarity rules weaken at the same rate as the modern state becomes dominant.

The beginning of the abandonment of traditional solidarity ties was a distributed phenomenon that occurred at the same time more or less everywhere in a broad cultural sphere from which a number of states later emerged. The process had no center or place of origin, but operated weakly at many points in obligation networks, slowly but surely changing the rules of solidarity and hostility. The phenomenon long remained silent and invisible: centuries went by before its effects were felt. What was at play was a slow transformation in people's attitudes. It was a change that can be described neither as properly cultural nor as political, but as a modification of the moral economics of relationships with others. We should not assume that, first, the changed relationships replaced the traditional forms of relationships with others, or that they prohibited them. At the beginning at least, the new way of interacting was not an alternative designed to replace them. Rather, it was something radically other, something on top of what was already there. The new way was "in addition" but not situated beyond what was normally required or demanded of each individual. Thus, it appeared to agents as an option that they were free to accept or reject.

The origin of the change in behavior was religious. The change flowed from transformations in religion caused by the Christian Revelation of the innocence of the scapegoat victim. It came, and this is not surprising, from a challenge to the sacred, in other words, to the ultimate principle of the distinction between legitimate violence and illegitimate violence in all societies that have not been secularized. The modern state, holder of the monopoly of legitimate violence, has seized the moral authority that states the difference between good and bad violence. It would thus not be surprising that an internal transformation of religion would be what has made this feat possible. According to René Girard, Christian Revelation hinders the functioning of the scapegoat mechanism that puts an end to the sacrificial crisis because it makes the innocence of the scapegoat victim public. We saw in chapter 1 that what puts an end to the convergence of all hatred onto a single victim is the abandonment of traditional bonds of solidarity. This abandonment makes it possible to be indifferent to the fate of others, to not care whether or not the victim is innocent, and this favors the pursuit of self-interest by each individual. The thesis that I am suggesting is that in the West, at least, Christianity played a fundamental role in the abandonment of traditional rules of solidarity.

In order to fully grasp the role of Christianity in this historical transformation, we need to focus on what people *do* rather than on what they *believe*. We need to keep our eyes on people's actions rather than on their beliefs. Indeed, I think it is neither necessary nor useful to interpret Christian Revelation exclusively, or primarily, in a cognitive manner, as Girard does in *Things Hidden since the Foundation of the World* and as many commentators and critics of his work have tended to do since then.[3] By "cognitive interpretation," I mean the apparent reduction of the Revelation to a belief, that of the innocence of the victim, that would make it impossible for the scapegoat mechanism to achieve closure. This interpretation does not make it possible to understand the historical action of the transformations introduced by Christianity. It distorts comprehension in two ways.

First, it gives disproportionate importance to agents' beliefs, as if what people think were an immediate explanation for social change. Such an explanation suggests that beliefs alone are capable of determining people's behavior.[4] However, on the contrary, the explanatory schemas that Girard uses generally take agents' beliefs to be so intimately linked with what they do that both are explained by the mimetic dynamic, rather than actions by beliefs. Thus, belief in a victim's guilt does not precede the killing, but on the contrary develops, takes shape, and gains strength in the process of unanimous convergence of hatred on the victim. According to Girard, it is the escalation of mimetic violence that explains the belief in the guilt of the victim, shared by those who perform the sacrifice; it is not the belief that explains their violence. In what sense did the maniacs in Hautefaye "believe" in the guilt of Alain de Monéys? To what degree does this belief explain their behavior? Clearly, trying to inform them, as his friends tried to do, that Alain de Monéys was not a "Prussian" was not sufficient to change their behavior. Their blindness was too closely linked with what they were doing. As in the case of the Khmer Rouge, belief in the victim's guilt was as much the result of the violent operation as it was the cause.

Second, since it identifies the historical efficiency of Christianity immediately with Revelation of the innocence of the scapegoat victim, the cognitive interpretation tends to dissimulate the differences that have existed (and that exist) between historical Christianity and the evangelical message itself. By reducing the historical work of the Revelation to a piece of cognitive content—the innocence of the scapegoat victim—this interpretation minimizes the role of institutions, such as churches, that have spread the evangelical message, and translated and betrayed it in various ways. It leads us to minimize violence and the role that churches have played in the violence that was fundamental to establishing the modern world. For, while the modern state was indeed, in a sense, made possible by the action of Christianity in history, the conflicts from which it emerged were religious wars in which the unity of Christianity disintegrated into an orgy of violence. The historical action of Christianity cannot be understood unless we take into account the distance between the evangelical message and its institutional "translation."

Charity and Forgiveness

In *charity*, we can first see a new attitude that, little by little, was to cause an upheaval in the traditional rules of solidarity/hostility and establish the conditions for their abandonment. Charity, conceived of as caring for the next person, in other words, for anyone, whoever that person may be, man, woman, child, or elderly person, free or slave, foreigner or neighbor. In this case, it is not a question of belief, for example, that of having an equal obligation to all without distinction. That comes much later, and the belief will never be, by far, universally shared. It is a question of what one does, the actions that one performs. It is in this sense only that charity can be a free option that agents can take or leave. This is not the case when it is seen as a belief. In the Middle Ages, and long after, it was impossible to join or leave Christianity as one wished, or to turn up one's nose at its dogmas. However, charity as a practice is rare. Many people are not charitable, and even those who are charitable are so only from time to time. This is why it makes sense to say that it is an option that agents can take or leave freely.

Consequently, if charity is an obligation, it is an "obligation" of a new type, for it is possible to fail to fulfill it without committing a serious wrong, a sin that requires atonement, and above all without the nonfulfillment being an insult to someone in particular. This is because charity is not a rule that identifies specific agents or duties. Rather, it corresponds to a general attitude that influences all relationships to others. In this, it is quite similar to what Hayek calls a negative rule. Charity does not prescribe anything, but it excludes certain forms of behavior. Moreover, it leaves it up to the context, and to the demands of the moment, to determine what is required and what one must not do. Such an obligation does not tie individuals to one another in the way that traditional solidarity ties do. It does not bind them together through reciprocal duties. Charity leaves each one free and, once the obligation is discharged, the charity that has been performed creates no obligations for the person who receives it; otherwise, precisely, it would not be charity. We could say that charity is an "additional obligation." It does not replace traditional ties, but adds to them. It acts upon the entire network. It is freely available to all, but binds no one.

Nonetheless, the practice of charity introduces a new recommendation into our interactions with those toward whom we have no reciprocal relations of solidarity. It teaches us that absence of reciprocity does not free us of all duties toward others, that it does not deliver the Other to us like prey into our hand. Charity disconnects obligation from reciprocity. It is an unconditional "obligation" that upsets the structure of the hostility/solidarity space based on social distance. It brings close what was distant.

While it does not replace traditional obligations, charity can nonetheless, and sometimes inevitably does, come into conflict with them because it rejects the exclusions that are the foundations of traditional duties. It undermines traditional solidarity groups from the inside, and refuses to see those groups or take them into consideration. It does not say that traditional obligations are useless, but rejects their limits. It does not weaken traditional obligations by contradicting them so much as by excess and *breaking bonds*. Just as it breaks the bond between obligation and reciprocity, charity separates help from hostility. Those whom one helps are no longer immediately those whose enemies one shares. In charity, "solidarity" is not the other side of a duty of violence, and this is why it is no longer exactly "solidarity," but something else, part of a different way to relate to others. In fact, we are required to be charitable even toward those against whom we are required to exercise violence. Charity can operate at any point in the network of obligations and on any form of behavior.

More or less the same thing applies with respect to forgiving. It transforms a transgression, a rejection or avoidance of one's duty to commit revenge, into the ideal of excellence and perfection. Just like charity, forgiving is an "obligation" that everyone knows is most often not fulfilled. It nonetheless remains a duty from which no one is ever, properly speaking, excused, notwithstanding the failure to fulfill it. Moreover, forgiving, like charity, is an "obligation" for which nothing is given in return. A person who does not forgive me does not commit an offense against me, and a person who forgives asks nothing of the person who has been forgiven.[5] Forgiving has in consequence *naturalized*, in other words, deritualized, vengeance. It has transformed the *obligation to take revenge* into a transgression that has to be explained, but that nonetheless calls for neither punishment nor retaliation. Vengeance thus tends to gradually become perceived as a spontaneous reaction in proportion to the seriousness of the offense. This twofold transformation of a transgression (avoiding one's duty to take revenge) into an ideal and of an obligation (to take revenge) into a transgression has made it possible for forgiving to accommodate vengeance and live with it. Rather than rejecting it out of hand, it gradually undermines it, condemning revenge all the more when the wrong was benign. Taken as model forms of behavior, charity and forgiving thus destroy, little by little, the traditional obligations of solidarity and violence. They neutralize them, reduce their ability to structure communities into distinct groups.

Yet neither one nor the other says that victims are innocent, that those whom we forgive are not guilty or that those with whom we share merit it. Forgiving teaches us to not make our foes into our victims. However, it does not proclaim that they are innocent. Charity recommends that we help even those to whom we are linked by no reciprocal obligation. Charity and forgiving are sufficient to break the unanimity against the victim because they place concern for the other before any obligation to engage in violence. They break the reciprocity of traditional obligations. Moreover, they have the advantage of being able to deconstruct unanimity after the fact, once the founding moment of mimetic enthusiasm has passed. Because they do not address agents' beliefs, but aim to reform their behavior, they can survive the mimetic illusion and assert themselves against it. They are models that offer people the possibility of acting otherwise. In order to accept the offer, to adopt these new forms of behavior, it is not necessary that agents first change their beliefs. On the contrary, we can forgive only those who have committed some wrong against us. Those who are innocent have no need to be forgiven. It is rather forgiving that will transform the meaning of what it is to be guilty or innocent. Forgiving and charity thus do not require that we reject in a single stroke all of our traditional obligations. It is only in case of conflict with what those obligations prescribe that the new models ask us to reject the exclusive forms of solidarity that the obligations define.

Charity and forgiving free people from their traditional obligations. They give people a moral justification that authorizes them not to fulfill them. In this, they are ambiguous because traditional obligations very often come into contradiction with personal interest. If we could, every one of us would abandon our obligations; not all of them and not in all circumstances, for they can also be to our advantage, but from time to time, when it is convenient and there is no danger. Charity and forgiving give agents an ideal that allows them to sneak out of fulfilling obligations without seeming to commit a fault. They provide an excuse, permission that makes it possible to abandon our solidarity obligations when they are not in our self-interest. This is why we must not reduce the historical consequences of charity and forgiving simply to what has been done out of charity or to acts of forgiving themselves. Agents will exploit to their own advantage the freedom that is offered by these new models of behavior, and while such exploitation may seem like a corruption of these ideals, that corruption nonetheless is an important dimension of their historical effect.

Charity and forgiving also have effects through what they authorize and permit indirectly. Their historical impact on the world comes as much, if not more, from the possibility they provide of renouncing, without committing a wrongdoing, our traditional solidarity obligations. Consequently, they introduce distance; they create a space where agents can refuse to honor, at least in part, their traditional obligations without becoming "foes" of the group to which they belong. Charity and forgiving give meaning and dignity to exteriority. They bring social externality closer. Through them, what is distant becomes close. The operation of bringing the distant close is made possible thanks to the recursive structure of traditional solidarity ties, which are repeated at each level: in the family, line, clan, and tribe we find the same action of exclusion and inclusion. At each of these levels, charity and forgiving can loosen and undo the ties.

However, their ambiguity remains. For example, while on one hand charity extends help beyond traditional bonds of solidarity, on the other hand it makes it possible to not fulfill those bonds. It authorizes agents to consider as superior and better what is done by charity rather than by obligation, and gives them the opportunity to neglect their traditional obligations. However, there may be many reasons why agents may want to take advantage of the authorization provided by charity and forgiving in order to avoid fulfilling their traditional obligations. The most obvious, and probably the most frequent, is that traditional ties are a burden, fetters that hinder agents and from which agents, big or small, always try to extricate themselves. What charity permits, namely, to give up fulfilling traditional obligations of help and support, is not always done out of charity, but on the contrary out of greed, resentment, or indifference. The renunciation of traditional obligations that charity permits will then prove to be both the biggest enemy of charity, in the sense of help and support for those in need, and its primary reason for being, what makes it necessary. Charity and forgiving are thus inseparable from their opposite: indifference to the misfortunes of others. The distance that they introduce fosters an increase in the number of what Joel Feinberg has in a famous article called "bad Samaritans,"[6] in other words, those who refuse to help persons in danger when they could do so with no threat to themselves and without excessive difficulty.

In fact, the expression "bad Samaritan" is a little unfortunate because it dissimulates the true nature of the innovation we call charity. In the Gospel parable, those who turn their heads and go on their way when they see the man who has been attacked and wounded by bandits are not Samaritans. They are Jews, like the victim, and Pharisees. In other words, they are people who should be immediately concerned by the misfortune of their compatriot and fellow believer. The Samaritan, who belongs to a foreign, "foe" group, is charitable. The help that he gives freely goes beyond any traditional obligation. His charity transgresses not so much an obligation, strictly speaking, as a behavioral expectation, for the traditional animosity between the two groups would have justified indifference. In this sense, it is rather the Good Samaritan, failing to do what is expected, who is a "bad Samaritan." His charity frees him from his "adversarial duty": if he had just passed by, he would have owed nothing to the one he chose to help.[7] In contrast, those who abandon the victim to his fate not only are not charitable but also fail to fulfill their duty of solidarity to one of theirs.[8] The Good Samaritan's charity is thus consistent with the indifference of those who, by abandoning the victim to his fate, avoid fulfilling their obligation. On both sides, there is a "failure," but they reveal different relationships to traditional obligations. Given this twofold "failing," we can say not only that charity transgresses and neutralizes traditional obligations, but that it simultaneously appears as a way of compensating for their weakening, their inevitable fatigue as we get further and further from their origin. The two phenomena go hand in hand. The weakening of traditional obligations, which is testified to by the indifference of those who pass by, is the condition of possibility for the Good Samaritan's charity, and his distance from his obligation of exclusive solidarity, which is indicated by his charity, is the condition of possibility for their indifference.

Rationalization of Violence

Understood in this way, charity and forgiving are local obstacles to the shift of violence. They do not prevent it, but they get in the way and create more or less hurdles in the paths that it spontaneously takes. As I said above, they do not form a complete set of rules that would replace those that turn violence away from the community by allowing it to be exercised on socially distant beings. Charity and forgiving are instead presented as alternate models of behavior that are in addition to existing rules and change the usual way that violence is shifted toward others. They take root in the hostility/solidarity space, of which they respect the structure. At first, they are all the more powerful as models of behavior when the social distance between agents is still limited because traditional obligations already forbid violence between those who are close and impose strong solidarity duties. Charity and forgiving thus only strengthen and confirm these dispositions. However, their influence tends to diminish as the distance between agents increases, for charity and forgiving then come into conflict with the exclusive nature of traditional solidarity and with the duty of vengeance that it entails. Nonetheless, with time, charity and forgiving prove to be easier to perform when the social distance separating us from the recipients of those actions is sufficiently great. Indeed, opportunities for conflict, rivalry, and frustration are all the more numerous when people rub elbows. The less there is to forgive, the easier it is to do, and we are more easily led to help those who have never wronged us.

Charity and forgiving thus operate on the two first circles of the solidarity/hostility space in a two ways. They create pressure in two opposite directions, which dilate and deform the circles. In the middle range, these two Christian virtues tend to minimize the animosity that is permitted between agents because they impose themselves all the more easily as models of behavior when those with whom we interact are not linked with us by too many obligations that they could fail to fulfill. However, when the social distance is reduced, offenses become to a certain degree more difficult to forgive because, given equal harm, the offense is greater if it is committed by someone close to us. Resentment makes charity more difficult. In both cases, charity and forgiving encourage agents to flee their traditional obligations whenever they can. In relation to those close to them, agents are subject to the twofold temptation to renounce their traditional obligations and to fail to forgive and be charitable. Animosity and resentment favor a certain degree of indifference, less attentiveness in interactions with those closest to us, who used to form the circle of unlimited solidarity. At the same time, more distant relationships become warmer under the influence of the new models of behavior. The complex effects of charity and forgiving tend to rationalize violence. They gradually render illegitimate the compensatory shift of violence toward sacrificable victims.

Forgiving as a model of behavior a fortiori delegitimizes gratuitous violence against people who have committed no offense, and given that it is easier to forgive when the social distance is greater, it makes the spontaneous shift of violence to the outside more difficult. In consequence, it drives the displacement of violence toward the center of the community, where violence is traditionally subject to the strictest rules. The ideals of forgiving and charity are then added to the weight of tradition to prohibit violence in that sphere and force agents to justify their misdeeds. Rationalization of violence is the result of this twofold pressure. It indicates nothing more than the difficulty in shifting violence onto sacrificable victims. Violence becomes rational insofar as it is increasingly called upon to be exercised against those who are the original targets, rather than against third parties: "scapegoats" who are completely innocent. This does not mean that the convergence of violence onto sacrificable victims does not take place any more, but that it becomes more difficult and almost impossible to express it openly. Rationalization of violence sends each of us back to our own conflicts, our own enemies. It deprives us all of a common outlet.

Such is the microsociological mechanism that facilitates the confusion of the circles of identity and adversariality in the space pacified by the holder of legitimate violence. Because it constantly increases the scope of the space where violence is contained, it requires violence to shift toward even more distant targets situated beyond the borders of the space where there is a monopoly of legitimate violence. However, at this greater scale, the influence of forgiving and charity, which helped to rationalize violence within the borders, fades away and the normal structure of the space of hostility regains its rights, so to speak. Use of violence becomes all the freer as the distance increases. The reason for this is that within international space, the agents of violence are not individuals freed of their duties of solidarity and violence, but states produced by the unanimous transfer of their subjects' violence.

How Should We Interact with Those to Whom We Owe Nothing?

On their own, charity and forgiving are incapable of managing all relations among agents because they do not form a complete system of rules. They are simply two "additional" models of behavior that, little by little, disrupt the functioning and effects of the existing system. They make different interactions with "Others" possible, but do not completely answer the question of what those interactions should be. In particular, while they make it possible to have peaceful relationships with those to whom we owe nothing, they do not say *how* we should interact with them. What rights and what duties do we have with respect to those with whom we are linked by no special bond?

The question is not entirely new. Even in the smallest traditional society, we sometimes encounter "Others" who escape the network of reciprocal obligations. How should we act toward them? What is new is not the question itself, but the manner in which it is asked, for the conditions that cause it to arise make the traditional answers less probable.

In a society that is still strongly structured by reciprocal ties of solidarity and hostility, a possible initial answer could be to extend our ties to "Others" to whom we are not linked. We can, for example, adopt strangers, introduce them into the family, and integrate them into our web of solidarity and hostility. We can establish matrimonial exchange relations or ritual exchanges with the strangers, which would reduce the otherness and make the strangers "the same." Ceremonial exchange can also establish new reciprocal obligations. For example, the oath as it is used in a feudal system creates new obligations and relations of dependency. In all of these cases, however, the problem is solved by putting an end, in a sense, to the situation out of which it arose. The Others are not abandoned in an exteriority where they have no ties to us. They are assimilated, absorbed into the network of solidarity/hostility relationships. In consequence the problem is dissolved rather than solved. We do not really answer the question: How should we act toward those to whom we are not related by any reciprocal obligations? This "solution" to the problem excludes in fact the possibility of relationships with "Others" unrelated to us by reciprocal obligations. However, there is another way to solve the problem: violence that exterminates the "Other." It puts a final end to the issue. In segmentary societies, the most outside circle of the solidarity/ hostility space, the home of those unattached to us by any reciprocal obligations, is where extreme violence is permitted toward those to whom we owe nothing, precisely because we owe them nothing.

These responses, which reject the question they are supposed to answer, prohibit the emergence of an area of relationships with people to whom we are linked by no reciprocal obligations. Violence or assimilation into the group prevents the creation of a space where such relations could emerge and become stable. It is precisely this space that charity and forgiving have permitted to emerge, but how has the slender opening that they authorized transformed into a vast area where people can live freely and which we call the "modern world?"

According to Marshall Sahlins, in segmentary societies there is a type of exchange that is a third form of behavior that can be adopted with respect to those to whom we owe nothing, those against whom it is also permitted to exercise the greatest violence. However, this form of exchange is of a special sort, different from the ceremonial exchange of gift and countergift that we find in such societies. It resembles modern economic transactions in that it concerns bartering, where each tries to maximize his or her own advantage, but at the other's expense.[9] Sahlins sees such exchange as a form of latent war, in which each party tries to gain the most possible to the detriment of the other. Lies and tricks are the rule, and violence is never very far away. While ceremonial exchanges, for example, the potlatch, sometimes resemble a meeting of two "adversaries" sizing each other up, the exchanges that occur in the third circle of the hostility/solidarity space are instead forms of predation. Sahlins implies that, in the modern capitalist economy, things may not be so different.

Yet, despite the rivalry to which it gives rise, modern exchange presents a very different picture. We all do indeed seek our own self-interest but, in principle, not at the expense of others. On the contrary, modern economic exchange is portrayed as a means by which *all* participants can maximize their own benefit, rather than one at the expense of the other. It suffices that it occur in conditions that ensure fairness. If an exchange is freely consented to and if the parties can be considered equal, then the transaction can be to the advantage of all. The question is thus how these conditions are "satisfied" in modern societies, and why they are not met in many other societies.

Exchange: A Rule of How to Behave for Those Not Bound by Reciprocal Obligation

According to Mark Anspach, one of the fundamental features of modern economic exchange is that it does not generate any reciprocal obligations between those who engage in it.[10] Indeed, we should not confuse the intrinsic reciprocity of mercantile exchange with the reciprocity typical of solidarity/

hostility relations. The reciprocity of exchange is that of the act itself. It is characterized by in-principle immediacy and radical autonomy. Once the goods have changed hands, all obligations cease. When I have paid for my car or my meal, I owe nothing more to the merchant, and the merchant owes nothing to me, aside from the car or meal that I have bought. I am owed neither courtesy nor assistance. It may be to the merchant's long-term advantage to not be too unpleasant to me, but the rational calculation that leads to a minimum of care and politeness is not an obligation. In modern exchange, once the transaction is finished, each party, as in Jean-Jacques Rousseau's social contract, remains "as free as before,"[11] but with no duty to unite with all. In economic exchange, each of us is free because we obey only ourselves, but in the proper sense this time, rather than through a form of association that requires that we each alienate ourselves completely to the whole community.

Ceremonial exchange produces social ties. It creates obligations that force agents to comply with reciprocity and subjugates them with duties to one another, whereas modern economic exchange, once it has been performed, puts an end to the relationship. Once the transaction is terminated, each goes on his or her way and, by definition, owes nothing more to the other with whom the exchange was performed. Once one has paid, in other words, as soon as one has given the "countergift," one is free of any debt, duty, or obligation.[12] In ceremonial exchange, the countergift does not put an end to exchange. On the contrary, it consolidates the relationship and calls for a new gift in return. This is one of the reasons ceremonial exchange should not be seen as a clumsy anticipation of modern merchant exchange. Rather than a primitive, rather inefficient form of commercial relations, ceremonial exchange is a form of reciprocal recognition, a means of renewing and maintaining the social bond.[13] It is a political rather than an economic phenomenon, and its purpose is precisely to manage certain "friends-foes" relationships, or more accurately certain relationships between "friends" and "adversaries." Exchanges that take place in the circle of warlike hostility that Sahlins talks about are also political: they reflect the hostility of "foe" groups between which there is no link except for reciprocal opposition. This is why, like modern exchange, they also do not create any lasting link between the parties. They are at best only temporary truces.

Exchange that, like modern transactions, creates no link between the parties can, for this very reason, become *a rule of behavior* between those who are not bound by any reciprocal obligations on the condition that the relationship of hostility between the unbound parties is suspended. As we will see, this twofold condition is *necessary*, but it is not sufficient. The special feature of this rule of behavior, which is at the origin of the flexibility that makes it generalizable, is the fact that the exchange relationship is its own rule unto itself. Rather than determining from the outside how agents should act, which is what law and traditional solidarity obligations do, exchange is regulated by itself.

> Man has almost constant occasion for the help of his brethren, and it is vain for him to expect it from their benevolence only. He will be more likely to prevail if he can interest their self-love in his favour, and show them that it is for their own advantage to do for him what he requires of them. Whoever offers to another a bargain of any kind, proposes to do this. Give me that which I want, and you shall have this which you want, is the meaning of every such offer; and it is in this manner that we obtain from one another the far greater part of those good offices which we stand in need of.[14]

Exchange, trade, is self-regulating, according to Adam Smith. It is subject to no outside obligation. As we each seek our own interest, the economy generates the rule of trade. Exchange finds its own just form on its own: it has no need for any external constraint. This is why this relationship can become established among those who owe nothing to one another, and why it is an answer, acceptable to all parties, to the question of how people who are not bound by any reciprocal obligations should act toward one another. The explanation for exchange's spontaneous regulation is that we would not voluntarily enter into such a relationship without the hope of receiving, if not as much as we give, at least as much as we need in order to voluntarily agree to the relationship. The spontaneity of exchange is nothing other than its rationality. It suffices that the agents' rational anticipations always be met for exchange to become a stable form of relationship between those who are not bound by any solidarity obligations. This is all that needs to be satisfied for the strategy of exchange to spread because it is to the advantage of everyone.

However, exchange cannot "self-regulate" unless agents are not bound by reciprocal obligations or hostility. They have to be "free." What we can call "breaking the bonds" of the agents is the necessary condition for the relationship to self-regulate, in other words, for it to be rational and fair. Perhaps you would lend money to your brother a second time, even though he is a bad payer and does not reimburse, but you would not be so generous with someone to whom you are bound only by the loan relationship. The condition of the exchange is that it be just and equitable. This is why it is self-regulating, for if it is not fair, the exchange will not take place. However, this self-regulation is possible only if agents are "free," in other words, if they are not bound by reciprocal obligations or duties to engage in violence. Moreover, the exchange can be fair only if agents are "equal" in a sense that will have to be defined below, but which is up to a certain point equivalent to the extent that their *bonds have been broken.*

As we have just seen, fairness of exchange is at the same time its condition of possibility. Exchange is a relationship that is its own law unto itself and constitutes a rule of action between those who are not bound by any reciprocal obligation because, when it is free, it is automatically fair. Free exchange, voluntarily consented to, brings an answer to the question: How should I act toward those who are not bound to me by any obligation of reciprocal reciprocity? It suffices to rely on and limit oneself to symmetry, to the immediate reciprocity of the freely consented to exchange relationship that entails no further obligation. Because the rule of the relationship is intrinsic to the relationship itself, compliance of each exchange with the rule is assessed independently of that of any other exchange relationship. This restriction of the rule of exchange to the relationship itself, isolated from any other commitment, ensures that those who exchange have no obligation to give, receive, or return. It also makes it possible for the exchange relationship to extend to all those who are ready to temporarily or partially suspend their traditional obligations.

Like charity, exchange is "in addition." It is not an alternative system of obligations. It progressively displaces former reciprocal obligations, but, at first at least, does not replace them. Because it is free and has no form other than that given to it by the participants in the exchange, it can occur anywhere in the network of relations and has no place of origin. Finally, because exchange is its own rule, it has no need to be taught or learned. It requires people be *unbound*, but does not depend on any of their specific beliefs. For all these reasons, it is a fixed point, an attractor for the behavior of individual agents as soon as certain constraints are removed.

Benevolence and Fraud

In Adam Smith's work, free, independent exchange does not take place in the circle of warlike hostility, where Sahlins believes he has found it.[15] It is not characteristic of relationships between "foes," but occurs between us, between "friends." It regulates the relationships between those who rub shoulders regularly. However, immediately after the passage cited above, the author of *The Wealth of Nations* adds this famous sentence: "It is not from the benevolence of the butcher, the brewer, or the baker that we expect our dinner, but from their regard to their own interest." A little later, he also says: "Nobody but a beggar chooses to depend chiefly upon the benevolence of his fellow-citizens."[16]

It is from the care that the butcher, brewer, and baker have for their own self-interest, rather than from a system of obligations to give, receive, and return, that we expect our dinner. They owe us nothing. This absence of reciprocal obligation is also what explains that beggars, even when forced by circumstances, *choose* to depend mainly on the benevolence of others. Benevolence, in other words, charity, is free. People who expect dinner from the benevolence of others beg for it; they do not demand it as a right. No own owes beggars anything. This is why begging is a choice, for no one can demand as owing what others give freely. Benevolence, or charity, as has been said above, is not an obligation in the proper sense. It is not a duty one is required to discharge under threat of punishment. Benevolence is "free." We even exercise it toward those to whom we owe nothing.

Just as Smith takes it for granted that the butcher, brewer, and baker have no special obligations that bind them to those who want to awaken their interest to their own advantage, he takes it for granted that the care that butchers and bakers have for their self-interest will not lead them to take advantage of the good faith of their clients. The father of economics supposes the existence of a minimum of benevolence between parties to exchange. In fact, what he says is that it is vain to hope to receive help from our brothers "from their benevolence only," and that only a beggar would decide to "depend chiefly on the benevolence" of others. Far from excluding benevolence, Smith supposes the existence of some minimal benevolence. What he says is that it is not sufficient to meet our needs; he does not say that it is useless or not necessary.

However, if nothing forces butchers and bakers to meet my needs, nothing guarantees that they will not take advantage of or exploit my weakness. As Daniel Finn reminds us, an economic market is a space of freedom protected by rules that prohibit certain abusive practices,[17] such as theft, trickery, fraud, and use of force, in short, all the real and latent violence the absence of which makes the difference between modern economic exchange and economic exchanges that, according to Sahlins, occur in the circle of hostility. In traditional societies, it is *because agents have obligations to one another* that they are required to abstain from violent practices that make free trade impossible, but these obligations simultaneously prevent the appearance of the "freedom" necessary for modern exchange. As soon as the strength of the obligations diminishes, as in the circle of hostility, violent practices reappear, and this is why the mercantile exchanges that we find there never manage to acquire sufficient "autonomy" to become established as rules of behavior. In such societies, reciprocal obligations apply only where free exchange does not occur. Consequently, they prohibit free trade in the circles of identity and adversariality, and fail to protect it in the circle of hostility. This is what happens in certain societies, such as in Fiji and Papua New Guinea, where it is extremely difficult for individuals of indigenous origin to establish themselves as modern entrepreneurs because traditional rules of solidarity oblige them to give away the goods they would like to sell, or force them to accord almost unlimited credit to a large proportion of their potential clients.[18]

If we remove these rules, as Adam Smith supposes, what prevents agents from resorting to practices that destroy exchange and the market system? In a sense, the answer is that there is nothing to prevent them since, by hypothesis, such obligations no longer apply. We can think, and experience shows this, that as soon as they have the opportunity to do so, agents often return to predatory practices. Why do they not always return to them? The manner in which traditional rules are removed can limit opportunities for the return to violence.

First, it is important that the parties to the exchange meet as isolated individuals rather than as representatives of distinct groups, "foes." This isolation of the agents makes it "rational" to have respect, or at least a certain form of respect, for our interest in the Other. Indeed, exchange is based on the fact that the interest of each of the parties depends on the interest of the other. As Adam Smith puts it so well: "Give me that which I want, and you shall have this which you want." Abandoning traditional ties of solidarity allows this reciprocal dependency to be expressed, to occupy, so to speak, center stage, for it separates my interest and the butcher's interest from the interests of the groups that could have something to gain if either I or the butcher were to suffer some harm. This unbinding of individual interests from group interests reduces the probability of recourse to open violence because it leaves each alone facing the other. It also limits opportunities for certain forms of trickery, namely, those that can easily lead to violence, but especially those that will make exchange impossible in the future. When agents meet in isolation, open fraud is not compatible with exchange except if the agents have no interest in engaging in the exchange relationship again in the future. Breaking the bonds does not, however, exclude another form of trickery that is more or less accepted by both parties and that leads to unequal exchanges.[19]

It is clear that neither benevolence nor enlightened self-interest is sufficient to ensure peace, yet they lay the foundations for a new order because they give birth to a *public* in the modern sense of the term, in other words, a collection of individuals, which is not properly speaking a group because the individuals are not bound by rules of reciprocal solidarity but simply share one or two common interests. In particular, they share "interest": the desire to want to pursue the interest that is common to them. In this sense, a public has the special feature of being a priori invisible. Aside from those that are accidental, there are no specific ties between those who are members of a given public—since those who share the same interest can be scattered across a vast territory and may not know one another. Therefore, a public can long remain invisible to both itself and others.[20] The emergence of publics within modern societies is the sign of the weakening of traditional groups in that publics are composed of collections of individuals who share similar interests independent of the groups to which they belong. Consequently, publics themselves have no special means of making themselves visible; their "emergence from the shadows," in other words, the fact that a public becomes socially visible at a certain time, indicates that the number of those who share the interest of the public and have taken distance with respect to their group obligations has become greater. A public is a *statistical group* in the sense in which this term was defined in chapter 2. As such, it cannot, so to speak, crystalize into a force, *into a visible social obstacle*, until it has reached a certain "density" in relation to the population as a whole. The slow development of a public within a community leads not only to the weakening of groups, but constitutes an obstacle, inertia, that opposes the formation of new groups. This is why in modern societies, where publics have dissolved traditional groups, setting up new groups, such as the proletariat or the nation, always requires using explicit means, such as propaganda, parties, and "movements."

The shared interest of the first public generated by the development of mercantile exchange was that each be able to pursue his or her individual interest. Among other things, this interest involved for each the desire to not be a victim of abusive practices that would make trade impossible. This meant that such a public spontaneously called for the establishment of a power capable of forcing agents to act according to their "enlightened self-interest," which meant able to prohibit them from meeting the obligations that they owed to their respective groups. This public (the bourgeoisie) was thus very naturally the social basis on which a group (the monarchy) could build when seeking to eliminate other groups (to reduce the power of the nobles). In other words, the group aimed not only to vanquish or replace its adversaries, but to conquer them, to become their master and destroy them *as groups*. To put it in Hobbes's words, such a group seeks "by force, or wiles, to master the persons of all men he can so long till he see no other power great enough to endanger him."[21]

This state of equilibrium is achieved when the public shows itself to be satisfied with the extent of the pacified area where it can "go about its business." The dismantling of traditional solidarity and hostility obligations under the slow pressure of charity and exchange is not just a prior condition for establishing a power that holds the monopoly of legitimate violence. It is a social transformation that makes it highly probable that a plurality of such powers will appear. They will be in more or less stable equilibrium with one another. The establishment of absolutist states in Europe was not the feat of only one invention, but the result of parallel developments that took place in different places more or less simultaneously. Rivalry among nascent states played an important role in the parallel developments.[22] For reasons that are contingent in relation to the logic of their development, such as geographical obstacles and the state of communication technology, all publics have a "natural" size. Moreover, the new division into larger groups, modern states, which are no longer structured by reciprocal reciprocity obligations, makes it possible for there to be exchange between individuals belonging to different states, so long as the animosity between the states is not too great. On both sides, the exchanges give rise to pressure on the states to agree to police them together. Montesquieu said: "Peace is the natural effect of trade," but he added: "if the spirit of commerce unites nations, it does not in the same manner unite individuals."[23]

Exclusion of Groups

Exchange as a solution leads to a deep upheaval in relations between those still bound, though always less perfectly, by reciprocal solidarity relations. The conception of justice that it embodies, namely, fairness, undermines the foundations of these obligations. It challenges the inherited solidarities, and motivates each to disappoint the expectations that they justify. The transformation into purely mercantile exchange of any set of services that used to be at least partially regulated by traditional solidarity—for example, lending seed, helping with the harvest, taking an apprentice or page into one's service—frustrates many agents, whose expectations were built on ancestral respect for these obligations. Simultaneously, the ideal of fairness that exchange contains offers each a degree of freedom of action that obligations used to prevent. Consequently, exchange is an unending source of conflict, vexation, and frustration. Moreover, while exchange offers everyone advantages, it also offers some people almost irresistible temptations that are contrary to its own ideal of justice. Indeed, the rule of exchange gives those who are well placed in the system of traditional obligations the ability to act like free riders in relation to their obligations. They have the advantage, on one hand, of not honoring their solidarity obligations to others and adhering strictly to the rule of exchange with them, and, on the other hand, of requiring others to honor their obligations to them. This temptation involves the risk of not being allowed to exchange in the future. However, it is a risk that some people have the luxury to take, in particular if what remains of the former system allows them to force others to honor their traditional obligations. This is because free, fair exchange appears in a society where inequality is still codified in traditional ties. On one hand, it challenges this inequality; on the other hand, this inequality gives some people the possibility of unequal exchanges that are to their advantage. For example, in England at the time of the enclosures, the inequality inherited from the former system allowed major landowners to divide common land to their advantage and to exclude all those who were not properly speaking landowners from having access to land, whereas they had been relatively protected by traditional obligations prior to that.[24] However, the possibility of inequality within exchange does not derive from inherited differences alone. It also comes from the many variations in individuals' abilities as well as simple luck. In addition to inequalities related to status, which are established by the system of traditional obligations, there are thus innumerable onetime, local inequalities that arise and disappear depending on the circumstances. Consequently, the temptation to take advantage of them in a way unjustified by the rules of fair trade is universal and, above all, such "hijacking" of trade cannot be distinguished from fair trade.

This phenomenon has three major consequences for the evolution of the modern political system. First, it hastens the abandoning of traditional solidarity obligations, not only because it is based in part on refusal to honor them, but above all because it corresponds to what can be called "asymmetrical respect for reciprocal relations," in other words, the fact that the "strong" require the "weak" to respect their traditional obligations while at the same time they try to avoid their own duties as much as possible. Consequently, these obligations are emptied of even more of their meaning and raison d'être. The second consequence is that this phenomenon thus paradoxically weakens the strong whom it benefits: it makes it increasingly difficult for them to establish their power on the basis of obligations for which they demand asymmetrical respect. It gradually destroys the foundation, the group that used to form the base for the power that allowed them to bend the rule of exchange to their advantage. They are thus forced to seek from the state protection for the advantages that they enjoy. Exchange from which they gain unequal advantage makes them more and more dependent on the state, for it makes their "natural" political base disappear. This is precisely what happened in France between Louis XIV's reign and the Revolution. Finally, the third consequence is that when it is based on status-related inequalities inherited from the system of traditional obligations, unequal exchange gives a political dimension to some of the innumerable conflicts that exchange generates. The social visibility of these inherited differences encourages such conflicts, which, though they result from free but unequal interactions among persons, acquire the form of group conflicts, for example, between the Third Estate and the nobility. In this sense, this visibility facilitates the convergence of resentment on the same targets. The targets of political violence, the aristocrats, thus oppose as a group the set of all the others united under the monopoly of legitimate violence.

However, they do not form a group in the proper sense of a set structured by ties of reciprocal reciprocity that distribute obligations of help and violence. "Nobility of the robe" and "nobility of the sword" were only collections of individuals torn apart by divisions and rivalries flowing from many different groups in which their ancestors sometimes used to occupy preferential positions in the networks of reciprocal obligations. They had become creatures of the state, on which they depended entirely in order to maintain their privileges. The convergence of violence onto them led to the need for the public emergence of parties, clubs, in other words, bodies that made the public visible to itself, as well as specialists to take charge of the exercise of violence.

Values and Moral Sentiments

Except in times of open political violence, such as wars and revolutions, the system of exchange gives rise to a form of sacrificial violence that we could call *violence by omission*. The victims of this violence most often appear to be the victims of no one, individuals against whom no one has committed an offense. First they are those who have been left behind as traditional solidarity obligations have withdrawn. The victims of violence by omission are those whom the abandoning of these obligations and the dismantling of the institutions that embodied them have left bereft and defenseless.[25] They are not victims of anyone in particular because their destitution flows from the fact that no one has any special duties with respect to them anymore.

Someone may have committed an offense against them, but it is generally incommensurable with the harm they suffer. It is the abandoning of obligations of help and support that transforms the offense into a tragedy. In this sense, they are the victims of widespread indifference, which should not be understood as a psychological disposition of certain agents, but as a new institutional arrangement. The isolation that protects us from the escalation of violence also leaves people defenseless. As exchange gradually spreads as a rule of behavior, all those who lose too much in the game of trade become victims of abandonment and indifference.

Such people are not simply abandoned to their fates; they are also the objects, in discourse and in reality, of a form of exclusion that reveals that they also have the value of substitute victims. The outcasts of exchange are not the victims of anyone, first, because exchange is by definition free and fair. It follows that, no matter what their present situation, if it is the result of exchange, no one has committed any injustice with respect to them. They thus have no right to ask for anything from anyone. They can of course address themselves to the free charity of their brothers and sisters, but no one has, properly speaking, any obligation to compensate them or ensure justice is done.[26] Given the preceding argument, it is natural that the suspicion should arise that they themselves are responsible for the misfortune that strikes them. Since evil never occurs without reason, and no one has wronged them, it seems more probable that the poverty they suffer comes either from a moral failing, or from a form of incompetency that makes them unfit for the market system, rather than from them being excluded. Consequently, as Hume says, helping them would be a mistake, a false form of charity: "Giving alms to common beggars is naturally praised, because it seems to carry relief to the distressed and the indigent. But when we observe the encouragement thence arising to idleness and debauchery, we regard that species of charity rather as a weakness than a virtue."[27] The poor and destitute, the outcasts of exchange, are here, in a second sense, the victims of no one. They are victims only of themselves, of their incompetency or their vices, and no one has any special responsibility with regard to them.

This twofold discourse, which expresses the guilt of the victims and the absence of everyone else's responsibility, transforms the misfortune that strikes them into justified punishment. It reflects, reveals, though not explicitly, their role as substitute victims. What changes bad luck in the game of exchange into definitive misfortune is not so much the incident of which an outcast has been the victim as the fact that no one has any obligation to him or her, and the fact that this absence of obligation and exclusion are later elevated into recommendations, moral norms. The outcasts of exchange are then delivered to the charity of "Good Samaritans," who most often continue on their way without stopping. Finally, the victims of no one reveal themselves to be the victims of everyone.

Indifference toward the outcasts of exchange, who are responsible for their misfortune and to whom no one owes anything, is the everyday, ordinary form of the banality of evil. This rational, and rationalized, indifference defines them as substitute victims. They are the sacrificed who provide us with consolation for our own failures. What prevents us from seeing their nature as substitute victims is precisely the fact that they are too banal and ordinary. Their sacrificial dimension is invisible, not because they are concealed but because they are disseminated everywhere. Unlike victims of ritual sacrifice, they are not at the focal point where all eyes in the community converge. They are indeed the victims of everybody, but because no one in particular is the victim of all, no one is the victim of anyone. They are destroyed neither by the hand of a sacrificer, nor with the unanimous agreement of all members of society, but by frequent individual failures disseminated like the victims themselves within the general population, in other words, by statistical facts, which for this very reason are not actions that anyone performs.

Through this, individual conflicts find private outlets, little local substitute victims. The violence that strikes them is legitimate and so it is not really violence. It is only justice, the fate that the victims have merited. This process strengthens the stability of the system and further encourages the abandonment of reciprocal obligations and the dissolution of the groups that the obligations used to structure. In the space pacified by the state monopoly of legitimate violence, where open violence in relationships between agents has lost any legitimacy, the shift of violence, resentment, and frustration onto substitute victims gives people an additional reason to sneak out of their obligations.

The Return of Groups

These local shifts of violence are the complete contrary of the convergence on a single victim. They make the transfers of violence diverge, rather than converge. The indirect violence by omission, as well as the direct violence that sometimes accompanies it, remain outside of politics so long as their victims do not form a group, so long as they remain socially invisible and do not become aware that they form a *public* with shared interests. However, as soon as they begin to be perceived as a distinct group within the nation pacified by the monopoly of legitimate violence, their presence alone threatens the monopoly and its legitimacy. The presence of a "victim" group within a community of "friends" is a challenge to the supposed equality and brotherhood, for in the world of rational violence, no one can claim to have victims who are not "foes," and under the monopoly of legitimate violence, there is no room for "foes."

The transformation of substitute victims into a group is in fact inevitable. As we have seen, the mechanism that engenders them and the discourse to which it gives rise make them carry the responsibility for their exclusion. The action that excludes them gives them shared features: it designates them as immoral, lazy, drunken, ignorant, in other words, "Other" and all the same. The indifference of which the outcasts are victims is justified by making them into and recognizing them as a new group, a set of individuals that has specific characteristics and is recognized as such. The monopoly of legitimate violence is thus unstable by definition, for the abandonment of traditional obligations that makes it possible, by weakening the ties that unite groups smaller than the state, simultaneously triggers the appearance of a different type of group, which initially forms only a statistical group, but rapidly turns into a *public*. Beginning at the time of the French Revolution, the sansculottes and then the various socialist and communist movements were the means of the transformation of this statistical group into an organized group, and the expression of the presence, within the space pacified by the monopoly of legitimate violence, of a relationship of hostility that justified recourse to violence: terrorist attacks, riots, assassinations, revolutions, civil wars, and finally wars between nations.

World War II was the last of an almost uninterrupted series of conflicts that had been tearing Europe apart since 1914. These conflicts, most often civil wars, were also expressions of the "universal" opposition between the Left and the Right. They extended beyond the borders of the nations where they took place, as can be seen from the involvement of various countries in the Russian and Spanish civil wars. The conflicts crossed the boundaries of the principle of territory-based hostility and transgressed its rules. Communism and Nazism challenged not only existing territorial arrangements, but also the mapping of national borders onto the opposition between "friends" and "foes." In the very process of excluding traditional groups, the monopoly of legitimate violence thus engendered new groups whose opposition could not be boiled down to the principle of territorial hostility. This is why we can see the two world wars and the many smaller conflicts that tore Europe apart as points in the same crisis of the territorial system. The end of World War I and that of World War II were marked in Europe by vast population shifts that were designed to expel and move "foe" groups into separate areas so as to re-create the territorial system.

However, only World War II was followed by lasting peace. In fact, it was the development of the destructive technology to which these conflicts led, in particular nuclear weapons, that made it possible to reestablish the territorial order. The opposition between the "Free World" and the "Communist World" reintroduced, within the space of nations, conflict in which the extreme form of hostility was expressed. The face-off between the Eastern bloc and the Western bloc, separated by the Iron Curtain, reterritorialized the opposition that had been bathing Europe and the world in blood for nearly fifty years. The threefold structure of the space of hostility was institutionalized in a new manner that distanced in time rather than in space the relationship of extreme hostility. The constantly looming threat of total destruction replaced the free space where unlimited violence was permitted.

The social conflict that had been dividing modern nations from the inside for over a century finally received a territorial form. The opposition between the Left and the Right became the confrontation between the East and the West. On both sides of this division, the Iron Curtain stood as the physical barrier on the other side of which "foes" lived. Simultaneously, we witnessed the development of social justice policies and the establishment of the welfare state. This has to be understood as an effort to reintegrate the "foe" group into the group of "friends." As we will see in the next chapter, this was meant to be seen as the ultimate achievement of the territorial order: the disappearance of all animosity relationships within the state.

The threat of mutual destruction made the Cold War the ultimate form of the relationship of enmity. This confrontation, always present and always looming, for which everyone was feverishly preparing, made possible the final disappearance of what remained of the free outside space. Decolonization, the creation of the United Nations, and the establishment of an international community composed uniquely of sovereign nation-states that were in principle equal simplified the hostility/solidarity space. The new arrangement, in which nuclear terror, *as a real possibility*, played the role of the third circle of hostility, apparently confined the relationship of enmity to relations between sovereign nations alone. Sheltered by nuclear terror, states even thought that they could exclude the relationship of enmity from relations between nations.

Consequently, every war that occurred was understood in the framework of the impossible confrontation between the "Communist World" and the "Free World," as the expression of the paradigmatic dichotomy that alone prohibited lasting peace. The omnipresence of this opposition between "friends" and "foes" was evidence of the success of the transformation of ordinary violence into political violence. However, the threat of total destruction had to fade only for a moment for wars of extermination to resurface in Europe, and for us to see new forms of conflict arise on the international scene. They may not take the form of wars between nations, but they nonetheless encompass entire regions.

CHAPTER 6

Social Justice and Territory

Modern redistribution policies and the institution of the welfare state have to be understood in the context of the reestablishment of the territorial order and restructuring of the space of hostility that took place after World War II. They were the results of the explicit desire of Western states to reterritorialize the "friends-foes" dichotomy, the confrontation between the revolutionary Left and the state that had divided them on the inside. It was a question of shifting the social conflict into an opposition defined in geographical space: the confrontation between the East and the West. The concern for social justice also went hand in hand with decolonization, the ultimate disappearance of the outside space of "non-nations," and the extension of the same type of "friends-foes" opposition between the inside and the outside of the state to the entire world, now composed uniquely of nation-states. Once again, what made this apparent simplification of the space of hostility possible was the existence of an absolute division between the East and the West, which embodied the most extreme form of violence: the total destruction of the planet, always possible, always put off to the future.

With the establishment of social justice and the welfare state, it was a question, in the end, of bringing the modern state's goal to fruition by making all members of the state truly "friends." Theories of social justice can be seen as sophisticated expressions of a desire for universal domestic solidarity, which is legitimized by the rejection of violence, a form of behavior that is left for the "foes" who live outside, on the other side of the Iron Curtain. The purpose of social justice is to revive the ideals of equality and well-being contained in past social claims, while disarming them, in the proper sense, though not rendering them powerless.

One of the fundamental theses of this book is that modern political institutions come from a transformation of the rules of reciprocal solidarity that structure relationships between agents, and that solidarity is inseparable from hostility. Historically, different forms of hostility have always corresponded to different rules of solidarity. In the first part of this chapter I will thus analyze some of the central concepts of social justice, more specifically, the relationships between the concepts of rationality and reciprocity. I argued above that, insofar as it is "the Other of violence," reason cannot exist except within the space pacified by the monopoly of legitimate violence. Outside of that territory, from which "foes" have been excluded, reason recommends the same actions as violence. Yet theories of social justice hope to create, on the basis of rationality, a system of reciprocity from which no one is in principle excluded. We thus need to see whether they really succeed in separating solidarity from hostility, and whether they can be at the foundation of truly global justice, in other words, whether they have managed to subvert the framework within which they emerged.

Theories of social justice do not presuppose the state. They see justice as the result of a free agreement among individuals in an original position. Institutions responsible for establishing justice and the state itself are also supposed to emerge from this agreement. Even though they do not advocate the idea of a universal state, these theories generally overlook the problem raised by the fact that there are many states. The extension of social justice to the entire planet then appears as a simple question of scale. It is only a question of looking a little further, of taking a broader approach, as if this expansion of the issue would not raise any problems other than technical ones. Can the ideal of social justice really be universalized in this way and extended to the planetary scale, as is sometimes suggested by theories of social justice? Or does the rationality on which this ideal is based presuppose some forms of exclusion?

Thus, in the second part of this chapter, I will discuss the phenomenon of globalization that underlies the global justice project. Globalization challenges the territorial order, the monopoly of legitimate violence and the formal equality of citizens. It not only leads to placing the "friends-foes" separation elsewhere than between nations, but also prevents "friends," "foes," and those destined for warlike hostility from being distributed in different spaces.

Social Justice

Since the end of World War II, social justice has tried to bring the modern state to completion by transforming all citizens into "friends" and preventing "foe" groups from resurfacing within the territory pacified through the state's monopoly of legitimate violence. Social justice is seen both as a way of reducing opportunities for violent political conflict, and as a way of reintegrating into the social body those whom the abandoning of traditional obligations has transformed into victims, outcasts of exchange. Yet the demand for social justice will have difficulty playing this irenic, unifying role so long as it remains formulated in terms of exploitation and class struggle or described as an expression of envy and resentment. Seen in either of these ways, the social justice requirement resuscitates political conflict between groups. It reveals the presence of "foes" within the state. Formulated in this way, the requirement of equality and social justice is inseparable from the desire to eliminate the "foes" of the people, nation, working class, and so on.

Social justice cannot become the means of eliminating enmity within the state rather than a means of violently excluding "foes" unless the link between injustice and social conflict is broken. This separation, the history of which we will not go back over here,[1] led to a radical transformation of the concept of justice as it had been understood until then, for it severed the notion of injustice from that of individual or collective fault. Just as there can be victimless crimes,[2] victims of social injustice would be victims of injustice not committed by criminals. The purpose of this transformation of the concept of justice, which frees the concern for social justice from its relationship with violence, is to establish a new order with no exclusions.

Thus, Rawls, for example, borrowed the idea of "social states" from economists,[3] and proposed to see whether a social state is just without taking into consideration the relationships between the agents within the state. According to him, it suffices to compare the results, in terms of resources or well-being, that different social states attribute to individual agents, in order to determine whether a given social state is just. Thus, in *A Theory of Justice*, Rawls took into account neither relationships between persons, nor relationships between organized groups, but only the final results distributed over various statistical groups, for example the worst off.[4] Statistical groups were then compared with one another in different social states so as to identify which social state best met the principles of justice that, according to Rawls, would have been chosen in the "original position." In fact, Rawls imagined an ideal original position in which individuals were called upon to choose the fundamental principles of justice that were to govern the way the society would be organized. One of the consequences of this way of presenting the question of justice is that justice and injustice are conceived of as intrinsic features of social states, independent of the specific relationships that there may be between agents. Of these relationships, there no longer remains anything but an obscure trace in the final distribution of goods, social roles, advantages and disadvantages. Justice and injustice become characteristics of social states rather than normative features specific to relations between people. Rawls said that justice is a virtue of institutions.[5] In other words, according to him, it does not directly concern real relationships between persons, but the rules and forms of institutions that structure those relationships.

In the writings of most authors, this transformation of the idea of justice, while real and fundamental, remains implicit because this aspect of the concept of social justice is rarely the object of explicit reflection. We have to thank Friedrich Hayek[6] for having made this clear, even if it was in order to criticize the inanity, according to him, of such a conception. Hayek points out that in the modern idea of social justice there is something extremely strange. Classical conceptions of justice and injustice refer to actions committed by specific persons, and to the consequences of those actions, rather than to results, to simple de facto states. If someone breaks your arm or steals your wallet, you are right to complain about having suffered injustice. In contrast, if you lose your wallet or fall and injure yourself, you have suffered a misfortune, but no one has committed any injustice toward you.

Hayek criticizes the modern concept of social justice for not taking into account what has always been at the heart of the idea of justice: the fact that only human behavior can be described as just or unjust.[7] He says that what is at issue in the social justice requirement are anonymous results of the economic market. Consequently, in relation to the worst off, for example, there is no answer to the question of who has been unjust to them for there is no one, no group, who can be considered as responsible for the outcome of a free market.[8]

Obviously, we can reply that it is naive to believe that the market is free or that agents meet one another there as equals whom nothing and no one forces to engage in trade or to accept the deals they are offered. This is not the essential point. Hayek clearly is right to think that the concept of social justice strays from the traditional notion of justice, and even contradicts it to a certain point. Yet it does not follow that this concept is inconsistent.[9] In a world that is no longer structured by reciprocal solidarity obligations, it may be legitimate for some to demand a form of redress, even if their situation does not result from an unjust action by anyone *in particular*. This is because the worst off are in the first place the victims of the abandoning of those obligations and the resulting indifference. The injustice that they suffer is a form of *violence by omission* that does indeed flow from human actions, even though it is very often the deed of no one in particular.

The modern conception of justice, because it considers the disadvantages that some individuals suffer as a structural feature of a social state, a feature that all can have reasons to want to avoid, rather than as the results of actions by other individuals, *makes it possible to dissociate the demand for social justice from denunciation of opposing groups within the state.* The reason the idea of social justice can lead toward social peace is because it also says that abandoning our traditional solidarity obligations does not free us from all of our duties to those whom the new dynamic of interactions puts at a disadvantage.[10] It refuses to turn the most disadvantaged into everybody's substitute victims for the frustrations that we all inevitably suffer, or to make the weakest and most vulnerable responsible for the misfortune that strikes them. Understood in this way, social justice aims to bring to completion what is best in the pacification of territory performed by the modern state's monopoly of legitimate violence: the equality of all members of society and the rejection of sacrificial violence.

Dialectic of Reason and Reciprocity: Solidarity and Voluntary Exclusion

The idea of social justice is meant to take the rational agreement of all as the basis for measures to help the outcasts of exchange. According to Rawls, such assistance policies can be based on a form of reciprocity, fairness, which is inseparable from rationality, to the point that it becomes difficult to distinguish one from the other: "People are reasonable in one basic aspect when, among equals say, they are ready to propose principles and standards as fair terms of cooperation and to abide by them willingly, given the assurance that others will likewise do so."[11]

In other words, between equals it is reasonable to propose fair rules of cooperation and to comply with them, "given the assurance that others will likewise do so." Inversely, it is fair to voluntarily comply with reasonable rules of cooperation *so long as others are inclined to do likewise.* It is reasonable to be fair when others are too, just as it is fair to act reasonably when others are also reasonable. We can call this *conditional reciprocity.* The solidarity of each depends on the solidarity of every other. It depends on the fact that each is assured that the other is also disposed to demonstrate solidarity. Since this dependence is by hypothesis true of all agents, obvious uncertainty follows and solidarity thus becomes possible only if the uncertainty can be removed.

Conditional reciprocity can be considered an answer to the question that we encountered in the preceding chapter: how should we behave toward those to whom we owe nothing, to whom we are tied by no reciprocal obligation? How can we create ties among us? What form should the bonds take? On what should we found obligations that free, equal agents, in other words, agents not bound by any reciprocal obligation, will be ready to honor? This is the problem solved by exchange, but it is also the one put in the spotlight by the social contract. In any case, the solution is formally the same, and the Rawlsian idea of conditional reciprocity is in a sense its formal expression. It consists in making fulfillment of the obligations of each dependent on the others fulfilling their own obligations.

Given this principle of rationality/reciprocity, my solidarity with the Other depends on the fact of knowing that the Other is disposed to behave with solidarity toward me, just as I am toward the Other on the condition that the Other is disposed toward me in the same way, and so on, to infinity.

Likewise, according to Rawls, it is reasonable to behave with solidarity if the Other is so disposed in return. Acting otherwise would be unreasonable. Not only is it not unreasonable to refuse to behave with solidarity toward those who are not disposed to behave with solidarity, it is unreasonable to think that rational individuals will agree to behave with solidarity toward others who are not inclined to do so in return. Solidarity is not rational in itself, but only conditionally. Likewise, rationality in itself does not lead to solidarity; it does so only conditionally. Conditional solidarity is different from charity, as described in the preceding chapter, first insofar as it is conditional. Charity is an unconditional injunction; it makes no distinction between persons. It does not take into account the group to which those in need belong. Above all, charity neither requires nor supposes any reciprocity, otherwise, precisely, it would no longer be charity.

Understood in this way, solidarity is no more of an obligation than is reason. Nothing requires me to act with solidarity. Everything depends on the other's attitude toward me. In fact, in this case, it is not even a question of a conditional obligation in the usual sense of the term, for while it is reasonable to accept fair terms of cooperation when others are willing to do likewise, no one is required to be reasonable. Instead, as Reiko Gotoh suggests, conditional reciprocity should be seen as a rational disposition that lightens the moral weight of the obligation. It gives agents a reason to act that relieves them of having to fulfill an unconditional moral obligation to help those in need.[12] Paraphrasing what Hobbes wrote about the laws of nature, we can say that conditional reciprocity is wise advice for those who want to and can maximize their own interest by taking advantage of cooperation.[13] Like exchange, to which it is related, conditional reciprocity is a rule of behavior toward those to whom no obligation of reciprocal solidary ties us. Like exchange, conditional reciprocity makes the rule of the relationship arise from the relationship; it is not imposed from the outside. However, applied to solidarity, conditional reciprocity is not its own law unto itself. It fails to be self-regulating because, contrary to exchange, conditional reciprocity does not correspond to a real relationship between agents, but to a possible relationship.

Exchange, bartering, comes to an end. The transaction closes the relationship. Once the purpose is achieved, it is possible to look back, so to speak, to assess whether the operation was successful or not, to take stock, to see whether or not we are ready to do it again. In contrast, conditional solidarity has no natural end. It is open to an indefinite future and ties us to others only by a form of *modality*, a condition that may not in fact be satisfied: "given the assurance that others will likewise do so." In truth, this is not a condition in the proper sense, but a disposition with a hypothetical aspect that cannot be eliminated. It is nonetheless conceived of as the prerequisite for all effective reciprocity, as the condition for the relationship itself. In other words, exchange is isolated, local, and links specific agents. It presupposes itself, as does conditional reciprocity, but the rational expectations on which it is based *may or may not be satisfied*, and in consequence agents can develop appropriate strategies. *Because it tries to link all agents in a form of commerce that encompasses an indefinite future, conditional solidarity requires knowing, beforehand, whether the expectations on which it is based will indeed by satisfied.* It requires an answer to the question: Will the others "likewise do so"? Are they disposed to prove to be rational and demonstrate solidarity?

This difficulty shines light on what remains implicit in Rawls's text: the fact that the Other may be neither fair nor reasonable. The conditional provision is a general rule of behavior between those who are not bound by any reciprocal obligations. What attitude and what behavior should we adopt when the conditional reciprocity requirement is not met? Hobbes' answer is the only consistent one in the framework of conditional reciprocity:

"A man that by asperity of nature will strive to retain those things which to himself are superfluous and to others necessary, and for the stubbornness of his passions cannot be corrected, is to be left or cast out of society as cumbersome thereunto."[14]

Owing to its nature, conditional reciprocity is open to all, and excludes only those who exclude themselves. Those who refuse to comply with fair rules of cooperation that others are disposed to follow thereby exclude themselves from the reasonable system of social cooperation. They are neither reasonable nor fair, and nothing forces us to be so toward them.

Dialectic of Reciprocity and Rationality: Time and Values

How can we know whether some exclude themselves? How can we know that some will not be tempted to speculate on unequal exchange? Is it sufficient, as Hobbes suggests, to observe whether they keep for themselves what they do not need when it is necessary for others? In other words, can we not simply see whether they comply with the rules of fair cooperation? The problem here is slightly different. The question is not to know whether individuals comply with the rule, but whether they are disposed to comply with it in an indefinite future. *How can an agent whose exclusion rests on failure to have a disposition, which is itself relative to a rule the existence of which supposes that the disposition will be had, self-exclude?* In truth, the agent can do this only after the fact, once the rule has been established. The difficulty is that the rule cannot be established unless we have already excluded "those who exclude themselves" because it sets as a "condition" that the disposition be had, and can exist only between those who do indeed have the disposition. Exclusion of "those who exclude themselves" is the condition for the emergence of a blueprint for rational, fair cooperation. This is the problem.

As Reiko Gotoh also points out, conceived of as conditional, reciprocity is not based on bilateral relations between agents, but on rules.[15] This is another way of saying that it is not a real relationship between individuals. Now, if this is the case, could we not, for example, base conditional reciprocity on the rule of reasonableness? In other words, could it not be based on the rule according to which it is reasonable to accept fair conditions of cooperation "given the assurance that others will likewise do so." This rule, insofar as it is conscious and explicit, places outside constraints on agents' behavior. In this, it is different from the rule of exchange, which is merely a regularity of behavior that emerges from exchange itself. In exchange, the agent needs neither to know nor to acknowledge the rule in order to comply with it. In contrast, the rule according to which it is reasonable to accept fair conditions of cooperation if others will also do so is presented to agents in an explicit manner, as a reason to make their behavior comply with the rule. As a reason for action, it establishes itself: it has to be self-evident in a way that imposes itself on agents. Is it possible to establish solidarity by getting agents to acknowledge the rational value of the rule of conditional reciprocity?

This "solution" to the problem of conditional reciprocity shifts the difficulty and changes the nature of the question. It can be formulated in the following way: What assures me that the Other will accept the rule of reciprocity? A priori nothing, unless I have reasons to think that he or she is rational or reasonable. However, the question is no longer whether the Other is inclined to accept the rule if I am likewise, but simply to know whether the Other accepts it. The question is no longer whether the Other is ready to be reasonable if I am too, but to know whether he or she is reasonable. Acceptance of the rule by one no longer has the condition of acceptance of the rule by the other. It becomes an internal, subjective action performed by each agent individually. It is a cognitive operation that places the agent in relation to independent intellectual content that is its own rationale: the rule of reciprocity. Thus, what establishes the rule is not the other's agreement to comply with it, but the rule's "intrinsic" rationality. This shift eliminates the conditional aspect and transforms a reciprocal rule into a value that self-perpetuates: reasonableness or fairness.

Values are intellectual content that is supposed to be self-motivating for agents. To recognize or accept a value, such as honesty, for example, is to accept that it is worthwhile in itself, independent of whether people are honest in general or on average. The same goes for fairness and solidarity considered as *values*, in other words, as independent intellectual content rather than as rational conditional forms of behavior. Since they are presented to us as intellectual objects or as independent ideals existing in themselves and pushing us toward certain actions without taking into account the behavior of others, could values not provide a solution to the problem of conditional solidarity? Hans Joas opposes "the affective experience of a value's unconditional validity to the insights achieved by rational deliberation."[16] Whether they are rational, ethnic, or cultural, values are absolutes that seem to escape the curse of conditionality. They establish us as autonomous subjects able to take action without taking into account the dispositions of others. However, is this really the case?

Of the Exclusion of Those Who Exclude Themselves

Socially, rather than at the level of each agent taken individually, recourse to values does not evade the difficulties of conditional reciprocity so easily. Even though they may be for each agent absolutes in relation to other agents, values do not put an end to the persistent doubt that undermines conditional reciprocity. Taken as a value, solidarity cannot be used to establish helping policies and practices unless it is shared socially. Its "transcendence" with respect to relationships between agents, its constitution as a pure ideal object offered to intellectual intuition as a subjective experience, in no way changes the fact that its real social efficiency depends on it being common to all, or to many people. Taken as a value, solidarity may solicit each person individually, but it cannot give birth to a cooperation scheme unless enough people elect it as a value. Adopting a value, whether rational, ethical, or cultural, does not on its own resolve the uncertainty concerning the dispositions of others. However, it suggests a way to do so, which consists in transforming the original question about the future into a question about the present. It is no longer a case of providing assurance that the other is disposed to demonstrate solidarity in the future given my own disposition to do likewise, but to know whether the Other shares the same value, namely solidarity.

Supposing that there is an external sign that an agent subscribes to a value, it would then become possible to answer the question we are interested in, and to know, before it is made real in action, whether the agent does or does not share the value in question. The problem is thus to find such a sign, if there is one. Now, the best way to solve this problem is to *institute* a sign as proof of sharing the desired value. The institution does not have to be official and conscious, and most often will be, at first anyway, the result of a spontaneous convergence on certain forms of behavior and certain features of individuals within a given populace. While the sign is presented as revealing agents' values, in reality it functions as a *convention* that "constrains" those who adopt it. A convention is by definition a social mechanism that regulates itself. Within a population where there is a convention, it is always to agents' advantage to comply with it, otherwise they will be excluded by the others, who will refuse to interact with them in the future.[17] The problem of recognizing who are those "who exclude themselves" is then solved: they are the ones who do not share the same values as us. The sharing is shown by certain external signs, which are chosen arbitrarily as meaning that the value in question is or is not shared. The signs can be, for example, religion, language or even a way of dressing. The best recent examples of such agreements are "negative" ones, such as the wearing of the Islamic veil or the burka. We suppose that these signs indicate that the agents who display them not only do not share, but *cannot share* the same values as we.[18]

"Universal" solidarity is possible only within a space from which are excluded those who do not share the same values as we, and whom by that fact exclude themselves. This is because the reciprocity requirement, of which conditional rationality is an expression, inevitably comes back to haunt solidarity. Contrary to charity, solidarity is possible only between those who recognize one another as united in one way or another. This is why, in the end, Rawls writes: "The essential point is this: as a practical political matter no general moral conception can provide a publicly recognized basis for a conception of justice in a modern democratic state. The social and historical conditions of such a state have their origins in the Wars of Religion following the Reformation and the subsequent development of the principle of toleration, and in the growth of constitutional government and the institutions of large industrial market economies. These conditions profoundly affect the requirements of a workable conception of political justice."[19]

The conditional reciprocity underlying the Rawlsian conception of justice as fairness is not possible everywhere. According to Rawls, it cannot exist and makes no sense except among those whom a shared history has led to share the same values of tolerance and rationality. Of this sharing, of this subscription to the values of tolerance and rationality, the shared history of states born from the Wars of Religion is supposed to be the proof. In the end, it is only among individual members of states shaped by that shared history that it is reasonable to agree to rules of fair social cooperation, when the others are disposed to do likewise. It is only among such fellow members with shared history that it is reasonable for us to suppose that others are disposed to do likewise, for we know they are the same as us.

Dialectic of Reason and Reciprocity: Anticipated Reciprocity

If any two men desire the same thing, which nevertheless they cannot both enjoy, they become enemies; and in the way to their end (which is principally their own conservation, and sometimes their delectation only) endeavour to destroy or subdue one another. And from hence it comes to pass that where an invader hath no more to fear than another man's single power, if one plant, sow, build, or possess a convenient seat, others may probably be expected to come prepared with forces united to dispossess and deprive him, not only of the fruit of his labour, but also of his life or liberty. And the invader again is in the like danger of another.

And from this diffidence of one another, *there is no way for any man to secure himself so reasonable as anticipation;* that is, by force, or wiles, to master the persons of all men he can so long till he see no other power great enough to endanger him.[20]

According to Hobbes, violence does not exist from the beginning: what comes first are the desires of two individuals converging on the same object that "they cannot both enjoy." Neither my violence nor that of the Other is original. Each person's aggression is transformed and justified by the rational justification of the Other's aggression. This anticipated reciprocity leads each of us to take the initiative, and do to the Other what we fear the Other will do to us. The distrust, the suspicion that the Other will display the anticipated behavior leads me to resort to the violence that I fear. According to Hobbes, violent reciprocity is also a form of conditional reciprocity. We resort to violence because we anticipate that the Other is disposed to do likewise. The problem of conditional reciprocity is thus, in a sense, "solved." Each agent's conditional disposition toward violence is inevitably made real, and the reality of the violence makes impossible the uncertain future to which conditional solidarity was designed to show the way.

In the present case, this "solution" is not based on an external sign functioning as a convention, or on the discovery that the Other has internal dispositions that would remove the uncertainty concerning his or her future action. In fact, the uncertainty is not removed. On the contrary, it is what leads each agent to make the violence of the Other a reality, and the anticipated presence of the Other justifies and provides grounds for the action by which the agent in question makes the Other's disposition toward violence real. It is a vicious cycle. The uncertainty is transformed into certainty of the worst. This time, as with exchange, we are dealing with a real relationship between agents: violence. It is a real relationship the goal of which is precisely to bring to a close the indefinite future opened by conditional reciprocity. However, that opening can be maintained only through the action of a superior force that, anticipating each individual's anticipation, is able to prohibit it and at the same time assure agents that the Others share the same values, the same rational disposition to conditional solidarity. This is why agents' rational anticipations cannot result in the conditional reciprocity of fairness except in the shadow of the monopoly of legitimate violence. Only the exclusions that make this monopoly possible can turn reasonableness into the "Other of violence."

Social Justice and Territory

Social justice as we know it, fairness understood as conditional reciprocity, has no place except in modern societies, for it supposes, within the space where it is deemed to be exercised, the disappearance of groups structured by ties of solidarity and hostility. Abandoning these ties of solidarity makes social justice necessary; abolishing duties of violence makes it possible. Social justice supposes a holder of the monopoly of legitimate violence and the territorial order that it imposes. It supposes agents who are not bound into groups by reciprocal obligations of solidarity. Conditional solidarity has no sense except in a world where solidarity *obligations* have ceased to be binding and have given way to the indifference that abandons each to his or her fate.

Today we are witnessing the dismantling of the territorial order on which social justice rests. The universalism of freedom, equality, and fraternity, as well as that of communism ("Workers of the world unite!"), seemed to challenge the territorial order because they transgressed the borders that structured it. In fact, both movements led to reestablishing it, to instituting, for different peoples or for the working class, specific territories that were exclusive of one another. The new foundations of territory were based on something "above" nations and the "friends-foes" relationship that both united and separated them. They required that there be a circle of hostility beyond the circle of simple adversarial relations. Each time after the territorial order was shaken, its reestablishment required a "space" where there was a relationship of enmity less constraining than that between opposing nations. This "space" was that of colonies or protectorates, or the "free space" of "non-nations," or the absolute confrontation between the Free World and the Communist bloc. The new establishment of the territorial order always required the institution of an area of conflict that reiterated the "friends-foes" relationship between nations. Globalization and the fall of the communist regimes indicate the (final?) disappearance of this external space. This is why they led to the dismantling of the territorial order and the emergence of a new enemy within, the terrorist, who is proof of the failure to institutionalize outside of the territory shared by "friends" the most extreme forms of the relationship of hostility.

Fragmentation of the "Friends-Foes" Dichotomy

The fall of the Berlin Wall and the Soviet Union signaled the disappearance of the space of hostility inherited from World War II. The paradigmatic opposition between the East and the West yielded to fragmentation of the relationship of hostility, the relationship of extreme enmity. The fragmentation has shown itself not only in the proliferation of weapons of mass destruction, but above all in the fact that the various conflicts, whether within or between states, now escape a form of supreme animosity that would situate and overdetermine them. The disorder characteristic of contemporary relations of hostility is revealed by the rise of special claims, multiculturalism, the return of religions as political players, and the fact that in many places it is becoming increasingly difficult to tell political groups apart from bands of criminals. It is not that this plurality and disorder are in themselves new, but we have lost the rule that made it possible to establish order in this jumble of confrontations and used to impose a shared vocabulary on the actors.

This fragmentation of the relationship of hostility is inseparable from what we call globalization. In a sense, it is its political dimension. However, an obvious but generally unnoticed essential characteristic of globalization is the absence of a space outside it. There is nowhere that is beyond it; no place escapes its laws and rules. By definition, globalization has no borders, no limits that say where it ends. It folds in upon itself like the surface of the Earth, of which it adopts the form and entirely encloses.

Until today, the outside has been the place where "Others" live, those who are not "us." In truth, it did not matter who they are, so long as they are not "us." The outside refers, first, to a separation in physical space such as used to be established by the territorial order. It exists in opposition to the interior, where those who are not "us" do not live, except by accident, with our permission and only for a limited time. This is the first thing that globalization has changed: "Others" are now among us. Globalization has put an end to the concurrence of political, social, and cultural divisions, on one hand, and distance in physical space, on the other hand. It is no longer true that those who are not "us" live elsewhere. We now share the same globalized space, into which we are all more or less integrated. In fact, it would be inaccurate to believe that in the past major social, cultural, and political differences always mapped onto differences in location. What has become impossible within globalization is to defuse, through an appeal to fundamental homogeneity, the differences that there are between us.

The problem is not so much the simple presence of "Others" among us, economic migrants, foreign workers, political refugees. The "globalized" world is certainly cosmopolitan, but that is not entirely new. What has disappeared is the capacity to unite those differences and others, such as sexual orientation, gender, ethnic, or linguistic origin and religion, in an overriding identity located in physical space. The concomitance of "relevant" political, social, and cultural differences with spatial remoteness is inseparable from the notion of territory, the existence of a plurality of exclusive territories and something beyond their interactions. Thus, as Bertrand Badie has seen clearly,[21] globalization corresponds to the end of territories, or, more accurately, the end *of territory* as a form of political and social organization, at both the national and international levels.

Of Territory

First, we could think that the territory of a state is limited to the physical (geographical) space over which it exercises its authority. All political organizations exist in physical space. It therefore seems that territories must have existed as long as such organizations, if not longer.[22] However, what is at play in territory as it has been instituted by the modern state is a social and political relationship to physical space that has existed neither eternally nor everywhere. While it may be true that political organizations are necessarily deployed in physical space, it does not follow that they must have a specific or special relationship with any given part of that space. Thus, a club, corporation, guild, or any system of alliances that comes into play anywhere a number of its members meet, a freemasonry or a terrorist network, for example, does not come into any special political relationship with any given part of physical space. This is equally true for political organizations that are based on ties of family or ethnic solidarity. The ties function as a principle for bringing "friends" together against "foes," independent of any territory. This is what makes it possible for these groups to adapt to radical social and economic changes and to remain political groups that have to be taken into account. Thus, in many countries formed through colonization, ethnic and clan solidarity remains a formidable force that the government cannot ignore except at its peril, despite the shift of a large portion of the population from the countryside to the city and their transformation from peasants into public servants, merchants, salaried employees, or laborers. Such political entities are not bound to any specific territory in physical space. Their functioning is independent of the location. Their reality as political formations comes from relationships between their members rather than the place where they are found.

In contrast, the territory of a modern state is a piece of physical space with which that state has a special political relationship. This political relationship transforms a given geographical area into a space characterized by certain features that are shared by all territories. First, except for a few rare exceptions that have generally proved unstable,[23] the territories of modern states are contiguous in the sense that every part of the territory touches some other part of the territory. Nothing separates one part of the territory of a state from some other part of its territory. All of the parts or divisions touch, and going from one to the next does not involve any qualitative difference with respect to the territory. Second, the territories of different states are exclusive, while a given place may be sacred for more than one religion. For example, Jerusalem is a sacred place for Islam and Judaism, but the city of Jerusalem cannot be part of both Israel and the kingdom of Jordan. Territories are mutually exclusive. They are external to one another, like parts of Euclidian space. Third, territory is isotropic in that no part of it is more "territory" than any other. Alsace and Lorraine are just as much parts of French territory as are Paris and Touraine. There may be major economic, cultural, linguistic, and ethnic differences between the various regions of a country, but nonetheless each is just as much a part of the national territory as any other one.

These characteristic features of territory reflect the political relationships typical of modern states. The monopoly of legitimate violence can be seen as a form of continuity of political power. It means that political power is exercised without any ruptures or gaps, with no stops or starts. The power of modern states is not only supreme, in the sense that there is no power that can stand up to it within the society: it is also sovereign. In other words, all local or subordinate power exists only through the authority of the state that institutes it. The formal equality of all citizens is the political equivalent of territorial isotropy. Just like parts of territory, citizens all have equal and the same value. We often consider that formal equality among citizens is insufficient, and this is certainly true. However, this criticism should not be interpreted, as it sometimes is, as implying a rejection of formal equality. On the contrary, it is based on what is promised and implied by formal equality.

Parts of mathematical space can be *really* identical to one another. The same is not true of human beings (or parts of geographical space). In both cases, the equality (or isotrophy) can only be formal (or metaphorical). Social actors are different in many distinct dimensions. Formal equality is a political decision to not take into account, in *certain* situations and in *certain* areas, *certain* differences among individuals. The criticism of formal equality can be conceived of as flowing from disagreements about specific purposes for which we shall not take into account major differences between agents or areas in which equality should be granted. Thus, with respect to the right to vote and the right to be elected, we do not take into account differences in income, education, gender, or sexual orientation, but we do take into consideration age and whether or not the individual is in jail. The form of equality within a given society is always the outcome of political debate. Which differences among agents will not be taken into account, for what purposes and in what areas: this depends both on power relationships within the state and on political history. The modern state is the institution thanks to which the "fiction" of equality has become real to a certain degree, but only within given borders and only for those who have a certain special relationship of "belonging" to the territory.

Membership: Territory and Culture

Membership is above all expressed through a legal relationship: citizenship. It is a political relationship defined in relation to space: place of birth. This relationship also has a cultural dimension that can come into contradiction

with the spatial definition of citizenship, and that can sometimes take precedence over it. Those who share the same culture are seen as "belonging" to
the same territory, and citizenship is more easily granted to "strangers" who
share the same language or religion, or come from the same ethnic group as
the majority of citizens. However, historically, those who live in the same
territory have been "led" to share the same culture. As Heather Rae[24] shows,
this has sometimes been accomplished by expelling or destroying minority
peoples. Most often, this cultural homogenization is the result of assimilation policies, public education, and repression of local dialects and minority
languages. However, in all cases, the people who live in what has become the
territory of a modern state, for example, France, have been *made* "homogenous" by explicit policies. The relationship to the territory precedes the
cultural belonging of which it is the condition.

Citizens are homogenous only with respect to certain dimensions,
for example, religion, ethnic group, language, or culture. The dimensions
are those that have been "chosen" to make the population homogenous. A
nation's culture is the result of these choices. Homogeneity, like equality, is
a "fiction" since the population is necessarily heterogeneous with respect to
many other dimensions, such as property and occupation. Homogeneity and
shared culture, like formal equality, overlook many major differences among
individuals, such as income and education. Those differences are considered
as not having any impact in relation to "what counts": being French, American, or Japanese.

A territory is the area where a state exercises its exclusive jurisdiction,
but it is in fact an international institution, the institutionalization of the
"friends-foes" dichotomy. This is why there cannot be one single territory,
but only many different mutually exclusive territories: an international
community. Territories determine a certain type of relationship among
states, which are founded on borders delimiting exclusive portions of political space. States claim exclusive jurisdiction over their territory, as if it were
something that flowed essentially from their own power and sovereignty.
However, the borders are real and have meaning only insofar as they are
recognized by other states. The central feature of the territorial order is that
it involves the existence of a number of states that are formally equal, in the
sense that each recognizes the exclusive sovereignty of every other over a portion of space. The territory of each state, the state's monopoly of legitimate

violence within its territory, exists only and insofar as it is recognized and accepted by other states. Outside of the territory of a state, there are other territories, the territories of other states, which have the same status and the same characteristics.

This plurality of territories is fundamental to the modern political order. Marches at the periphery of an empire, beyond which barbarian tribes roam, delimit the empire as a sanctuary in a hostile, and largely unknown, world. Borders, in contrast, separate states that are formally equal and form a community of political entities that exclude one another.

This community of territories is a special way of institutionalizing the "friends-foes" relationship, of which the central feature is that it makes this relationship coincide with the distinction between the inside and the outside of the territory. It is not that those who live outside the territory are now or are always "foes," but that those who live inside are "friends." Between them, resorting to violence is illegitimate. Conflicts arising between them have to be resolved by appealing to a third party, with whose decision they agree to comply. Achieving this "friendship" among all citizens is the goal of social justice. The division between political friendship and enmity is inseparable from citizens' equality and homogeneity. Formal equality and a degree of cultural homogeneity are *normal* characteristics of states constituted by the monopoly of legitimate violence within a given territory.

The "War on Terror"

To say that there are "enemies" among us means that, in the space pacified by the state monopoly of legitimate violence, there are groups that consider themselves as authorized to use violence against others whom they consider their "foes." We now call the enemies among us "terrorists." The "War on Terror" undertaken by Western states is a sign of the end of the territorial order. It is not simply a response to a challenge to their monopoly of legitimate violence. In fact, it is part of the dismantling of this monopoly and the emergence of new ways of managing hostility and solidarity, which can be seen above all in the disappearance of wars in the form that we have learned to know them, in other words, either as armed conflicts between sovereign states or as civil wars: confrontations in which factions fight one another to seize the monopoly of legitimate violence. In both of these forms, war is an event of limited duration, with a clearly marked beginning and end. There are winners and losers, and once the war is over, peace returns. However, there are many indications that armed conflicts of this type are disappearing and being replaced by what Frédéric Gros has called "states of violence."[25]

In *Neverending Wars*, Ann Hironaka shows that since 1944 the number of civil wars around the world has grown dramatically. What has increased even more is the number of conflicts occurring simultaneously, a sign that hostilities are lasting longer.[26] However, the sometimes extremely long conflicts are no longer exactly "civil wars," for the combatants are not aiming simply to seize or keep state power. The struggle continues, even once that goal has been attained. This means that in these conflicts no one manages to establish the monopoly of legitimate violence. In truth, very often that is no longer what is in question.

Let us take the example of Afghanistan. The "civil war" began in 1978. The following year, the country was invaded by the USSR. Soviet occupation lasted ten years, during which the fighting never stopped, and it continued after the Russian troops left. Then, even after Kabul was taken by the Taliban, the latter had gained power over virtually all Afghan territory and the international community had recognized the regime, the struggle continued and was still raging in some areas in 2001. The country was then invaded again, this time by the Americans, who hoped to capture bin Laden and destroy al-Qaeda. Today, Germany, France, Canada, England, Italy, Poland, and the United States have soldiers in Afghanistan. NATO has just asked its member states for a long-term commitment because the conflict is far from over and there has been resurgence in attacks by the Taliban and their allies.

Over thirty years have gone by since 1978: enough time to live a whole life: to be born, grow up, get married, have children and die . . . in combat. An entire life "at war." Such a never-ending conflict is not a war but a "state of violence." The violence in such a situation is not a means to a specific end, a means that will be abandoned once the end is achieved. The violence no longer corresponds to a crisis point and time of decision. It is a permanent reality.

Today, there are many areas that seem to have fallen into such "states of violence," for example, Palestine, Iraq, Afghanistan, Somalia, Pakistan, Congo, and Colombia, to name only a few places where violence seems to have been transformed in to a *way of being*. These states of violence are not civil wars or clashes between sovereign nations, but violence transformed into a way of life, not only for certain groups or certain individuals, for example, mercenaries, criminal associations and illegal armed bands, but for whole areas and populations. In fact, these states of violence very often do not concern the whole state or country that they affect, but are limited to certain specific areas, confined to only part of the state's territory. In the surrounding areas, outside of those regions, life continues, more or less "as usual."

These enclaves of violence can also play a major economic role or have great strategic value.[27] Moreover, in general, a number of different types of players participate in the relationship of hostility: government troops (and more or less official paramilitary units), rebel combatants, private security firms, local warlords, tribal forces, troops from neighboring countries and members of international peacekeeping forces. This incomplete list of typical players involved in conflicts reveals two important features of states of violence.

The first is their internationalization. It is very rare that the participants in a conflict are limited to the citizens of only one state. Most of the time, foreign elements and outside influences play important roles in the evolution of the conflict and are the main reasons it lasts.[28] The second is the presence of nonstate players, such as rebel troops of course, but also private security firms and the major corporations that employ them, as well as organized crime.[29] In fact, it is often difficult to distinguish between a political conflict and large-scale criminal activities in that insurgents often develop criminal activities in order to fund their fighting. Consequently, victory sometimes ceases to be the goal. The struggle turns into an economic undertaking of a specific type. The violence becomes a means of monopolizing drug production or trafficking, trade in diamonds or any other form of contraband. Little by little, the conflict is integrated into the world economy. So long as the violence remains confined to certain areas and the hostilities do not overflow too much, continuation of the conflict can also serve the interests of groups other than those of insurgents transformed into entrepreneurs. For example, it may make it possible for some, such as the army, to keep control over state power.

States of violence are *holes* in the fabric of international relations and the territories of various nations. They are holes that can be incorporated perfectly into the world economy.[30] In consequence, these conflicts are neither accidents nor anomalies. They are instead aspects of the new face of the international order. The expression "War on Terror" indicates that the major powers have largely accepted this transformation of the international scene.

Territories and Sanctuaries

Declaring war on terror is not an official act, an international legal action. This "declaration" does not create any special legal responsibilities or obligations. The U.S. government does not recognize terrorists as enemy combatants, and does not give them the protection of the Geneva Convention. It refuses to be bound by the rules of international law in its interactions with terrorists, and insofar as possible excludes them from American law. In various countries, whether they are friendly or hostile (and with or without the agreement of local authorities), it kidnaps individuals suspected of terrorism or of having ties to terrorists, and takes them to other countries where torture is practiced. In other words, it exploits to its advantage the different rules and practices elsewhere, a little as do multinationals when they take advantage of opportunities offered by different labor or environmental protection laws. It violates the airspace of independent states to attack terrorist installations (or structures that it believes are such) wherever they may be found. In short, the War on Terror does not recognize the validity of the borders between states. It belongs to a "friends-foes" dichotomy that is different and more extreme.

It would be naive to think that only the American government adopts such practices or that electing a new president of the United States would suffice to put an end to them. France in Africa, England in Afghanistan, Israel in Arab countries, Russia in bordering ex-USSR republics, Rwanda in the Democratic Republic of the Congo: all countries that are able to intervene outside of their borders, and have reasons to do so, employ more or less the same practices.

The War on Terror does not recognize the structure of the international community made of independent states separated by clear borders. The space within which this "war" unfolds is not that of territories. It is not composed of parts that are external to one another. It is neither homogenous nor isotropic. This space is divided between "hot spots," which are marked by violence and conflicts, and other "cooler" spots, where peace and order more or less reign. The primary goal of those who conduct the "War on Terror" is not to reestablish peace in the "hot spots," but to establish *sanctuaries*, protected spaces that are sheltered from violence.

The new organization of international space into protected sanctuaries and an outside world abandoned to disorder has a fractal aspect. The space in which we live has the same structure at a number of different scales and levels. For example, at the smallest scale, or at a higher degree of resolution, there is the Green Zone in Baghdad, where relative security reigns in comparison with the rest of the city. There, attacks, kidnappings and arbitrary arrests are much rarer. A few Western journalists can even be found there. On a much larger scale, there is "Fortress America," protected by biometric identification technology, by strict immigration rules and conditions for admittance that are becoming more stringent, as well as by an enormous quantity of personal information about citizens of other countries who enter the United States or simply fly over its territory.[31] It reproduces the same separation between a protected space and an external world more or less abandoned to disorder. At an intermediate level between these two extremes, we find, for example, the wall that Israel is building to protect its territory from suicide attacks, and the kilometers of metal fences that separate the United States from Mexico in the hope of preventing the entrance of illegal immigrants from Latin America. At a smaller scale, we find the housing complexes surrounded by walls, sometimes even barbed wire, and protected by private guards in cities where law and order is supposed to reign. Likewise, there are entire neighborhoods that people cannot enter unless they are residents or can explain what brings them there.

We no longer have the territorial order, a continuous isotropic space of which each part is external to each other. Moreover, a sanctuary can contain other, safer, or more closed sanctuaries. The limits of these zones of peace and relative security are not marked by borders, imaginary lines that exist insofar as they are recognized by the community of nations. The extent of these secure spaces is not determined by international agreements, but by the relation of power between adversaries. In fact, the protection, fortified walls, innumerable identity checks, and biometric security measures are there precisely because borders have ceased playing a role. "Foes" cannot be recognized on the basis of their passport alone. Borders and visas are no longer adequate tools for keeping them outside the space we share.

Territory's disappearance goes hand in hand with disappearance of equality and the rule of law, features of the territorial order. The "others," the "foes," are different from "us," and they are not always reasonable. There is thus no reason for us to give them the protection of law, which they are ready to break. In part, this is not entirely new. Strangers, potential "foes," have always been subject to different regulations. However, the territorial order gave this different treatment an obvious reason, just as it provided a simple, public procedure for determining who was subject to the special rules. It was in consequence possible to maintain a degree of equality among us, "friends," and up to a certain point between "us" and "them" because we knew who "we" were and who "they" were. Now that "enemies" are among us, hidden everywhere and anywhere, they can be anyone. Consequently, on the basis of a simple suspicion, we can suspend the rule of law for certain people who, until they were pointed out, were exactly like everyone else, and had no obvious characteristic distinguishing "them" from "us."

"Foes," contrary to those who commit criminal acts, are not apprehended after the fact, and they are not presumed innocent. They have to be arrested before they can act. Disappearance of the territorial order means that there is no longer any simple, public procedure to tell the difference between "friends" and "foes." We are already getting used to not everyone being treated equally on the basis of suspicions that are sometimes justified and sometimes unfounded.

It is important to remember that the reign of suspicion is the contrary of the rule of law. According to law, you can be punished only for a crime that you have already committed, the broken law must be public, and the punishment has to be in proportion to the crime. However, "foes," whose bad intentions we suspect, are not properly speaking convicted for crimes they have committed. They are rendered inoffensive, incapable of doing harm, before they are able to act. The objective is not justice, which seeks to maintain a degree of proportion between the crime and the punishment, but efficiency, at the cost of a few "unfortunate mistakes," as can be seen from the tragic death of Jean-Charles de Menezes.[32] Suspicion is to law what a preemptive attack (such as on Pearl Harbor) is to a declaration of war.

The "War on Terror" cannot have any obvious end. No official act can restore the preceding order and proclaim that the war is over, that we can now live in peace. Depending on the point in time, the danger can be considered more or less great, and terrorist attacks may become less frequent. We can be more successful in ensuring the sanctuary is safe. However, the "War on Terror" is not a "war" that can be won, properly speaking. This "war" is a state of violence inseparable from the existence of other states of violence in the world. It is an expression of the new way that conflicts are institutionalized in the "globalized" world where we live.

The end of territories has not led to the end of violence, much to the contrary—it has augmented and distributed it in a new way. The global world is a world of global violence, as René Girard said in *Battling to the End*. It is a world of violence without borders, and it is also a world where political violence fails to protect us and becomes itself the greatest form of violence. Today's crumbling of politics as a moral authority able to state the difference between good and bad violence results from the same transformation that made politics possible: the abandonment of reciprocal ties of solidarity facilitated by Christian Revelation.

Epilogue

This right to present themselves to society belongs to all mankind in virtue of our common right of possession on the surface of the earth on which, as it is a globe, we cannot be infinitely scattered, and must in the end reconcile ourselves to existence side by side: at the same time, originally no one individual had more right than another to live in any one particular spot.

—Immanuel Kant, *Perpetual Peace*

Political violence is a form of violence that legitimizes itself, a form of violence that becomes legitimate through the simple fact that it occurs. Such violence divides: it designates "foes," acceptable victims, but it also brings people together. It brings together all those who consider legitimate the violence exercised against the "foes" in question and identify with it. This is why political violence is always a way of forming groups by dividing the community between those who are "friends," namely, people, good citizens, and those who are "foes": traitors, terrorists, or members of some minority. In order for the transfer of violence to be successful, so that it can last and give rise to a stable institution, "foes" have to be eliminated from the group, expelled to the outside, where they remain available as "foes" and potential victims. Opposition to the "foe" also has to give rise to solidarity, and establish helpful, supportive relationships among "friends." Indeed, solidarity and hostility are two faces of the same reality. Each is a condition for the other. While the failure to transfer violence makes solidarity impossible, absence of solidarity in return undermines the transfer of violence and brings conflict back inside the community.

The modern state, holder of the monopoly of legitimate violence, results from a successful transfer, from a "unanimous" shift of every individual's violence onto "foes," for it manages to impose only its violence as legitimate. This monopoly is by definition limited in space. It supposes an outside inhabited by "others" who are "foes." The success of the transfer entails that the state's violence, because it alone is legitimate, ceases to be violence, whether it is exercised inside or outside. In the former case, it becomes the coercive power of law, in the latter, legitimate defense.

The eruption of political violence within the space pacified by the monopoly of legitimate violence is always a challenge to the monopoly of legitimacy. The return of political violence is the sign of a breakdown in the mechanism that engenders the state. It reveals the state's failure to provide substitute victims. The violence of a state against its citizens is the expression of attempts to re-create its monopoly. The state then designates an internal group as responsible for the violence, and turns that group into a set of sacrificable victims so that it can try to legitimize itself by the violence it exercises against them. The growth in the number of victims is a sign of the failure of these attempts at reestablishing its foundation, an even more definitive failure of the mechanism for transferring violence. It demonstrates the inability to transform each individual's violence into legitimate violence. The genocides perpetrated by governments against their own nationals is the ultimate form of this incapacity.[1]

This failure of the political transfer of violence toward substitute victims comes, paradoxically, from what makes the state possible, namely, the abandonment of reciprocal obligations of solidarity and the rejection of duties to engage in violence. The modern state has been able to acquire the monopoly of legitimate violence because solidarity groups have fragmented into individuals as traditional obligations have lost their power. Actors gradually ceased considering as legitimate the violence that obligations imposed on them, and became disposed to identify with the state's superior power.

However, this was only a negative condition for establishing a monopoly of legitimate violence: that solidarity groups no longer constitute obstacles to its formation. In order to hold the monopoly of legitimate violence, one need only hold the monopoly of violence, but in order to hold onto that monopoly, one must still succeed in imposing one's violence as a substitute for the violence of all. It is not sufficient to remove the obstacles that would normally prevent the formation of unanimity against the same "foes": one has to succeed in pointing out those "Others" to each, and leading the violence of all to converge on them.

It follows that the success of the political transfer of violence onto substitute victims supposes a limit on the fragmentation of members of society. This transfer requires that certain ties of solidarity remain among them. Initially, in the absolutist state, traditional solidarity was weakened but had not entirely disappeared, and the state received, so to speak, the homage with which the great are honored. Each individual's loyalty to the state passed through each individual's loyalty to his or her immediate superiors. So long as the two legitimacies reinforced each other, so long as they did not pull in different directions, the monopoly of violence was stable. The French Revolution put an end to the interlocking relationships that had integrated the various levels in the social hierarchy. It placed the state face to face with isolated individuals. Recourse to political propaganda in the broad sense then became necessary as a means of reaching actors individually, outside of the social relationships in which they were involved. Political propaganda is a tool that makes it possible to reach each citizen without going through the network of his or her social interactions and, if necessary, to get him or her to oppose the solidarity that structures those interactions. Means of communication, such as newspapers, and organs of opinion such as salons, clubs, and various associations, allow individuals to become *publics*[2] that share similar interests. Media and associations, as well as public meetings, parades in uniform, social movements, and political parties, can become means of transforming these *publics*, in other words, these statistical groups, into organized groups. To put it in the now antiquated language of Marxist philosophy, they are means of transforming the *class in itself* into a *class for itself*. These various communications practices are ways to create solidarity ties between people who are not bound by any reciprocal obligations, and to make it possible for them to engage in common action, political action.

However, although it may be necessary, propaganda is not sufficient to produce the political shift in violence. The transfer of each individual's violence onto victims outside the community requires real violence able to ensnare and disorient hatred and resentment.

These two initial conditions for political violence, namely, first, the fragmentation of members of society through the abandonment of traditional obligations followed by their aggregation into statistical groups, and, second, the necessity of real violence, entail that, contrary to what occurs at the time of the resolution of the sacrificial crisis as described by René Girard, we are never dealing with a unique victim. Isolated, alone, defenseless and rejected by all perhaps, the victim nonetheless still belongs to a group. He or she falls into a general category: Jews, bourgeois, Shiites, women, homosexuals, "Prussians," agents of imperialism, and so on. It is impossible to make a single victim the point of convergence of the violence of members of a statistical group or *public* that is, by definition, an imagined community that, to speak like Kant, cannot be the object of possible experience. For the shift in violence to be able to take place everywhere members of the imagined community are found, it suffices that there be numerous potential victims who, while necessarily different from one another, are nonetheless "the same victim": members of a group.

The growth in the number of victims of political violence occurs when the transfer mechanism is derailed. Two forces contribute to this malfunction. Both result more or less directly from exacerbation of the process of fragmentation of members of society and their aggregation into different *publics* owing to the ever more complete abandonment of reciprocal obligations. The first is exploitation of political violence by individual agents. By hijacking political violence for private ends in order to resolve personal disputes, agents prevent the shift of violence onto substitute victims and confine its exercise to precisely where it should be most distant: the heart of the community. This individual exploitation of political violence shows the violence's failure to establish a group of "friends" united in their opposition to common "foes." It bears witness to the violence's inability to transcend the isolation of individuals. The second force contributing to the malfunction is the temptation, owing to the difficulty in overcoming the agents' separation, to have recourse to greater violence in order to more clearly mark the difference between "them" and "us." Here also the shift in violence fails because the growth in the number of substitute victims does not attract onto them the violence of those who do not participate in it. The sacrificial mechanism is, properly speaking, an economical form of violence. All exercise their violence against "the same victim." Its social efficiency is proportional to this thrift, to the "savings," to the reduction in the number of victims. In contrast, the greater the number of victims, the less efficient the mechanism is and the less the transfer occurs.

We then witness the total failure of the sacrificial mechanism and its modern substitute: political violence. There are indeed still shifts in violence and substitute victims, but the convergence of all against the victims no longer occurs. On one hand, individual exploitation of collective violence tends to reduce the average distance of the shift of violence: we no longer sacrifice "others," but assassinate "the same." On the other hand, the shift of violence onto an innocent victim no longer quenches the resentment of many simultaneously. The abandonment of reciprocal obligations of solidarity creates indifference, disinterest in the fate of those whose death does not concern us. It is the indifference of those who continued to do business while under their eyes others were giving patriotic speeches as Alain de Monéys burned. The fairgoers of Hautefaye were indifferent to the fate of someone who was for them only an unknown, but they were just as indifferent to whether or not the victim was a "Prussian." Like Sartre, they did not assign much importance to whether the member of the group whose lynching they were witnessing was simply "thought to be a traitor" or "really a traitor."

Rather than political violence, in other words, violence that is legitimized by the simple fact that it occurs, violence appears in such situations *because it is legitimate*, authorized, encouraged, recommended, or even simply accepted and tolerated by the authorities. Such violence does not require murderers to hate their victims. Imitation is enough. The fact of knowing that killing Jews or Tutsis can be done with impunity, and that it may even be profitable in the form of a cow to roast or alcohol to be distributed once the "work" is done, is enough to lead people to kill neighbors for whom they feel no hatred. Mimesis is the imperceptible transformation of the social and moral worth of a form of behavior by the simple fact that others are doing it and it has become acceptable.

Political violence is a means of dealing with this indifference and protecting us from the unlimited violence that it makes possible.[3] It is an attempt to create ties of solidarity among agents who are not bound by any reciprocal obligations and to redirect them away from their single-minded concern with their "self-interest." The modern state protects us against our own violence by directing it onto "others" who are external to the area where it exercises its authority. The "others" are all the more sacrificable when they are far away. *Territory* establishes physical distance and cultural strangeness as measures of remoteness that authorize recourse to greater violence, and it makes these two measures coincide. Its stability implies a dual relationship of enmity (adversariality and hostility) in which growing distance makes greater violence permissible. Interactions between territorialized nation-states give rise to measured conflicts, to wars regulated by shared law. Outside of that circle there is the area of "non-nations," political entities of a different type that are more distant both in space and culture. The conflicts that occur there are not so limited in the use of violence, and the wars that take place there are of a different type.[4] The racism that was omnipresent in the West in the nineteenth century and most of the twentieth century was the cultural expression of this threefold division of international space.

The enemy within violates this spatial organization of hostility. Such enemies bring the most intense violence back as close as possible to the community. The enemy within tears apart the area unified by the monopoly of legitimate violence, and inverts the relationship between violence and externality. However, until recently, the violence of the enemy within did not entirely escape the territorial system. For example, while it may have drawn the line separating "friends" from "foes" differently, for example, between social classes, the *public* that this violence sought to form into a new group of "friends" shared the same physical and social space as those whom the violence struck. The notables and police officers whom the Red Brigades and Prima Linea murdered were neighbors and fellow citizens, "friends" in the territorial order, of the workers, students, and proletarians whom they wanted to incite to revolt. The violence aimed to reestablish a different territory rather than reject territory as a form of organization of political space. Finally, the struggle against the enemy within, in the form of the *traitor*, always seeks to give the clash a territorial dimension and make it "normal" in a sense. Not only is a traitor an agent from outside, but that outside is a territory, another state to which the traitor has sworn allegiance.

The image of the Islamic terrorist that haunts the West today is very

different. He or she is not a traitor, but a stranger among us. His or her allegiance is not to another state or nation, not to Saudi Arabia, Pakistan, or
Afghanistan, but to a nonterritorialized ideal: Islam or the community of
believers. More than place of birth or nationality, this is what makes him or
her "foreign." Al-Qaeda, the organization considered responsible for terrorist attacks, does not correspond to a specific territory. It has at least as many
enemy states (and certainly many more terrorist activities) in the Muslim
world as in the West. This is why, despite the clumsy attempts of Western
political propaganda, al-Qaeda cannot be associated with any location in
particular in the space of international relations. Al-Qaeda is a network of
exchanges, communication, and power that links agents beyond and despite
states, and creates ties of solidarity between them independent of any territorial anchoring.

The Islamic terrorist appears to us both as the most foreign, because
capable of the most extreme violence, and as the most similar, because he or
she is invisible, the same as everyone else: an unknown among others until
the fatal detonation. This invisibility distresses us. We would like to send the
"foe" back to an identifiable elsewhere, give him or her visible foreignness, as
can be seen from the obsession with veils and scarves that, commencing in
France, is spreading everywhere in Europe. Terrorists' duplicity transgresses
the territorial order. The same goes for the war we conduct against them.
We violate the borders of countries with which we have friendly relations to
bomb places that are supposed to shelter terrorists and schools where they
are indoctrinated. This war disregards the nationality of agents and assas-
sinates nationals of countries with which we are not in conflict. Moreover,
in many countries such as Canada and the United Kingdom, the War on
Terror authorizes the discretionary, indeterminate imprisonment of citizens
and foreigners on the basis of suspicions of which the intelligence services are
the only judges. It in no way takes into account equal rights or presumption
of innocence.

Because it territorializes the "friends-foes" opposition, the modern state,
the nation-state tends toward equality among citizens. This equality is the
normal form of solidarity in states built on the abandonment of reciprocal
solidarity obligations. It is like an attractor toward which they are "naturally"
drawn. In contrast, the abandonment of territory as a structure underlying
conflict management reduces the pressure toward equality. Contrary to what

one might think, this renunciation of territory is not dictated by the enemy who has to be fought—Islamic terrorism—but by the internal evolution of modern states. The reason the confrontation between groups is now taking on a new form is the new structure of states, which remain fundamental political players.

Modern states have become networks. They are networks of services that extend beyond their borders. Within national borders, they often provide access to their services to residents who are not citizens and even to foreigners who are passing through. They are above all resource distribution and production networks grafted onto other shipping, communications, commercial, and financial networks. It is not only that states have interests everywhere in the world: it is that states no longer depend on their territory in the same way as before. Territory is no longer the fundamental reservoir of labor, raw materials, soldiers, know-how, basic industrial production, capital, or even financial resources.[5] Thus, the United States does not produce enough graduates to meet its needs in most scientific areas. The needs are met by importing foreign brains. Likewise, some rich countries, for example, the United Kingdom, "purchase" from poor countries entire graduating years of nurses and laboratory technicians.[6] The wealth and power of privileged states depends less and less on their national territory, and more and more on the strategic location they occupy in these networks of exchange and communication, as well as their ability to exploit them to their advantage.

The material basis of the most powerful modern states no longer corresponds to their national territory in two distinct manners. First, they have to seek beyond their territory to obtain their wealth and power, in terms of natural resources and economic markets, obviously, but also in terms of know-how, skills, workers, technology, and industrial capacity. Second, some parts of their territory are losing more and more of their economic and political interest. They are becoming dead weight that costs but does not pay. States need both more and less than their territory. Above all, they do not need territory. Certainly, they need some anchor points in physical space, which explains the growing importance of large cities, but it is no longer indispensable to them to exercise authority in a homogenous way everywhere in the country. While a territory is a plane or surface, a network is made of nodes and communication lines that link those nodes beyond the empty space separating them. States no longer have the same interest in defending their territory, or, if one prefers, they no longer have interest in protecting it in the same way. For them, it is no longer a question of protecting an area and ensuring their authority over each of its points, but of defending the integrity of a network. For that, it suffices to control certain points in particular and the communications between them. All the rest can be abandoned if it does not disturb the functioning of the network.

The passage from the territorial system to that of the sanctuary illustrates this transformation of our political space. Moreover, the flows and networks that are indispensable to the wealth of countries such as Canada and the United States are also those that create the wealth of France and Japan. A network space, unlike that of a territory, is not exclusive. Of course, it may be advantageous to prohibit some from having access to a network, but by definition the purpose of all networks is to include and bring into communication. It follows that many countries have interest in protecting and developing the networks on which they depend and with which, to a certain extent, they identify. Increasingly strict controls at borders, more stringent requirements concerning residency, and deportation of foreigners in irregular situations suggest an attempt to reterritorialize the face of the enemy, to assimilate terrorists with foreigners from the outside. However, this attempt is doomed to fail because there is no longer an outside.

We have to consider that Islamic terrorism is telling the truth when it portrays itself in the framework of an opposition between the Christian world and Islam. This is how it understands itself, and this is how we have to understand it. Of course, the call to throw the "crusaders" out of the lands of Islam appears to us to be simplistic and to be hiding more complex political stakes. Moreover, we are no longer quite sure that we are still "the Christian world." Yet what is at issue is very clear: the designation of an enemy par excellence against which the community of believers, divided by conflicts and split into different nations, can be marshaled. The violence directed against the Western world operates as a means of unifying the Muslim world by turning the violence that is tearing it apart toward the outside. We are that outside, just as we want it to be our outside. It follows that, on both sides, the public to which this violence is intended to give form does not share the same physical and social space as those on whom the violence is exercised. Certainly, the operation has not been very successful so far, despite all the efforts to encourage it and to portray us as the paradigmatic enemy of Islam.

With respect to Islamic terrorists, we occupy the place that we want them to occupy for us. We are doubles. This is why it is impossible to reterritorialize the conflict.

Things did not used to work like this. The Hereros of Namibia, who were exterminated by the German army's expeditionary force in 1904, never set off bombs in Berlin or Frankfurt. Between them and the German Empire, there was a fundamental asymmetry. Their territorial exteriority in relationship to those who had decreed their destruction was equivalent to their incapacity to become the Germans' doubles, to eliminate the difference that made them victims rather than enemies. This asymmetry and externality are today in the process of disappearing now that the war that the West takes to others suddenly continues in New York and in the subways of London and Madrid.

Indeed, there is no longer any exterior able to limit our confrontation, for the nonterritorial nature of the adversaries makes nuclear weapons inefficient. Transcendent violence, the threat of total destruction that protected us until the fall of the Soviet bloc, is now unable to limit or constrain the violence of our confrontations. The asymmetry or imbalance of power that used to separate countries with nuclear weapons from those who did not have them has been replaced by a new asymmetry of a different form. The asymmetry between the nuclear powers and the others was territorial in that the weapons of mass destruction were designed to guarantee that the security of certain lands and territory is the only appropriate target for nuclear weapons. An "appropriate target" is a target that the nuclear weapon can destroy completely and for which it is an absolute threat. Nuclear weapons can be used as supreme violence against such targets. Those who have such weapons are, in relation to those who do not, in positions of absolute exteriority, and they can exercise on the latter the violence of warlike hostility. This asymmetry, this radical imbalance of power between nations, gave to those who had nuclear weapons the advantage of intensifying the relationship of enmity and provided the threefold division of the space of hostility with a geographical, territorial embodiment.

In contrast, there is no sense in trying to destroy a terrorist network using nuclear weapons. Such a network can use such weapons, but it cannot be their target. This new asymmetry has no possible spatial translation. The modern political order is born of territorialization of the relationships of solidarity and hostility. Its two fundamental institutions have been the modern state, holder of the monopoly of legitimate violence, and European colonial expansion. The fact that it is now impossible to reterritorialize these relationships threatens us in ways we have never before experienced. It also opens the way to political developments that we are unable to imagine.

◆　◆　◆

The entire time that Alain de Monéys was being beaten and tortured to death by the enraged crowd, some of his friends stayed with him. They attended him throughout his suffering, interceded on his behalf, pleaded with his torturers, proclaimed his innocence, and denounced the terrible misunderstanding that doomed him. Unlike the priest, who tried with revolver in hand to put an end to the riot using violence that he believed greater, and who ended up lifting a glass with the murderers, the friends of the victim did not try to oppose violence with violence. They simply denounced the meaningless violence. We can regret the powerlessness of their protests, their incapacity to put an end to the violence, and their inability to protect the victim. However, we can also think that those friends played, perhaps unintentionally, a fundamental role in the transformation of the "patriotic act" into an atrocious crime. Their stubbornness in defending the victim and affirming his innocence against all hope, even when all was lost, neutralized the conspiracy of silence that very naturally becomes established between the murderers and "those who let them do it." Alain de Monéys's friends made it impossible to say to those who were absent, to others, to those who were not there, to those who would come later either that "nothing happened" or that "he was a Prussian spy." Their powerless presence deconstructed both lies: of violence and of indifference. We have to acknowledge and accept the strength of this weakness.

Notes

Introduction

1. Paradox: "para-doxa," what is exterior, contrary to doctrine.

2. Max Weber, "Politics as a Vocation," in *The Vocation Lectures*, ed. David Owen and Tracy B. Strong, trans. Rodney Livingstone (Cambridge, MA: Hackett, 2004), 32–94.

3. Claude Bruaire, *La Raison politique* (Paris: Fayard, 1974), 13 [our translation].

4. René Girard, *Violence and the Sacred*, trans. Patrick Gregory (Baltimore: Johns Hopkins University Press, 1977).

5. René Girard, *Things Hidden since the Foundation of the World*, trans. Stephen Bann and Michael Metteer (New York: Continuum, 2003), 51–57.

6. The theory of the modern state reveals the transfer of violence only imperfectly. It portrays the shift of violence as the renunciation by each of his or her own violence (right to protect himself or herself) rather than as the acceptance by all of sovereign violence. It portrays as abandonment of violence what is in reality (and necessarily according to the theory) agreement to the exercise of violence by the sovereign. The fact that the operation consists in shifting the violence of all to third-party victims is even less visible. Yet, since it is a shift of violence, rather than an abandonment, the operation necessarily implies that the violence is indeed exercised against someone.

7. Thomas Hobbes, *Leviathan*, ed. Edwin Curley (Indianapolis: Hackett Publishing Company, 1994), 75.

8. Alain Corbin, *The Village of Cannibals*, trans. Arthur Goldhammer (Cambridge, MA: Harvard University Press, 1992).

9. Hannah Arendt, *Eichmann in Jerusalem* (New York: Viking Press, 1963).

10. Nancy Scheper-Hughes, "The Genocidal Continuum: Peace-time Crimes," in *Power and the Self*, ed. Jeannette Marie Mageo (Cambridge: Cambridge University Press, 2002), 29–47; "Coming to Our Senses: Anthropology and Genocide," in *Annihilating Difference: The Anthropology of Genocide*, ed. Alexander Laban Hinton (Berkeley: University of California Press, 2002), 348–81.

11. This was justly pointed out by Seyla Benhabib, *The Rights of Others: Aliens, Residents and Citizens* (Cambridge: Cambridge University Press, 2004).

12. Carl Schmitt, *The Concept of the Political*, trans. George D. Schwab (Chicago: University of Chicago Press, 1996).

13. Schmitt, *Concept of the Political*, 36.

14. René Girard, *Battling to the End: Conversations with Benoît Chantre*, trans. Mary Baker (East Lansing: Michigan State University Press, 2010).

15. Carl Schmitt, *The Nomos of the Earth in the International Law of the Jus Publicum Europaeum*, trans. G. L. Ulmen (New York: Telos Press, 2006).

16. Jean-Paul Sartre, *Critique of Dialectical Reason*, trans. Alan Sheridan-Smith, vol. 1 (London: Verso, 2004).

17. Girard notes that in order to play his or her role properly, the sacrificial victim has to be at an optimal distance from the community, neither too close, nor too far. In *Violence and the Sacred*, Girard says that the victim has to be both inside and outside the community. If too close, the murder will set violence off again; if too far, the transfer of violence will be less effective and the victim will not play the role of substitute. This is why there are always preparation rituals for sacrificial victims that are designed to render the victim closer to or further from the community, depending on the case.

18. For example, Henri Atlan, "Founding Violence and Divine Referent," in *Violence and Truth: On the Work of René Girard*, ed. Paul Dumouchel (Stanford: Stanford University Press, 1988); and Christiane Frémont, "De la croyance et du savoir," in *Stanford French Review* 10 (1986): 197–201. By "cognitive interpretation," I mean, as I explain in greater detail in chapter 5, the apparent reduction of Revelation to a belief, namely, that the victim is innocent, which would make closure of the sacrificial mechanism impossible.

19. Benhabib, *Rights of Others*, 15.

20. Ernst Nolte, *Der europäische Bürgerkrieg 1917–1945: Nationalsozialismus und Bolschewismus* (Munich: Herbig, 2000).

21. Frédéric Gros, *States of Violence*, trans. Krysztof Fijalkowski and Michael Richardson (London: Seagull Books, 2010).

Chapter 1. Solidarity and Enmity

1. Jean Hatzfeld, *Machete Season*, trans. Linda Coverdale (New York: Farrar, Straus and Giroux, 2005), 214. [The English translation of Hatzfeld's book employs "a really bad helper" for "mauvais concurrent." We have preferred "no competition."]

2. Christopher Browning, *Ordinary Men: Reserve Police Battalion 101 and the Final Solution in Poland* (London: Penguin Books, 2001).

3. Harald Welzer, *Les Exécuteurs: Des hommes normaux aux meutriers de masse* (Paris: Gallimard, 2007).

4. Jan T. Gross, *Neighbors: The Destruction of the Jewish Community in Jedwabne, Poland, 1941* (Princeton, NJ: Princeton University Press, 2003).

5. Welzer, *Les Exécuteurs*.

6. On this, see Jacques Sémelin, Claire Andrieu, and Sarah Gensburger, eds., *La Résistance aux génocides: De la pluralité des actes de sauvetage* (Paris: Presses de la Fondation nationale des sciences politiques, 2008).

7. Genesis 4.9.

8. Alain Corbin, *The Village of Cannibals*, trans. Arthur Goldhammer (Cambridge, MA: Harvard University Press, 1992), 85.

9. Corbin, *The Village of Cannibals*, 62.

10. Corbin, *The Village of Cannibals*, 64.

11. This is confirmed clearly in texts by Girard other than those directly focusing on analysis of the resolution of the crisis, for example, the reading of Peter's denial in *The Scapegoat*, trans. Yvonne Freccero (Baltimore: Johns Hopkins University Press, 1986), 149–64.

12. Corbin, *The Village of Cannibals*, 63.

13. Corbin, *The Village of Cannibals*, 55.

14. Corbin, *The Village of Cannibals*, 49.

15. Corbin, *The Village of Cannibals*, 118.

16. Corbin, *The Village of Cannibals*, 97–98.

17. Benedict Anderson, *Imagined Communities* (London: Verso, 2006).

18. We know that, according to René Girard, all sacrificial rites are based on two substitutions. First, the founding violence substitutes the scapegoat victim for all members of the community. Second, in the rite, the sacrificial victim is substituted for the scapegoat victim. In the first case, the choice of victim results from spontaneous convergence of violent mimetism, and so it necessarily follows from the convergence of violence. In contrast, the victim of a sacrifice is chosen and is the object of ritual preparations prior to the rite, which then causes the violence to converge on him or her. See René Girard, *Violence and the Sacred*, , trans. Patrick Gregory (Baltimore: Johns Hopkins University Press, 1977), in particular, chapter 10, "The Gods, the Dead, the Sacred, and Sacrificial Substitution."

19. See Paul Dumouchel, "The Ambivalence of Scarcity," in *The Ambivalence of Scarcity and Other Essays* (East Lansing: Michigan State University Press, 2014), 3–96.

20. Hannah Arendt, *Eichmann in Jerusalem* (New York: Viking Press, 1963), 252.

21. See Paul Dumouchel, "La technique et la banalité du mal," in *Jean-Pierre Dupuy, dans l'oeil du cyclone: Colloque de Cerisy*, ed. Marc Anspach (Paris: Carnets Nord, 2009), 67–102. This antisacrificial dimension is perhaps what explains the violence of the reactions that this expression generated. What was scandalizing was Arendt's refusal to make either the victims or the torturers sacred.

22. We find this same desanctification—a veritable secularization—of the executioner in Primo Levi, in particular in chapter 2, "The Grey Zone," of *The Drowned and the Saved*, trans. Raymond Rosenthal (London: Abacus, 1989), 22–51.

23. René Girard, *Things Hidden since the Foundation of the World*, trans. Stephen Bann and Michael Metteer (New York: Continuum, 2003), 51–57.

24. Marcel Granet, *La Civilisation chinoise* (Paris: La Renaissance du livre, 1929).

25. Concerning the links between sanctification of victims and of masters of violence, see Dumouchel, "From Scapegoat to God," in *Ambivalence of Scarcity*, 259–74.

26. Today, nearly fifty years after Hannah Arendt forged this expression, the possibility—that the most terrible evil is now within anyone's reach—has become literally true since it is technically possible for an isolated individual to procure and explode a nuclear device.

27. Arendt, *Eichmann in Jerusalem*.

28. Arendt, *Eichmann in Jerusalem*, 22.

29. Arendt, *Eichmann in Jerusalem*, 29.

30. Hannah Arendt, *The Human Condition* (Chicago: University of Chicago Press, 1958).

31. Thucydides, *The History of the Peloponnesian War*, translated by Richard Crawley, book 3, chapter 9 for Mytilene, and book 5, chapter 17 for Melos. Online at http://www.gutenberg.org/files/7142/7142-h/7142-h.htm.

32. Raphael Lemkin, *Axis Rule in Occupied Europe* (Washington, DC: Carnegie Endowment for International Peace, 1944), 79: "a coordinated plan of different actions aiming at the destruction of the essential foundations of the life of national groups, with the aim of annihilating the groups themselves."

33. Bernard Eck, "Essai pour une typologie des massacres en Grèce classique," in *Le Massacre, objet d'histoire*, ed. David El Kenz (Paris: Gallimard, 2005), 72–120.

34. Nancy Scheper-Hughes, "The Genocidal Continuum: Peace-time Crimes," in *Power and the Self*, ed. Jeannette Marie Mageo (Cambridge: Cambridge University Press, 2002), 27–49; Scheper-Hughes, "Coming to Our Senses: Anthropology and Genocide," in *Annihilating Difference: The Anthropology of Genocide*, ed. Alexander Laban Hinton (Berkeley: University of California Press, 2002), 348–81.

35. Franco Basaglia and Franca Basaglia Ongara, *Crimini di pace* (Milan: Baldini Castaldi Dalai, 2009).

36. Scheper-Hughes, "The Genocidal Continuum," 30.

37. In fact, courts that hear cases involving crimes against humanity generally do not allow the accused to invoke as a defense the fact that the action was legal when it was committed. They counter this defense with the so-called manifest illegality clause, according to which even if the action was performed in response to an order given by a legally constituted authority, if the order—for example, to kill innocent women and children—was manifestly illegal, the accused cannot use the claimed legality as a reason for his or her action. On this, see Mark J. Osiel, *Mass Atrocity, Ordinary Evil, and Hannah Arendt* (New Haven: Yale University Press, 2001), especially 149–64.

38. See http://www.prisonsucks.com.

39. With respect to this, it is instructive to consider the case of Margaret Haywood, an English nurse who was struck from the nursing register because she had made public a video filmed in state homes and institutions illustrating the poor treatment inflicted daily on elderly people. See Jenni Russell, "To Sack a Nurse for Exposing Cruelty Is a Farcical Injustice," *Guardian*, April 28, 2009.

40. Contrary to what Günter Anders suggests in *Nous, fils d'Eichmann*, trans. Sabine Cornille and Philippe Ivernel (Paris: Rivage, 1999).

41. In 1937, the Gestapo had only 7,000 employees of all ranks in a country with a population of nearly 70 million, and in 1941 it had no more than 7,700 employees in the *Altreich*, in other words, prewar Germany. See Robert Gellately, *Backing Hitler: Consent and Coercion in Nazi Germany* (Oxford: Oxford University Press, 2001), 72.

42. The greater number of instrumental denunciations in relation to strictly political denunciations is not a phenomenon reserved to Nazi Germany. It was also the case in the Soviet Union and the German Democratic Republic. See Sheila Fitzpatrick and Robert Gellately, "Introduction to the Practices of Denunciation in Modern Europe," in *Accusatory Practices: Denunciation in Modern European History, 1789–1989*, ed. Sheila Fitzpatrick and Robert Gellately (Chicago: University of Chicago Press, 1996), 231.

43. Robert Gellately, "Denunciations in Twentieth-Century Germany: Aspects of Self-Policing in the Third Reich and the German Democratic Republic," in Fitzpatrick and Gellately, *Accusatory Practices*, 184–221.

44. Vandana Joshi, *Gender and Power in the Third Reich: Female Denouncers and the Gestapo, 1933–1945* (New York: Palgrave Macmillan, 2003).

45. Gellately, "Denunciations," 218.

46. Götz Aly, in *Hitler's Beneficiaries, Plunder, Racial War, and the Nazi Welfare State* (New York: Metropolitan Books, 2007), shows that political denunciations were also most often motivated by self-interest. Denouncing a Jewish merchant or neighbor could be an excellent way to eliminate a competitor or obtain a new apartment.

Chapter 2. The State, Violence, and Groups

1. Étienne de La Boétie, *The Politics of Obedience: The Discourse of Voluntary Servitude*, trans. Harry Kurz (Auburn, AL: Ludwig von Mises Institute, 2008). The first edition of the *Discours de la servitude volontaire* dates from 1574, in other words, ten years after La Boétie's death, but it is generally agreed that it was written around 1548, thus before the French Wars of Religion.

2. La Boétie, *Politics of Obedience*, 46.

3. Jean Jacques Rousseau, "The Social Contract," in *The Major Political Writings of Jean-Jacques Rousseau*, trans. and ed. John T. Scott (Chicago: The University of Chicago Press, 2012), 161–272.

4. Just as did those who, for personal and private, rather than ideological and political, reasons denounced the real or invented "crimes" of their relatives, colleagues, and neighbors to the Gestapo.

5. According to Marx, it is the very nature of the state to exercise violence against the majority. This is why the solution requires its abolition and decline, and the establishment of a classless society. The problem is the same, but the solution is different.

6. One of the famous theses that Locke set out in *The Second Treatise of Civil Government* is that people have the right to depose a sovereign who abuses his or her power and they will be acting rationally if they do so. John Locke, *Two Treatises of Government* (Cambridge: Cambridge University Press, 1963), chapters 17 and 18 of the Second Treatise, in particular paragraphs 218, 219, and 220.

7. On this, see David Boucher and Paul Kelly, "The Social Contract and Its Critics: An Overview," in *The Social Contract from Hobbes to Rawls*, ed. David Boucher and Paul Kelly (London: Routledge, 1994), 1–34.

8. Joseph Raz, *The Morality of Freedom* (Oxford: Clarendon Press, 1986). See in particular chapter 7, "The Nature of Rights."

9. Larry May, *Crimes against Humanity: A Normative Account* (New York: Cambridge University Press, 2005).

10. May, *Crimes against Humanity*, 83.

11. In fact, May considers that this plurality of meanings may be a source of confusion, but thinks that crimes against humanity are an issue that is important enough for him to allow himself to not take this analytical difficulty into account. It seems to me that, on the contrary, the twofold meaning of the word "group" is, in this context, revealing of certain fundamental aspects of political violence.

12. The Khmer Rouge considered that wearing glasses was a sign of belonging to the bourgeoisie or intellectual class, and that this made it possible to identify individuals on whom they should be especially hard.

13. Antoine Garapon, *Des crimes qu'on ne peut ni punir ni pardonner* (Paris: Odile Jacob, 2002), 128.

14. In fact, May's condition is excessively weak. The disjunction "one or the other" makes it possible to consider as a crime against humanity both the violence of hooligans in a soccer stadium—even if the victim is not a member of a group, the hooligans constitute an organized group in a minimal sense at least—and an ordinary racist attack—the attacker may not be part of an organized group, but the victim belongs to a well-defined set, for example, that of North Africans. However, because May's definition is broader, it makes it possible to consider that state torture of citizens who seem to have been selected randomly is a crime against humanity.

15. Garapon, *Des crimes*, 128 [our translation].

16. In fact, if the universal characteristics of the victims were targeted, they would not be able to form a group, a distinct set. They could do so only by mistake or chance since, by definition, the features motivating their persecution would be common to all individuals. If the victims had been chosen because of the characteristics that they share with all, anyone could have been chosen. If victims of crimes against humanity have to belong to a group, then it is logically necessary that they not be chosen as victims because of the characteristics that they share with all.

17. Cf. Paul Dumouchel, "Persona: Reason and Representation in Hobbes' Political Philosophy," in *Public Space and Democracy*, ed. Marcel Hénaff and Tracey B. Strong (Minneapolis: University of Minnesota Press, 2001), 53–65. This is also asserted by Max Weber in "Politics as a Vocation," in *The Vocation Lectures,* ed. David Owen and Tracy B. Strong, trans. Rodney Livingstone (Cambridge, MA: Hackett, 2004), 34: "If the state is to survive, those who are ruled over must always *acquiesce* in the authority that is claimed by the rulers of the day."

18. Thomas Hobbes, *Leviathan* (London: Andrew Crooke, 1651), chapter 10.

19. Hobbes, *Leviathan*, chapter 21.

20. Hobbes, *Leviathan*, chapter 21.

21. Hobbes, *Leviathan*, chapter 20.

22. Hobbes, *Leviathan*, chapter 20.

23. Hobbes, *Leviathan*, introduction.

24. Hobbes, *Leviathan*, chapter 13.

25. Such a power may be an assembly of all members of the community (democracy), an assembly of a few (oligarchy), or an assembly reduced to one (monarchy). Hobbes's preference for the third form of government flowed from the fact that he found the institution of monarchy more consistent with the logic of the unanimous consent of the original contract.

26. Hobbes, *Leviathan*, chapter 13.

27. Carl Schmitt, *The Concept of the Political*, trans. George D. Schwab, expanded edition (Chicago: University of Chicago Press, 2006), 19.

28. Schmitt, *Concept of the Political*. [The English version, unlike the French translation, does not contain the 1932 postface, which is the source of this quotation. The translation quoted here comes from a review by Robert D. Rachlin: "Review of Schmitt, Carl, *The Concept of the Political*," H-German, H-Net Reviews, October 2007, http://www.h-net.org/reviews/showrev.php?id=13761, but we have altered it slightly after consultation with Wolfgang Palaver.]

29. Schmitt, *Concept of the Political*, 38. [The English version used here has been altered slightly after consultation with Wolfgang Palaver.]

30. In order to indicate that we are talking about groups, not individuals, I have used "friends" and "foes" rather than "friend" and "foe."

31. Schmitt, *Concept of the Political*, 28.

32. Schmitt, *Concept of the Political*, 27. Schmitt did not claim that no conflict between "friends" and "foes" could be resolved using established rules or thanks to a neutral third party, but that "in the extreme case" conflicts that cannot be resolved through such means are always possible.

33. Schmitt, *Concept of the Political*, 46.

34. Schmitt, *Concept of the Political*, 46.

35. Carl Schmitt, *Political Theology: Four Chapters on the Concept of Sovereignty*, trans. George D. Schwab (Chicago: University of Chicago Press, 1985), 13.

36. Raymond Verdier, ed., *La Vengeance: Études d'ethnologie, d'histoire et de philosophie*, 4 vols. (Paris: Cujas, 1980–84). See in particular R. Verdier, "Le Système vindicatoire," 1:24–25; "Une Justice sans passion, une justice sans bourreau," 3:149–53; see also Lucien Scubla, "La Place de la nation dans les sociétés individualistes," *Droit et Cultures* 39, no. 1 (2000): 191–210.

37. For example, Edward Evans-Pritchard, *The Nuers* (Oxford: Oxford University Press, 1940); Ernest Gellner, *Muslim Society* (Cambridge: Cambridge University Press, 1981); Edmund Leach, *Political Systems of Highland Burma* (London: Athlone, 1970); Robert Montagne, *Les Berbères et le Makhzen dans le sud du Maroc* (Paris: Alcan, 1930); Simon Simonse, *Kings of Disaster* (Leiden: E.J. Brill, 1992).

38. "Family" needs to be understood in the social, rather than the simply biological, sense. The term thus refers to all organizations in which links between agents are thought of or represented using kinship categories, even when the ties are not strictly genealogical. See Meyer Fortes, *Kinship and the Social Order* (Chicago: Aldine, 1969).

39. We find traces of these rules in ancient Athens, for example, where there was no theft between immediate kin. See Louis Gernet, *Recherches sur le développement de la pensée juridique et morale en Grèce* (Paris: Albin Michel, 2001).

40. Marshall Sahlins, "On the Sociology of Primitive Exchange," in *Stone Age Economics* (Chicago: Aldine, 1972), 185–276.

41. Bronislaw Malinowski, *The Argonauts of the Western Pacific* (London: Routledge, 1922).

42. Sahlins, "Sociology of Primitive Exchange," 194.

43. Marshall Sahlins, *Tribesmen* (Englewoods Cliffs, NJ: Prentice Hall, 1968), 4–13.

44. On the role of conflicts as sources of social cohesion, see Jacob Black-Michaud, *Feuding Societies* (Oxford: Basil Blackwell, 1970).

45. Since often the same word means "person" and "member of the group."

46. Sahlins, "Sociology of Primitive Exchange," 195.

47. Simonse, *Kings of Disaster*, 27.

48. Simonse, *Kings of Disaster*, 26–30.

49. See in particular Evans-Pritchard, *The Nuers*.

50. Segmented societies are those made up of many different groups that interlock with one another and have relationships of opposition that resolve into alliances at higher levels. For example, in a society divided into families, clans, and tribes, families many be in opposition to one another, but at the same time part of the same clan, which opposes other clans, etc. This organization through hierarchical interlocking and complementary opposition does not require a centralized power. Since membership in a segment is generally determined by an individual's, family's, clan's, etc., genealogical status, an individual has as many point of reference as there are levels of segmentation.

51. Cf. René Girard, *Violence and the Sacred*, trans. Patrick Gregory (Baltimore: Johns Hopkins University Press, 1977), chapter 10.

52. Alfred Métraux, "L'Anthropophagie rituelle des Tupinamba," in *Religions et magies indiennes d'Amérique du Sud* (Paris: Gallimard, 1967), 45–78.

Chapter 3. Territory and War

1. Carl Schmitt, *The Leviathan in the State Theory of Thomas Hobbes*, trans. George Schwab and Erna Hilfstein (Westport, CT: Greenwood Press, 1996).

2. Carl Schmitt, *The Concept of the Political*, trans. George D. Schwab, expanded edition (Chicago: University of Chicago Press, 2006). [These quotes are from the preface published in the French translation (not part of the English translation): *La notion de politique: Théorie du partisan*, trans. Marie-Louise Steinhauser (Paris: Calmann-Lévy, 1972), 45 [our translation].

3. On this, see Robert Muchembled, *Le Temps des supplices: De l'obéissance sous les rois absolus* (Paris: Armand Colin, 1992). In fact, as Muchembled shows, the establishment of a central power leads first to strengthening of intermediary groups, which becomes one of the causes of future conflict.

4. Emmanuel-Joseph Sieyès, *Qu'est-ce que le tiers état?* (Paris: Flammarion, 2009).

5. It is this same act of expelling from the state fellow citizens who were reputed to be foes or foreigners that Léon Mugesera, vice president of the National Republican Movement for Democracy and Development, the party of President Habyarimana, repeated at the beginning of the genocide when he advised his fellow Hutu citizens to send the Tutsis back to Ethiopia, which,

legend had it, they had come from. See Gérard Prunier, *The Rwanda Crisis 1959–1994: A History of a Genocide* (London: Hurst, 1995), 171–72.

6. Lucien Scubla, "La Place de la nation dans les sociétés individualistes," *Droit et Cultures* 39, no. 1 (2000): 199–200 [our translation.].

7. Marcel Hénaff, *The Price of Truth: Gift, Money, and Philosophy*, trans. Jean-Louis Morhange (Stanford, CA: Stanford University Press, 2010).

8. This is how Sun Yat-sen, still revered today as the father of modern China, understood nationalism. In *San Min Chu I: The Three Principles of the People*, trans. Frank W. Price (Shanghai: Commercial Press, 1929), he wrote that the Chinese lack the principle of nationalism because until now they have understood loyalty only to the family and clan, but not the necessity to make the supreme sacrifice for the nation (4–7).

9. It is interesting (and we will come back to this) that the "distancing" can be measured on several "levels" that are at first sight very different, for example, physical (geographical) distance, social milieu, and kinship ties. On each of these levels, the distancing leads to similar weakening of obligations.

10. "Blood" and "biologicalized" culture and language can play a role similar to that of territory. Contrary to territory, blood does not correspond to a physical space, but like it, it is a principle of solidarity that is completely separated from agents' social relations, and, like territory, blood naturalizes bonds of solidarity and hostility.

11. Concerning this, see Dominique Poulot, *Musée, nation, patrimoine: 1789–1915* (Paris: Gallimard, 1997).

12. Cf. Benedict Anderson, *Imagined Communities* (New York: Verso, 2006), especially chapter 2.

13. Heather Rae, *State Identities and the Homogenization of Peoples* (New York: Cambridge University Press, 2002).

14. Schmitt, *Concept of the Political*, 27.

15. Concerning this paradox of democracy, see Jean Hampton, *Hobbes and the Social Contract Tradition* (New York: Cambridge University Press, 1986), especially chapter 9, 281–85.

16. Donald L. Horowitz, *Ethnic Groups in Conflict* (Berkeley: University of California Press, 2000), 697.

17. Francis Fukuyama, *The End of History and the Last Man* (New York: Free Press, 1992).

18. Kok-Chor Tan, *Justice without Borders: Cosmopolitanism, Nationalism and Patriotism* (New York: Cambridge University Press, 2004).

19. Schmitt, *Concept of the Political*, 33.

20. Schmitt, *Concept of the Political*, 49.

21. Schmitt, *Concept of the Political*, 49.

22. On this topic, see, for example, Georg Simmel, *Der Krieg und die Giestigen Entscheidungen* (Munich: Duncker & Humblot, 1917), and *Lebensanschauung: Vier Metaphysische Kapitel* (Munich: Duncker & Humblot, 1922), and also Hans Joas, *The Genesis of Values* (Cambridge: Polity Press, 2000), chapter 5, 69–83.

23. Schmitt, *Concept of the Political*, part 5.

24. See René Girard, *Battling to the End: Conversations with Benoît Chantre*, trans. Mary Baker (East Lansing: Michigan University Press, 2010).

25. Schmitt, *Concept of the Political*, 36.

26. Schmitt, *Concept of the Political*, 28–29.

27. Carl Schmitt, *The Nomos of the Earth*, trans. G. L. Ulmen (New York: Telos Press, 2006), 161.

28. Schmitt, *Nomos of the Earth*, especially 140, 183–84, 199, 220.

29. Rabindranath Tagore, *Nationalism* (New Delhi: Rupa, 1992). The book is a collection of lectures on nationalism that Tagore gave in the United States and Japan during World War I.

30. Emmanuel Kant, *Perpetual Peace*, trans. M. Campbell Smith (London: George Allen & Unwin, 1903), 138; we have to admit that Schmitt is aware of this danger.

31. Hannah Arendt, *Imperialism: Part Two of* The Origins of Totalitarianism (New York: Harcourt Brace and World, 1951).

Chapter 4. The Traitor and Reason

1. Alain Corbin, *The Village of Cannibals*, trans. Arthur Goldhammer (Cambridge, MA: Harvard University Press, 1992), 84.

2. Corbin, *The Village of Cannibals*, 111.

3. Corbin, *The Village of Cannibals*, 115.

4. Sartre added the following note, which should be included here: "Indeed, it goes without saying that, down to its last member, the group is characterised by its transcendent relation to the other group, that is to say, to the hostile group; we shall return to this." Jean-Paul Sartre, *Critique of Dialectical Reason: Theory of Practical Ensembles*, trans. Alan Sheridan-Smith, vol. 1 (London: Verso, 2004), 438.

5. Sartre, *Critique of Dialectical Reason*, 438–39.

6. Sartre, *Critique of Dialectical Reason*, 362.

7. Sartre, *Critique of Dialectical Reason*, 438.

8. Sartre, *Critique of Dialectical Reason*, 430.

9. As Sartre noted. See *Critique of Dialectical Reason*, 431–32.

10. Sartre, *Critique of Dialectical Reason*, 443

11. Alexander L. Hinton, *Why Did They Kill? Cambodia in the Shadow of Genocide* (Berkeley: University of California Press, 2005).

12. *Angkar* was the termed used by the Khmer Rouge to refer to the state and the party organization, including the army.

13. René Girard, *Violence and the Sacred*, trans. Patrick Gregory (Baltimore: Johns Hopkins University Press, 1977), 2.

14. Stathis N. Kalyvas, *The Logic of Violence in Civil War* (New York: Cambridge University Press, 2006). Kalyvas's investigation is both empirical and theoretical. The civil war that tore Greece apart after World War II is his research specialty.

15. This seems to be confirmed by Abderrahmane Moussaoui's analyses in *De la violence en Algérie: Les lois du chaos* (Arles: Actes Sud, 2006). He suggests that very often the real motive for massacres is far from political or religious, but has its roots in debts of honour and family or village rivalries.

16. Robert Gellately, *Backing Hitler: Consent and Coercion in Nazi Germany* (Oxford: Oxford University Press, 2001); Sheila Fitzpatrick and Robert Gellately, eds., *Accusatory Practices: Denunciation in Modern European History, 1789–1989* (Chicago: University of Chicago Press, 1996).

17. Of course, this was not the case with respect to the raids and group arrests that targeted categories of individuals who were considered asocial.

18. I would like to thank Daniel Bougnoux for drawing my attention to these points.

19. Paul Dumouchel, "Voir et craindre un lion," *Rue Descartes: Passions et politique* 12–13 (May 1995): 92–105.

20. In particular, Leo Strauss, *The Political Philosophy of Hobbes* (Chicago: University of Chicago Press, 1952) and, nearer to our time, Quentin Skinner, *Reason and Rhetoric in the Philosophy of Hobbes* (New York: Cambridge University Press, 1996). For a criticism of this analysis of the role of passions, see Paul Dumouchel, "Rhetoric et passions chez Hobbes," in *Penser les passions à l'âge classique*, ed. Lucie Desjardins and Daniel Dumouchel (Paris: Hermann, 2012), 53–66.

21. Thomas Hobbes, *Leviathan* (London: Andrew Crooke, 1651), chapter 13, "Of the Natural Condition of Mankind as Concerning Their Felicity and Misery."

22. Hobbes, *Leviathan*, chapter 5, "Of Reason and Science."

23. Russell Hardin, *One for All: The Logic of Group Conflict* (Princeton, NJ: Princeton University Press, 1995); Ronald Wintrobe, *Rational Extremism: The Political Economy of Radicalism* (New York: Cambridge University Press, 2006).

24. Georg Wilhelm Friedrich Hegel, *Lectures on the Philosophy of World History*, trans. H. B. Nisbet (New York: Cambridge University Press, 1975), 177.

25. Hegel, *Lectures*, 184.

26. Hegel, *Lectures*, 185.

27. Hegel, *Lectures*, 186.

Chapter 5. Indifference and Charity

1. There is an analysis and description of this phenomenon, though centered on its relationship with the market economy rather than on the constitution of modern politics, in "The Ambivalence of Scarcity" (24–59) in the eponymous book (East Lansing: Michigan State University Press, 2014). In fact, I say "in Europe" because it is not certain that this phenomenon occurred in the same way elsewhere, especially where the cultural influence of Christianity was less strong, for example, in Japan.

2. When we read a classical author, such as Fustel de Coulanges in *The Ancient City*, trans. Willard Small (Boston: Lee and Shepard, 1877), the persistence of these rules and obligations in the civilizations of classical antiquity is very clear, but rules and obligations were also maintained in China, for example. As we have seen, this is precisely what Sun Yat-sen criticized his compatriots for in *San Min Chu I: The Three Principles of the People*, trans. Frank W. Price (Shanghai: Commercial Press, 1929): to have maintained rules of solidarity based on the family and clan.

According to him, this was the reason the Chinese were unable to create a modern state. See Jacqueline Stevens, *States without Nations* (New York: Columbia University Press, 2010) concerning the persistence of family ties systems in modern states.

3. Cf. Henri Atlan, "Founding Violence and Divine Referent," in *Violence and Truth: On the Work of René Girard*, ed. Paul Dumouchel (Stanford, CA: Stanford University Press, 1988), 192–208; and Christiane Frémont, "De la croyance et du savoir," in *Stanford French Review* 10 (1986): 197–201.

4. This is exactly the criticism that Henri Atlan makes of Girard: that he takes at face value the psychoanalytical hypothesis that the "revelation of things hidden" will inevitably change the behavior of agents and cause their symptoms to disappear.

5. This is true even though it is also true that in a sense forgiving is not "successful" unless the person who has been forgiven accepts being forgiven. This is, however, another question, and it shows that forgiveness as an action remains marked by our fragility and dependency on the Other.

6. Joel Feinberg, "The Moral and Legal Responsibility of the Bad Samaritan," *Criminal Justice Ethics* 3, no. 1 (1984): 56–69. Feinberg points out that in countries influenced by the common-law tradition in particular, abandoning people in danger may receive moral condemnation, but no legal sanction. Moreover, everywhere that refusal to help persons in danger is a legal offense, it is so owing to recent legislation. The oldest examples of it date back barely one hundred years.

7. In *The Rivers North of the Future: The Testament of Ivan Illich*, ed. David Cayley (Toronto: House of Anansi Press, 2005), 51, Ivan Illich compares the Good Samaritan's action with that of a Palestinian helping a wounded Israeli.

8. As James Alison pointed out to me (in a personal communication), in Luke 10:30–37, the first two to pass by are a priest and a Levite who are going to a temple to perform a sacrifice. If they had gone near the wounded victim, they would have been in contract with blood and would not have been able to perform the sacrifice before going through a purification ritual. In their case, it is thus respect for their traditional obligations that prevented them from being charitable and helping the victim. They turned away from the wounded man in order to avoid becoming impure. They were thus in a situation that was in a sense similar to that of the Good Samaritan in that, in order to be charitable, they would have had to, to some degree, go against their traditional obligations. The partial resemblance between the situation of the Samaritan and the two others make the radical difference in their respective attitudes much clearer.

9. Marshall Sahlins, "On the Sociology of Primitive Exchange," in *Stone Age Economics* (Chicago: Aldine, 1972), 185–230, especially 195.

10. Mark Anspach, *À charge de revanche* (Paris: Seuil, 2002), 59–60; "Les fondements rituels de la transaction monétaire, ou comment remercier un bourreau," in *La Monnaie souveraine*, ed. Michel Aglietta and André Orléan (Paris: Odile Jacob, 1998), 53–83; see also Davis Baird, *Thing Knowledge: A Philosophy of Scientific Instruments* (Berkeley: University of California Press, 2004), chapter 10, "The Gift," especially 223–24.

11. Jean-Jacques Rousseau, "The Social Contract," in *The Major Political Writings of Jean-Jacques Rousseau*, trans. and ed. John T. Scott (Chicago: The University of Chicago Press, 2012), 172.

12. Money plays a fundamental role in this phenomenon. It establishes, among all those who have it, abstract relations that can at any time be made real and that allow people to take distance from any specific exchange relation.

13. Marcel Hénaff, "Gift, Market and Social Justice," in *Against Injustice: The New Economics of Amartya Sen*, ed. Paul Dumouchel and Reiko Gotoh (New York: Cambridge University Press, 2009), 112–39.

14. Adam Smith, *An Inquiry into the Nature and Cause of the Wealth of Nations* (London: Everyman's Library, 1975), book 1, chapter 2, 13.

15. As we have seen, Sahlins thinks that there is exchange of this type in traditional societies, in other words, that there is exchange between agents who are not bound by any reciprocal reciprocity obligations, and he explicitly associates it with modern mercantile exchange rather than with ceremonial exchange, though he thinks that in such societies, exchanges of this type occur in the third circle of warlike hostility.

16. Smith, *Wealth of Nations*, book 1, chapter 2, 13.

17. Daniel K. Finn, *The Moral Ecology of Markets* (Cambridge: Cambridge University Press, 2006).

18. See David Akin and Joel Robbins, eds., *Money and Modernity: State and Local Currencies in Melanesia* (Pittsburgh: University of Pittsburgh Press, 1999), 284; Jonathan Parry and Maurice Bloch, eds., *Money and the Morality of Exchange* (Cambridge: Cambridge University Press, 1989), 276.

19. On this, see Paul Dumouchel, "Rational Deception," in *Deception in Markets*, ed. C. Gerschlager (New York: Palgrave, 2005), 51–71.

20. This is one of the reasons why we have developed refined methods for conducting opinion polls in order to make different publics visible.

21. Thomas Hobbes, *Leviathan* (London: Andrew Crooke, 1651), book 1, chapter 13.

22. Charles Tilly, *Coercion, Capital and European States, A.D. 990–1990* (Cambridge, MA: B. Blackwell, 1992).

23. Montesquieu, Charles-Louis de Secondat, Baron de, *The Spirit of Laws*, trans. Anne M. Cohler, Basia C. Miller, and Harold S. Stone (Cambridge: Cambridge University Press, 1989), part 4, book 20, 2.

24. See Dumouchel, "The Ambivalence of Scarcity."

25. Concerning this, see my analysis of the enclosures in England at the end of the eighteenth century in "The Ambivalence of Scarcity," 83–96. For converging indications with respect to the agrarian property reform in Russia in the years preceding the Revolution, see Orlando Figes, *A People's Tragedy: The Russian Revolutions 1891–1921* (London: Pimlico, 1996), 236–37.

26. Sophisticated versions of this argument can be found in works by authors such as Robert Nozick (*Anarchy, State and Utopia* [New York: Basic Books, 1974]), and Friedrich Hayek (*Law, Legislation and Liberty*, vol. 2, *The Mirage of Social Justice* [Chicago: University of Chicago Press, 1976]).

27. David Hume, *An Inquiry Concerning the Principles of Morals* (New York: Bobbs-Merrill, 1957), 13.

Chapter 6. Social Justice and Territory

1. Though it is not at the heart of his inquiry, specific information on this topic can be found in Samuel Fleischacker, *A Short History of Distributive Justice* (Cambridge, MA: Harvard University Press, 2004).

2. See Ruwen Ogien, *L'Éthique aujourd'hui: Maximalistes et minimalistes* (Paris: Gallimard, 2007).

3. In this sense, a social state is a depiction of a possible state of a society in which certain conditions

are satisfied, for example, equal distribution of resources or compensation for the most needy, or, on the contrary, a society where the distribution of wealth comes uniquely from the operation of the market. Understood in this way, a social state is thus neither a sociological or political concept, nor a normative concept that would apply to certain societies but not to others. It is in fact an abstract model of a possible distribution, within a society, of resources, wealth, freedom, political rights, etc.

4. John Rawls, *A Theory of Justice* (Cambridge, MA: Harvard University Press, 1971). The worst off form a statistical group in the sense defined in chapter 2 of the present book insofar as the individual members of the group do not necessarily know or, in general, have relationships with one another.

5. John Rawls, "Justice as Fairness," in *Collected Papers*, ed. Samuel Freeman (Cambridge, MA: Harvard University Press, 1999), 47.

6. Friedrich Hayek, *Law, Legislation and Liberty*, vol. 2, *The Mirage of Social Justice* (Chicago: University of Chicago Press, 1976). To a lesser degree, we should also acknowledge Robert Nozick, *Anarchy, State and Utopia* (New York: Basic Books, 1974), for his criticism of Rawls implies the rejection of such a conception of justice.

7. Hayek, *Mirage of Social Justice*, 31.

8. Hayek, *Mirage of Social Justice*, 69.

9. Hayek's position is in fact more complex than this. His thesis can more accurately be described as the following: The classical notion of justice is inseparable from the birth of modern societies and their economic success; the requirement of social justice, guided by an inconsistent conception of justice, risks undermining the foundations of these societies.

10. Sergio Manghi, "Nessuno escluso," *Pluriverso* 4–5 (1999): 204–18.

11. John Rawls, *Political Liberalism* (New York: Columbia University Press, 1993), 49.

12. Reiko Gotoh, "Justice and Public Reciprocity," in *Against Injustice: The New Economics of Amartya Sen*, ed. Reiko Gotoh and Paul Dumouchel (New York: Cambridge University Press, 2009), 157.

13. On the laws of nature, Thomas Hobbes wrote: "These dictates of reason men used to call by the name of laws, but improperly: for they are but conclusions or theorems concerning what conduceth to the conservation and defence of themselves; whereas law, properly, is the word of him that by right hath command over others" (*Leviathan* [London: Andrew Crooke, 1651], chapter 15).

14. Hobbes, *Leviathan*, chapter 15.

15. Gotoh, "Justice and Public Reciprocity," 154–55.

16. Hans Joas, *The Genesis of Values* (Cambridge: Polity Press, 2000), 75.

17. On this, see David Lewis, *Convention* (Cambridge, MA: Harvard University Press, 1969); Brian Skyrms, *The Evolution of the Social Contract* (New York: Cambridge University Press, 1996); Don Ross and Paul Dumouchel, "Emotions as Strategic Actions," *Rationality and Society* 16, no. 3 (2004): 251–86.

18. See Paul Dumouchel, "Faut-il interdire la burqa?" *Esprit*, October 2010.

19. John Rawls, "Justice as Fairness: Political Not Metaphysical," in *Collected Papers*, ed. Samuel Freeman (Cambridge, MA: Harvard University Press, 1999), 390.

20. Hobbes, *Leviathan*, chapter 13 (my emphasis).

21. Bertrand Badie, *La Fin des territoires* (Paris: Fayard, 1995).

22. Robert Ardrey, *The Territorial Imperative* (New York: Kodansha, 1997).

23. For example, Pakistan before the civil war that led to the creation of Bangladesh, and Germany between the two wars, when it was separated from East Prussia by the Danzig Corridor. Alaska, which is divided from the rest of the United States by Canadian territory, constitutes the only apparent counterexample to this rule.

24. Heather Rae, *State Identities and the Homogenization of Peoples* (New York: Cambridge University Press, 2002).

25. Frédéric Gros, *States of Violence*, trans. Krysztof Fijalkowski and Michael Richardson (London: Seagull Books, 2010).

26. Ann Hironaka, *Neverending Wars: The International Community, Weak States and the Perpetuation of Civil War* (Cambridge, MA: Harvard University Press, 2008).

27. This was likely long the case of Afghanistan, where the Americans hoped to establish a regime that would be the enemy of both Russia and Iran.

28. According to Ann Hironaka, civil wars in which other states intervene last much longer than those in which there is no interstate intervention (*Neverending Wars*, 51).

29. Paul Richards, "Emotions at War: A Musicological Approach to Understanding Atrocity in Sierra Leone," in *Public Emotions*, ed. Susannah Radstone, Corinne Squire, and Amal Treacher (London: Palgrave, 2007), 62–84; Loretta Napoleoni, *Terror Incorporated* (New York: Seven Stories Press, 2005).

30. Napoleoni, *Terror Incorporated*, 143–224.

31. Ian Traynor, "Bush Orders Clampdown on Flights to US," http://www.theguardian.com/world/2008/feb/11/usa.theairlineindustry.

32. Jean-Charles de Menezes was killed in the London subway in 2005 by police officers from the London Metropolitan Police. Following a tragic series of mistakes, they took him for a terrorist who was preparing to commit an attack.

Epilogue

1. This is at least the case of genocides perpetrated by states against their own citizens, such as those that occurred in Anatolia, Germany, Cambodia, and Rwanda. When genocide is committed by an outside power, the phenomenon is different and requires a different type of explanation.

2. In the sense of the term defined in chapter 3.

3. The reason the torture and murder of Alain de Monéys never became a political act and remained the Hautefaye crime is precisely because of its failure to overcome this indifference.

4. On this, see Isabel V. Hull, *Absolute Destruction: Military Culture and the Practices of War in Imperial Germany* (Ithaca, NY: Cornell University Press, 2005).

5. As Dambisa Moyo shows in *Dead Aid: Why Africa Is Not Working and How There Is Another Way for Africa* (London: Allen Lane, 2009), this is just as true in poor countries, in particular in Africa, except that those countries depend on international aid that, according to her, is largely what prevents them from improving their positions in the networks of international trade.

6. Gillian Brok, *Global Justice: A Cosmopolitan Account* (Oxford: Oxford University Press, 2009), 200–202.

Bibliography

Ajy, Götz. *Hitler's Beneficiaries, Plunder, Racial War, and the Nazi Welfare State*. New York: Metropolitan Books, 2007.

Akin, David, and Joel Robbins, eds. *Money and Modernity: State and Local Currencies in Melanesia*. Pittsburgh: University of Pittsburgh Press, 1999.

Anders, Günter. *Nous, fils d'Eichmann*. Translated by Sabine Cornille and Philippe Ivernel. Paris: Rivage, 1999.

Anderson, Benedict. *Imagined Communities*. New York: Verso, 2006.

Anspach, Mark. *À charge de revanche*. Paris: Seuil, 2002.

———. "Les fondements rituels de la transaction monétaire, ou comment remercier un bourreau." In *La Monnaie sourveraine*, ed. Michel Aglietta and André Orléan. Paris: Odile Jacob, 1998.

Ardrey, Robert. *The Territorial Imperative*. New York: Kodansha, 1997.

Arendt, Hannah. *Imperialism: Part Two of* The Origins of Totalitarianism. New York: Harcourt Brace and World, 1951.

———. *Eichmann in Jerusalem*. New York: Viking Press, 1963.

———. *The Human Condition*. Chicago: University of Chicago Press, 1958.

Atlan, Henri. "Founding Violence and Divine Referent." In *Violence and Truth: On the Work of René Girard,* ed. Paul Dumouchel, 192–208. Stanford: Stanford University Press, 1988.

Badie, Bertrand. *La Fin des territoires*. Paris: Fayard, 1995.

Baird, Davis. "The Gift." In *Thing Knowledge: A Philosophy of Scientific Instruments*, 211–37. Berkeley: University of California Press, 2004.

Basaglia, Franco, and Franca Basaglia Ongara. *Crimini di pace*. Milano: Baldini Castaldi Dalai, 2009.

Benhabib, Seyla. *The Rights of Others: Aliens, Residents and Citizens*. Cambridge: Cambridge University Press, 2004.

Black-Michaud, Jacob. *Feuding Societies*. Oxford: Basil Blackwell, 1970.

Boucher, David, and Paul Kelly. "The Social Contract and Its Critics: An Overview." In *The Social Contract from Hobbes to Rawls*, ed. David Boucher and Paul Kelly, 1–34. London: Routledge, 1994.

Brok, Gillian. *Global Justice: A Cosmopolitan Account*. Oxford: Oxford University Press, 2009.

Browning, Christopher. *Ordinary Men: Reserve Police Battalion 101 and the Final Solution in Poland*. London: Penguin Books, 2001.

Bruaire, Claude. *La Raison politique*. Paris: Fayard, 1974.

Césaire, Aimé. *Discours sur le colonialisme*. Paris: Présence africaine, 2004.

Corbin, Alain. *The Village of Cannibals*. Trans. Arthur Goldhammer. Cambridge, MA: Harvard University Press, 1992.

De Coulanges, Fustel. *The Ancient City*. Trans. Willard Small. Boston: Lee and Shepard, 1877.

Dumouchel, Paul. "Faut-il interdire la burqa?" *Esprit* (October 2010).

———. "From Scapegoat to God." In *The Ambivalence of Scarcity and Other Essays,* 259–74. East Lansing: Michigan State University Press, 2014.

———. "La technique et la banalité du mal." In *Jean-Pierre Dupuy: Dans l'oeil du cyclone: Colloque de Cerisy*, ed. Marc Anspach, 67–102. Paris: Carnets Nord, 2009.

———. "Persona: Reason and Representation in Hobbes' Political Philosophy." In *Public Space and Democracy,* ed. Marcel Hénaff and Tracey B. Strong, 53–65. Minneapolis: University of Minnesota Press, 2001.

———. "Rational Deception." In *Deception in Markets,* ed. C. Gerschlager, 51–71. New York: Palgrave, 2005.

———. "Rhetoric et passions chez Hobbes." In *Penser les passions à l'*âge classique, ed. Lucie Desjardins and Daniel Dumouchel, 53–66. Paris: Hermann, 2012.

———. "The Ambivalence of Scarcity." In *The Ambivalence of Scarcity and Other Essays,* 3–96. East Lansing: Michigan State University Press, 2014.

———. "Voir et craindre un lion." *Rue Descartes: Passions et politique* 12/13 (May 1995): 92–105.

Eck, Bernard. "Essai pour une typologie des massacres en Grèce classique." In *Le Massacre, objet d'histoire,* ed. David El Kenz, 72–120. Paris: Gallimard, 2005.

Evans-Pritchard, Edward. *The Nuers*. Oxford: Oxford University Press, 1940.

Feinberg, Joel. "The Moral and Legal Responsibility of the Bad Samaritan." *Criminal Justice Ethics* 3, no. 1 (1984): 56–69.

Figes, Orlando. *A People's Tragedy: The Russian Revolutions 1891–1921*. London: Pimlico, 1996.

Finn, Daniel K. *The Moral Ecology of Markets*. Cambridge: Cambridge University Press, 2006.

Fitzpatrick, Sheila, and Robert Gellately, eds. *Accusatory Practices: Denunciation in Modern European History, 1789–1989*. Chicago: University of Chicago Press, 1996.

Fleischacker, Samuel. *A Short History of Distributive Justice.* Cambridge, MA: Harvard University Press, 2004.

Fortes, Meyer. *Kinship and the Social Order.* Chicago: Aldine, 1969.

Frémont, Christiane. "De la croyance et du savoir." *Stanford French Review* 10 (1986): 197–201.

Fukuyama, Francis. *The End of History and the Last Man.* New York: Free Press, 1992.

Garapon, Antoine. *Des crimes qu'on ne peut ni punir ni pardonner.* Paris: Odile Jacob, 2002.

Gellately, Robert. "Denunciations in Twentieth-Century Germany: Aspects of Self-Policing in the Third Reich and the German Democratic Republic." In *Accusatory Practices: Denunciation in Modern European History, 1789–1989,* ed. Sheila Fitzpatrick and Robert Gellately, 184–221. Chicago: Chicago University Press, 1996.

———. *Backing Hitler: Consent and Coercion in Nazi Germany.* Oxford: Oxford University Press, 2001.

Gellner, Ernest. *Muslim Society.* Cambridge: Cambridge University Press, 1981.

Gernet, Louis. *Recherches sur le développement de la pensée juridique et morale en Grèce.* Paris: Albin Michel, 2001.

Girard, René. *Battling to the End: Conversations with Benoît Chantre.* Trans. Mary Baker. East Lansing: Michigan State University Press, 2010.

———. *The Scapegoat.* Trans. Yvonne Freccero. Baltimore: Johns Hopkins University Press, 1986.

———. *Things Hidden since the Foundation of the World.* Trans. Stephen Bann and Michael Metteer. New York: Continuum, 2003.

———. *Violence and the Sacred.* Trans. Patrick Gregory. Baltimore: Johns Hopkins University Press, 1977.

Gotoh, Reiko. "Justice and Public Reciprocity." In *Against Injustice: The New Economics of Amartya Sen,* ed. Reiko Gotoh and Paul Dumouchel, 140–60. New York: Cambridge University Press, 2009.

Granet, Marcel. *La Civilisation chinoise.* Paris: La Renaissance du livre, 1929.

Gros, Frédéric. *States of Violence: An Essay on the End of War.* Trans. Krysztof Fijalkowski and Michael Richardson. London: Seagull Books, 2010.

Gross, Jan T. *Neighbors: The Destruction of the Jewish Community in Jedwabne, Poland, 1941.* Princeton: Princeton University Press, 2003.

Hampton, Jean. *Hobbes and the Social Contract Tradition.* New York: Cambridge University Press, 1986.

Hardin, Russell. *One for All: The Logic of Group Conflict.* Princeton, NJ: Princeton University Press, 1995.

Hatzfeld, Jean. *Machete Season.* Trans. Linda Coverdale. New York: Farrar, Straus and Giroux, 2005.

Hayek, Friedrich. *Law, Legislation and Liberty.* Vol. 2, *The Mirage of Social Justice.* Chicago: University of Chicago Press, 1976.

Hegel, Georg Wilhelm Friedrich. *Lectures on the Philosophy of World History.* Trans. H. B. Nisbet. New York: Cambridge University Press, 1975.

Hénaff, Marcel. "Gift, Market and Social Justice." In *Against Injustice: The New Economics of Amartya*

Sen, ed. Reiko Gotoh and Paul Dumouchel, 112–39. New York: Cambridge University Press, 2009.

———. *The Price of Truth: Gift, Money, and Philosophy.* Trans. Jean-Louis Morhange. Stanford, CA: Stanford University Press, 2010.

Hinton, Alexander L. *Why Did They Kill? Cambodia in the Shadow of Genocide.* Berkeley: University of California Press, 2005.

Hironaka, Ann. *Neverending Wars: The International Community, Weak States and the Perpetuation of Civil War.* Cambridge, MA: Harvard University Press, 2008.

Hobbes, Thomas. *Leviathan.* Ed. Edwin Curley. Indianapolis: Hackett Publishing Company, 1994.

Horowitz, Donald L. *Ethnic Groups in Conflict.* Berkeley: University of California Press, 2000.

Hull, Isabel V. *Absolute Destruction: Military Culture and the Practices of War in Imperial Germany.* Ithaca: Cornell University Press, 2005.

Hume, David. *An Inquiry Concerning the Principles of Morals.* New York: Bobbs-Merrill, 1957.

Illich, Ivan. *The Rivers North of the Future: The Testament of Ivan Illich.* Ed. David Cayley. Toronto: House of Anansi Press, 2005.

Joas, Hans. *The Genesis of Values.* Cambridge: Polity Press, 2000.

Joshi, Vandana. *Gender and Power in the Third Reich: Female Denouncers and the Gestapo, 1933–1945.* New York: Palgrave Macmillan, 2003.

Kalyvas, Stathis N. *The Logic of Violence in Civil War.* New York: Cambridge University Press, 2006.

Kant, Immanuel. *Perpetual Peace.* Trans. M. Campbell Smith. London: George Allen and Unwin Ltd., 1903.

La Boétie, Étienne. *The Politics of Obedience: The Discourse of Voluntary Servitude.* Trans. Harry Kurz. Auburn, AL: Ludwig von Mises Institute, 2008.

Leach, Edmund. *Political Systems of Highland Burma.* London: Athlone, 1970.

Lemkin, Raphael. *Axis Rule in Occupied Europe.* Washington, DC: Carnegie Endowment for International Peace, 1944.

Levi, Primo. "The Grey Zone." In *The Drowned and the Saved,* trans. Raymond Rosenthal, 22–51. London: Abacus, 1989.

Lewis, David. *Convention.* Cambridge, MA: Harvard University Press, 1969.

Locke, John. *Two Treatises of Government.* Vol. 2, *The Second Treatise of Civil Government.* Cambridge: Cambridge University Press, 1963.

Malinowski, Bronislaw. *The Argonauts of the Western Pacific.* London: Routledge, 1922.

Manghi, Sergio. "Nessuno escluso." *Pluriverso* 4–5 (1999): 204–18.

May, Larry. *Crimes against Humanity: A Normative Account.* New York: Cambridge University Press, 2005.

Métraux, Alfred. "L'anthropophagie rituelle des Tupinamba." In *Religions et magies indiennes d'Amérique du Sud,* 45–78. Paris: Gallimard, 1967.

Montagne, Robert. *Les Berbères et le Makhzen dans le sud du Maroc.* Paris: Alcan, 1930.

Montesquieu, Charles-Louis de Secondat, Baron de. *The Spirit of Laws.* Part 4, Book 20. Trans. Anne M. Cohler, Basia C. Miller, and Harold S. Stone. Cambridge: Cambridge University Press, 1989.

Moussaoui, Abderrahmane. *De la violence en Algérie: Les lois du chaos.* Arles: Actes Sud, 2006.

Moyo, Dambisa. *Dead Aid: Why Africa Is Not Working and How There Is Another Way for Africa.* London: Allen Lane, 2009.

Muchembled, Robert. *Le Temps des supplices: De l'obéissance sous les rois absolus.* Paris: Armand Colin, 1992.

Napoleoni, Loretta. *Terror Incorporated.* New York: Seven Stories Press, 2005.

Nolte, Ernst. *Der europäische Bürgerkrieg 1917–1945: Nationalsozialismus und Bolschewismus.* Munich: Herbig, 2000.

Nozick, Robert. *Anarchy, State and Utopia.* New York: Basic Books, 1974.

Ogien, Ruwen. *L'Éthique aujourd'hui: Maximalistes et minimalistes.* Paris: Gallimard, 2007.

Osiel, Mark J. *Mass Atrocity, Ordinary Evil, and Hannah Arendt.* New Haven: Yale University Press, 2001.

Parry, Jonathan, and Maurice Bloch, eds. *Money and the Morality of Exchange.* Cambridge: Cambridge University Press, 1989.

Poulot, Dominique. *Musée, nation, patrimoine: 1789–1915.* Paris: Gallimard, 1997.

Prunier, Gérard. *The Rwanda Crisis 1959–1994: A History of a Genocide.* London: Hurst, 1995.

Rachlin, Robert D. "Review of Schmitt, Carl, *The Concept of the Political.*" H-German, H-Net Reviews: October 2007. http://www.h-net.org/reviews/showrev.php?id=13761.

Rae, Heather. *State Identities and the Homogenization of Peoples.* New York: Cambridge University Press, 2002.

Rawls, John. "Justice as Fairness." In *Collected Papers,* ed. Samuel Freeman, 47–72. Cambridge, MA: Harvard University Press, 1999.

———. "Justice as Fairness: Political not Metaphysical" in *Collected Papers*, ed. Samuel Freeman, 388–414. Cambridge, MA: Harvard University Press, 1999.

———. *A Theory of Justice.* Cambridge, MA: Harvard University Press, 1971.

———. *Political Liberalism.* New York: Columbia University Press, 1993.

Raz, Joseph. *The Morality of Freedom.* Oxford: Clarendon Press, 1986.

Richards, Paul. "Emotions at War: A Musicological Approach to Understanding Atrocity in Sierra Leone." In *Public Emotions,* ed. Susannah Radstone, Corinne Squire, and Amal Treacher, 62–84. London: Palgrave, 2007.

Ross, Don, and Paul Dumouchel. "Emotions as Strategic Actions." *Rationality and Society* 16, no. 3 (2004): 251–86.

Rousseau, Jean-Jacques. "The Social Contract." In *The Major Political Writings of Jean-Jacques Rousseau,* trans. and ed. John T. Scott, 161–272. Chicago: The University of Chicago Press, 2012.

Russell, Jenni. "To Sack a Nurse for Exposing Cruelty Is a Farcical Injustice." *Guardian,* April 28, 2009.

Sahlins, Marshall. "On the Sociology of Primitive Exchange." In *Stone Age Economics,* 185–230. Chicago: Aldine, 1972.

———. *Tribesmen*. Englewoods Cliffs, NJ: Prentice Hall, 1968.

Sartre, Jean-Paul. *Critique of Dialectical Reason*. Vol. 1, *Theory of Practical Ensembles*. Trans. Alan Sheridan-Smith. London: Verso, 2004.

Scheper-Hughes, Nancy. "Coming to Our Senses: Anthropology and Genocide." In *Annihilating Difference: The Anthropology of Genocide,* ed. Alexander Laban Hinton, 348–81. Berkeley: University of California Press, 2002.

———. "The Genocidal Continuum: Peace-time Crimes." In *Power and the Self,* ed. Jeannette Marie Mageo, 29–47. Cambridge: Cambridge University Press, 2002.

Schmitt, Carl. *La notion de politique: Théorie du partisan*. Trans. Marie-Louise Steinhauser. Paris: Calmann-Lévy, 1972.

———. *Political Theology: Four Chapters on the Concept of Sovereignty*. Trans. George D. Schwab. Chicago: University of Chicago Press, 1985.

———. *The Concept of the Political*. Trans. George D. Schwab. Chicago: University of Chicago Press, 1996.

———. *The Concept of the Political*. Trans. George D. Schwab. University of Chicago Press, 2006.

———. *The Leviathan in the State Theory of Thomas Hobbes*. Trans. George Schwab and Erna Hilfstein. Westport, CT: Greenwood Press, 1996).

———. *The Nomos of the Earth*. Trans. G. L. Ulmen. New York: Telos Press, 2006.

Scubla, Lucien. "La Place de la nation dans les sociétés individualistes." *Droit et Cultures* 39, no. 1 (2000): 191–210.

Sémelin, Jacques, Claire Andrieu, and Sarah Gensburger, eds. *La Résistance aux génocides: De la pluralité des actes de sauvetage*. Paris: Presses de la Fondation nationale des sciences politiques, 2008.

Sieyès, Emmanuel-Joseph. *Qu'est-ce que le tiers état?* Paris: Flammarion, 2009.

Sigler, Carl. *Essai sur la colonisation*. Paris: Mercure de France, 1907.

Simmel, Georg. *Der Krieg und die Giestigen Entscheidungen*. Munich: Duncker and Humblot, 1917.

———. *Lebensanschauung: Vier Metaphysische Kapitel*. Munich: Duncker and Humblot, 1922.

Simonse, Simon. *Kings of Disaster*. Leiden: E.J. Brill, 1992.

Skinner, Quentin. *Reason and Rhetoric in the Philosophy of Hobbes*. New York: Cambridge University Press, 1996.

Skyrms, Brian. *The Evolution of the Social Contract*. New York: Cambridge University Press, 1996.

Smith, Adam. *An Inquiry into the Nature and Cause of the Wealth of Nations*. London: Everyman's Library, 1975.

Stevens, Jacqueline. *States without Nations*. New York: Columbia University Press, 2010.

Strauss, Leo. *The Political Philosophy of Hobbes*. Chicago: University of Chicago Press, 1952.

Tagore, Rabindranath. *Nationalism*. New Delhi: Rupa, 1992.

Tan, Kok-Chor. *Justice without Borders: Cosmopolitanism, Nationalism and Patriotism*. New York: Cambridge University Press, 2004.

Thucydides. *The History of the Peloponnesian War.* Trans. Richard Crawley. http://www.gutenberg.org/files/7142/7142-h/7142-h.htm.

Tilly, Charles. *Coercion, Capital and European States, A.D. 990–1990.* Cambridge, MA: B. Blackwell, 1992.

Traynor, Ian. "Bush Orders Clampdown on Flights to US." http://www.theguardian.com/world/2008/feb/11/usa.theairlineindustry.

Verdier, Raymond, ed. *La Vengeance. Études d'ethnologie, d'histoire et de philosophie.* 4 vols. Paris: Cujas, 1980–1984.

Weber, Max. "Politics as a Vocation." In *The Vocation Lectures,* ed. David Owen and Tracy B. Strong, trans. Rodney Livingstone, 32–94. Cambridge, MA: Hackett, 2004.

Welzer, Harald. *Les Exécuteurs: Des hommes normaux aux meutriers de masse.* Paris: Gallimard, 2007.

Wintrobe, Ronald. *Rational Extremism: The Political Economy of Radicalism.* New York: Cambridge University Press, 2006.

Yat-sen, Sun. *San Min Chu I: The Three Principles of the People.* Trans. Frank W. Price. Shanghai: The Commercial Press, 1929.

Index

A

action and selfhood, 20–23, 26, 28–29
adversarial relations. *See* "friends-foes"
    dichotomy; solidarity
Aeschylus, 52
Afghanistan, xxxi, 76, 163, 165, 195n27
Africa, 111–12, 165, 178, 195n5
al-Qaeda, xxxi, 163, 175
Alison, James, 192n8
Aly, Götz, 30
Anderson, Benedict, 71
Anspach, Mark, 127
Arendt, Hannah, xix, 15–16, 18–21, 28, 85, 183n21
Atlan, Henri, 192n4

B

Badie, Bertrand, 158
"banality of evil," xix, 15–22, 30, 88–89, 139,
    184n26
Basaglia, Franco, 23
benevolence, 131–33
Benhabib, Seyla, xxix, 182n11
bin Laden, Osama, 163
Browning, Christopher, 2–3
Bruaire, Claude, xiii

C

Cambodia, xi, xxiv–xxv, 39, 110, 195n1; crisis of
    differences and, 105–6; dismantling of
    traditional institutions of, 96–103, 115; guilt
    of traitors to revolution and, 93, 100–102,
    118. *See also* denunciations; equality;
    feudalism; traitors
capitalism, 13, 54, 127–28, 147; predatory practices
    of, 132. *See also* exchange: mercantile
charity and forgiveness, xxvi–xxvii, 118–25, 149,
    154, 192n5; Good Samaritan parable and,
    122–23, 139, 192nn7–8; Hume on, 138
China, 17, 24, 189n8, 191n2
Christianity, xxvi, 116–19, 168, 177
citizenship, 160–61
civil wars, xiv, 45, 104–5, 141, 163, 190n14, 195n28
class struggle, 85, 145
Clausewitz, Carl von, xxiii, 77–81. *See also*
    "friends-foes" dichotomy; solidarity:
    hostility and; wars
Cold War, 140–41
colonies, 83; as "safety valves," 61, 82
colonization, xxxi, 111–12, 159, 179
Corbin, Alain, 4–9, 13, 87–88, 90. *See also*
    Hautefaye Fair murder

crimes against humanity. *See* group crimes
criminal organizations, 157, 164
crowds, 9–15

D

decolonization, 142, 143
democracy, 72–75; "democratic paradox," 73
denunciations, 27–30, 105, 185n42; in Cambodia,
    96, 101; in Nazi Germany, 27–28, 105,
    185n46, 185n4
doubles, xxi, 7. *See also* Other, the

E

East/West opposition, 141–44, 156–57, 177–78
Eck, Bernard, 22
Eichmann, Adolf, xix, 15–16, 18–20, 21, 23, 26–27
elderly care, 25–26, 184n39. *See also* exclusion;
    indifference
enclosures, 54, 136, 193n25
"end of history" concept, 75
"enemy within" concept, xx–xxi, xxiii, xxx, 40,
    50–51, 57, 59–60, 64–65, 85, 89, 174; during
    War on Terror, 162, 167
England, 45, 136, 165, 175
enmity. *See* "friends-foes" dichotomy; solidarity
equality: in Cambodia, 97–98; disappearance
    of, 167; formal, 70, 84, 97–98, 140, 145,
    160–62, 175; ideal, xxx, 62, 66, 68, 75,
    79, 144, 147, 156, 160. *See also* French
    Revolution; "friends-foes" dichotomy;
    solidarity; territory
exchange, xxvii–xxviii, 13, 126–36, 149–51, 193n15;
    ceremonial, 53, 67, 126, 127, 128; mercantile,
    54, 127–35, 192n12; outcasts of, 137–39, 145
exclusion: of groups, xx, xxi, 25, 42, 46–48, 50,
    59, 62–64, 74, 83–84, 115, 119, 122, 135–37,
    140–41, 144–45, 156; of those who exclude
    themselves, xxviii, xxix, 148, 150–54; of
    victims, 138–40. *See also* exchange: outcasts
    of; "friends-foes" dichotomy; Hobbes,
    Thomas; indifference; solidarity; territory

F

Feinberg, Joel, 122, 192n6
feudalism, xiii, 62, 65–66; Cambodian, 97, 102
Final Solution. *See* Holocaust
Finn, Daniel, 132
forgiveness. *See* charity and forgiveness
France: mob violence in, 9–13; premodern, 71,
    137; warfare and, 78, 165

Franco-Prussian War, 4–5, 9
fraud, 131–35. *See also* reason
French Revolution, 66, 68, 78, 84, 140, 171
"friends-foes" dichotomy, xx–xxvi, xxix, xxxii,
    48–63, 79, 81, 85, 89, 94, 187n32; exchange
    and, 128; fragmentation of, 157–59;
    institutionalization of, 161–62, 169–70;
    modern state and, 64–70, 72–77, 140–45,
    156, 175; in segmented societies, 56–57, 81,
    188n50
Fustel de Coulanges, Muna Denis, 191n2

G

Garapon, Antoine, 40
Gellately, Robert, 27–29, 105
genocide, xi–xii, 1–2, 22, 100–101, 103–4, 109,
    170, 191n15, 195n1; "genocidal continuum,"
    xix, 23, 26; nineteenth-century precursors
    of, 8–9
Germany: genocide of Hereros, 178; genocide of
    Jews, xi, xix, 2–3, 6–7, 15, 21, 22, 27–30, 105,
    195n1
Girard, René, xv, xvii, xviii–xix, xxi, 192n4; on
    Christianity, xxvi, 117–18; on conflict,
    57–58; on global violence, 168; on sacred
    violence, 17–18, 92, 117–18, 172, 182n17,
    183n18; on war, xxiii, xxx. WORKS: *Battling
    to the End*, 168; *The Scapegoat*, 183n11;
    *Things Hidden since the Foundation of the
    World*, xxvi, 117; *Violence and the Sacred*, 5,
    7, 101–2, 182n17
globalization, xxxi, 145, 156–58, 168
Gotoh, Reiko, 149, 151
Granet, Marcel, 17
Greece, ancient, 21–22, 187n39, 191n2
Gros, Frédéric, 163
group: expulsion by state, xv, xxi, 46–48, 50–51,
    59, 63–64, 68–69, 74–75, 84, 115; statistical,
    39–40, 42, 134, 140, 146, 171, 172, 194n4;
    weakening of, xxvi, xxvii, xxxii, 12, 120,
    133–34, 139, 156, 170. *See also* "friends-foes"
    dichotomy; Khmer Rouge; sacrificial
    mechanism; solidarity
group crimes, xx, 38–42, 59, 184n37, 186n11,
    186n14, 186n16

H

Habyarimana, Juvénal, 188n5
Hardin, Russell, 109–10
Hatzfeld, Jean, 1–3

Hautefaye Fair murder, 4–13, 29, 40–41, 92, 95, 179, 195n3; guilt of Monéys and, 5, 93, 118; indifference and, xviii, xxiv, 7, 19, 23, 27, 87, 173; unanimity and, 87–91. *See also* sacrificial mechanism; solidarity; traitors; violence: political
Hayek, Friedrich, 119, 146–47, 194n9
Haywood, Margaret, 184n39
Hegel, Georg Wilhelm Friedrich, 111–12
Hénaff, Marcel, 67
Hinton, Alexander Laban, 96, 100–103, 104
Hironaka, Ann, 163, 195n28
Hitler, Adolf, 22
Hobbes, Thomas, 33, 34, 35, 42–48, 50, 61–62, 187n25; on group exclusion, xx–xxi, 45–47, 51, 59, 63, 74; on power, 42–48, 134, 154–55; on "right reason," 108–10, 113; on self-exclusion, 150–51; on state of nature, 44–45, 53, 63, 106–8, 110, 149, 194n13; on state violence, xii, xvii
Holocaust, xxix, 2–4, 15–16, 19–21, 173
Horowitz, Donald, 74
hostility: and exchange, xxviii, 54, 127–32, 134, 193n15; warlike, 54, 56, 58, 64, 70, 80–83, 91, 110, 128, 131, 178, 193n15. *See also* "enemy within" concept; solidarity
Hume, David, 138

I
illegal immigrants, xxx, 166. *See also* "enemy within" concept; "friends-foes" dichotomy
Illich, Ivan, 192n7
indifference, xxv–xxvi, 6, 23, 26–27, 88, 117, 139; charity and, 115, 122–23; Eichmann and, xix, 15, 19; Hautefaye Fair murder and, 7, 19, 87; sacrificial mechanism and, xviii; solidarity and, 69
individual interest. *See* self-interest
Iraq, xxxi, 76, 163, 166
Islam, 153, 159, 174–76, 177–78
Israel, 76, 159, 165–66

J
Joas, Hans, 152
justice, 8, 50, 66, 75, 135, 145, 147, 194n9; social, xxviii–xxx, 112–13, 143–48, 154, 156

K
Kalyvas, Stathis, 103–5
Kant, Immanuel, xvii, 14, 84, 169, 172

Khmer Rouge, xxv, 96–103, 105–6, 115, 118, 186n12. *See also* Cambodia

L
La Boétie, Étienne de, xix–xx, 30, 31–34, 37
Lemkin, Raphael, 22
Livy, 17
Locke, John, 34, 185n6
Lon Nol, 98

M
Maillard, Camille de, 5
Malinowski, Bronislaw, 53
Marx, Karl, 34, 171, 185n5
May, Larry, 38–41, 49, 186n11, 186n14
Menezes, Jean-Charles de, 167, 195n32
mimesis, 14–15, 173
mimetic crisis. *See* sacrificial mechanism
mimetic theory, 18, 57–58, 103. *See also* Girard, René
Monéys, Alain de. *See* Hautefaye Fair murder
Montesquieu, Charles-Louis de Secondat, 135
Moussaoui, Abderrahmane, 191n15
Muchembled, Robert, 188n3
Mugesera, Léon, 188n5
myths, 17–18, 57

N
Nolte, Ernst, xxx
Nozick, Robert, 194n6
nuclear annihilation threat, 22, 141–42, 178. *See also* Clausewitz, Carl von

O
Oedipus myth, 92
Other, the, xvii, xxi, xxiii, xxiv, xxix, 49, 54, 57, 58, 63, 91, 110–13, 125–26, 155, 171; colonial, 80, 82; outcasts as, 140, 148–52; spatial relationship, 157–58; terrorists as, 167

P
Pakistan, 163, 195n23
Palestine, 76, 163
participation in massacres: in Cambodia, 101–5; Eichmann and, 15, 19, 21; by German reserve, 2–4, 173; Hautefaye Fair murder and, 11–12, 88; in Rwanda, 1–4, 6, 173, 188n5. *See also* denunciations; Eichmann, Adolf; group crimes; traitors
patriotism and violence, xxxii, 5–6, 87–89, 179

"peacetime crimes," 23–27, 30. *See also* indifference
politics: and "banality of evil," 22, 30; defined,
    20–21, 49
Pol Pot, 100, 103
propaganda, 171–72, 175
public discussion, 21–23, 28, 171
publics, 133–35, 140, 171, 174, 193n20

R

racism, 24, 27, 29, 174; Hegel's, 111
Rae, Heather, 161
Rawls, John, xxviii–xxix, 145–46, 148–50, 154
reason, xv–xvii, xx, 144; Others and, xvii, xxv,
    75, 110–13, 144, 156; political conflict
    and, 75–77, 106–13; political submission
    and, 34–37; reciprocity and, 144, 148–50,
    154–56; traitors and, xxiv–xxv, 87–113
rights violations, xx, xxviii, 23, 25, 35
rituals, 13
Rousseau, Jean-Jacques, 32–33, 34
Russia, xi, 163, 165
Rwanda, xi, 1–2, 4, 6, 165, 173, 188n5, 195n1

S

sacrificial mechanism, xiv–xvi, xviii–xix, xxi, xxii,
    58, 125, 182nn17–18, 183n18; breakdown of,
    xxiv, xxxii, 23, 117, 173; Christianity and,
    117–18, 182n18; divinization and, 17–18;
    Hautefaye murder and, 5–7, 10, 88–89;
    outcasts of exchange and, 137–40, 147;
    politics and, 63–64, 90; torture and, 101–2;
    traitors and, 92–95. *See also* doubles; wars
Sahlins, Marshall, 52–54, 127, 128, 131–32, 193n15
sanctuary concept, xxx–xxxi, 162, 166, 168, 177
Sartre, Jean-Paul, xxiv, 91–95, 99–100, 173, 190n4
scarcity, 15
Scheper-Hughes, Nancy, xix, 23–24
Schmitt, Carl, xx–xxi, xxii, xxix, 48–50, 54, 59,
    65, 75–77, 79–84, 187n32; on democracies,
    72–73; on Hobbes, 62–63; *The Nomos of the
    Earth*, 81–82, 84; on war, 79–81, 85
Scubla, Lucien, 67
self-interest, 44, 117, 127, 134, 185n46; and fraud,
    131, 133; and political violence, 103–6; and
    rationality, 37, 74; and state of nature,
    106–7; and solidarity, xxvii, 121, 174
Sieyès, Emmanuel-Joseph, 66
Sigler, Carl, 61
Simonse, Simon, 54–55
Smith, Adam, xxviii, 129, 131–33

Social Contract (Rousseau), 32, 128. *See also*
    Hobbes, Thomas: on state of nature
social contract theories, xiii, xvii, xxviii, 35–37, 59,
    61, 64, 112; Hobbes on, 46
social justice. *See* justice
social states, 145–46, 147, 193n3
solidarity, xiii, xviii–xix, xxi–xxii, xxv–xxx, 10–15,
    26–27, 65–69, 116–22, 133, 135–37, 144,
    171–74; distance and, 69, 189n9; ethnicity
    and, 71–72; hostility and, 51–58, 63, 65, 68,
    70, 80, 116, 118, 123–28, 134, 142, 144, 156,
    170; mercantile exchange and, 132, 134;
    nationalism and, 67, 189n8; reciprocity and,
    148–53, 168, 170, 175; universal, 153–54
Somalia, 163
state, the: homogeneity of, xx–xxi, xxviii–xxix,
    63, 72, 75, 158, 161; legitimacy of, xvii, xxxi,
    29, 33–37; modern, 62–63, 116, 134–35;
    nation vs., 67; as network, 176–77, 195n5;
    protective function of, xi–xii, 30, 34–35,
    43, 46–47; shared history and culture
    (identity) in, 70–71; source of power of,
    31–34, 42–46; violence of, 24–25, 29, 34,
    170, 185n5; violence monopoly, xi–xvii, xx,
    xxii, xxviii–xxxii, 48, 59, 62, 67, 75, 90–91,
    94, 103, 110, 113, 115, 117, 140, 145, 159,
    161–62, 170–71, 179; welfare, 141, 143
state of nature, xiii, xvii, 44–45, 53, 63, 106–8,
    110–11. *See also* Hobbes, Thomas
"states of violence," xxx–xxxi, 163–64, 168

T

Tagore, Rabindranath, 83
territory, xxii, xxix–xxx, 64, 69–72, 75, 82–85,
    141, 156–62; blood relations and, 189n10;
    growing irrelevance of, 167–68, 174–78
terrorism, xiv, xxi, xxx–xxxi, 109, 140, 157, 162,
    165–68, 174–75, 177–78; Sartre on, 95
Thirty Years' War, 63
Thucydides, 21–22
traitors, xxiv–xxv, xxx, 28, 99–100, 106, 110, 169,
    173–75; Sartre's theory of, xxiv, 91–95,
    99. *See also* Cambodia; denunciations;
    Hautefaye Fair murder
Tuol Sleng Prison (S-21), 100–102. *See also*
    Cambodia

U

unanimity, 6, 41–42, 87–89; Hobbes on, 42–48;
    rationality and, 34–38; violence and, xiv, xv,

xxvii, 7, 100, 121, 171
United States: "friends-foes" dichotomy and, 165,
175; penitentiary industry, 24–25, 26

V
values: defined, 152; shared, 153–54
vengeance and vendettas, xii, xxvi, 12, 34, 51,
53–54, 120. *See also* doubles
Verdier, Raymond, 51, 54
Vietnam War, 96
Village of Cannibals, The (Corbin). *See* Hautefaye
Fair murder
violence: anticipated, 154–55; collective, 4–13;
compensatory, 101–2; contagious quality,
xviii, 7–8, 12–14; excessive, 100–101, 103;
"existential justification" for, 75–76; good
(legitimate) vs. bad (illegitimate), xii–xvii,
xxiv–xxvi, 55–56, 63, 77, 83, 115, 117, 168,
169; kinship and, 52–53; "by omission,"
137–40, 147; political, xiv, xxiv–xxv, xxxii,
8, 90–91, 95, 103–6, 168–74; rationalization

of, 107–13, 123–25; routinized, 23;
self-protection and, xiii, 54; transfer of,
xiv–xvi, xxv, xxxii, 90–91, 101–2, 124–25,
140, 170–72, 181n6. *See also* group crimes;
sacrificial mechanism; state, the

W
"War on Terror," 162–68, 175
wars, xxiii–xxiv, 77–84; Clausewitz on, 77–81;
disappearance of conventional, 162–63;
Napoleonic, xxiii, 78–81, 83–84; religious,
62–63, 118, 154. *See also* civil wars
Weber, Max, xii
Welzer, Harald, 3
Wintrobe, Ronald, 109–10
World War I, 80–81, 85, 140–41
World War II, 80–81, 85, 96, 140–41, 157, 167

Y
Yat-sen, Sun, 189n8, 191n2